Gotcha Again!

Gotcha Again!

**More Nonfiction
Booktalks to Get Kids
Excited About Reading**

Kathleen A. Baxter
Marcia Agness Kochel

2002
Libraries Unlimited
Teacher Ideas Press
A Division of Greenwood Publishing Group, Inc.
Greenwood Village, Colorado

For Maud Hart Lovelace, author of the Betsy-Tacy books, without whom we never would have written this book together.

Teacher Ideas Press/Libraries Unlimited
A Division of Greenwood Publishing Group, Inc.
7730 East Belleview Avenue, Suite A200
Greenwood Village, CO 80111
1-800-225-5800
www.lu.com

Library of Congress Cataloging-in-Publication Data

Baxter, Kathleen A.
    Gotcha again! : more nonfiction booktalks to get kids excited about reading / Kathleen A. Baxter, Marcia Agness Kochel.
       p. cm.
    Includes bibliographical references and indexes.
    ISBN 1-56308-940-8
    1. Children--Books and reading--United States. 2. Children's literature, American--Book reviews. 3. Book talks--United States. I. Kochel, Marcia Agness. II. Title.

Z1037.A1 B35 2002
028.1'62--dc21
                                                           2001050859

Contents

List of Figures

Acknowledgments

Chapter 1

Cover from *The Perilous Journey of the Donner Party* by Marian Calabro. Jacket front illustration copyright © 1999 by Leslie Evans. Reprinted by permission of Clarion Books/Houghton Mifflin Company. All rights reserved.

Cover from *Digging for Bird-Dinosaurs: An Expedition to Madagascar* by Nic Bishop. Jacket photograph copyright © 2000 by Nic Bishop. Reprinted by permission of Houghton Mifflin Company. All rights reserved.

Cover from *Sir Walter Ralegh and the Quest for El Dorado* by Marc Aronson. Jacket illustration copyright © 2000 by Kayley Le Faiver. Reprinted by permission of Clarion Books/Houghton Mifflin Company. All rights reserved.

Cover from *SEAL Teams* (U.S. Navy Special Forces) by Michael Burgan. Copyright © Capstone Books, an imprint of Capstone Press, Mankato, MN, 2000. Used by permission of Capstone Press.

Chapter 2

Cover from *The Weimaraner* by Charlotte Wilcox. Copyright © Capstone Books, an imprint of Capstone Press, Mankato, MN, 1999. Used by permission of Capstone Press.

Cover from *Mountain Gorillas* by Karen Kane. Photographs by Gerry Ellis. Copyright © 2001 by Karen Kane. Published by Lerner Publications, a division of Lerner Publishing Group. Used by permission of the publisher. All rights reserved.

Cover from *Cockroaches* by Patricia Kite. Copyright © 2001 by Patricia Kite. Published by Lerner Publications, a division of Lerner Publishing Group. Used by permission of the publisher. All rights reserved.

Cover from *Ducks!* by Gail Gibbons. Copyright © Holiday House, 2001. Used by permission of Holiday House.

Cover from *Bill Nye the Science Guy's Big Blue Ocean* by Bill Nye. Copyright © Hyperion Books for Children, 1999. Used by permission of Hyperion.

Chapter 3

Cover from *Toasting Marshmallows: Camping Poems* by Kristine O'Connell George. Jacket Illustration copyright © 2001 by Kate Kiesler. Reprinted by permission of Clarion Books/Houghton Mifflin Company. All rights reserved.

Cover from *Sit on a Potato Pan, Otis! More Palindromes*. Copyright © 1999 by Jon Agee. Used with the permission of Farrar, Straus & Giroux.

Chapter 5

Chapter 6

Chapter 7

Introduction

NONFICTION BOOKTALKING MADE EASY

This, our second book of nonfiction booktalks, is once again written for people who want to encourage children to read. Since the 1999 publication of *Gotcha! Nonfiction Booktalks to Get Kids Excited About Reading*, we have heard from librarians, teachers, and parents about how useful it is to have high-quality nonfiction to recommend to young readers. In addition to using our book to create booktalk programs, many librarians use our bibliographies for book-purchasing suggestions, and parents use our suggestions to select books for their children's pleasure reading.

Educational testing and national standards are starting to emphasize reading for information, yet many teachers and librarians continue to promote and value fiction as somehow superior to nonfiction. We hope to change that by showing well-written and eye-catching choices that will enthrall and open the minds of the readers in your life.

In *Gotcha Again!* we present ideas for approximately 350 booktalks, some so short that they simply entail showing illustrations, others somewhat longer—but none so long that you will have to spend hours memorizing them. We tell you which illustrations are good to show a crowd, and we place books together so that you don't have to come up with your own groupings. Our goal is to make it easy for you.

This book is divided thematically into seven high-interest chapters and is written in a conversational style, as if we were talking to a group of children. Browse through and find a mix of books that interests you—it doesn't take special skill to get kids excited about reading, just high-quality books and a lot of enthusiasm on your part.

SELECTION CRITERIA

Since sending the manuscript of *Gotcha!* to the publisher in August 1998, we have read dozens of new (and some previously undiscovered) books that we felt were equally deserving of attention. This is the product of that reading.

In this work you will find booktalks for almost all of the American Library Association's nonfiction Notable Children's Books and a large selection of others that, for one reason or another, appeal to us as books about topics kids would like. Many of the books were exceptionally well reviewed in standard library reviewing sources, and others were ignored. In cases where there were no reviews, or only a few, we read the books and found them to be worthy of inclusion.

When doing your own booktalks, you don't necessarily have to read every word of every book, although many of these books are so good you will not be able to put them down. But rest assured, we have read every page of each book included here and believe them to be worth your time and money.

HOW TO PUT TOGETHER A BOOKTALK PROGRAM

How do you put together a surefire booktalk program? I follow three rules—use lots of variety, only booktalk books that you are excited about, and make your booktalks personal whenever you can.

My number one rule is variety. My best talks contain booktalks from every chapter of this book. I am a great believer in hurtling fun information about many topics at my audiences. I almost never do "themed" booktalks. My motto is that if you don't like what I am talking about now, you won't have to wait long for it to change. At least one of the books I describe will appeal to every member of the audience.

Another important element of a good booktalk is your own enthusiasm. Choose books that you think are fascinating, and let your interest show. If you aren't crazy about the books, how can you expect kids to be excited? Chances are, if something intrigues you, you will convey that to your audience.

Finally, personalize your booktalks whenever you can. If your grandfather fought in World War II, mention that when you booktalk *Attack on Pearl Harbor*. Have you been to Africa and seen mountain gorillas like the ones in *Gorilla Walk*? Did you do your sixth-grade biography report on Helen Keller? When you talk about *The World at Her Fingertips*, mention this and tell what an impact Keller had on your life. Any tidbits you can throw in make your booktalks more interesting (and make you seem more human to the kids).

My specific choices for a booktalk include the following:

- Start off with a couple of adventure/disaster books. *Mystery on Everest: A Photobiography of George Mallory* and *Triumph on Everest: A Photobiography of Sir Edmund Hillary* make a good pair. Also from Chapter 1, talk about how great adventurers have to do a lot of reading and mention *How to Find Lost Treasure in All 50 States*. Jim Murphy's *Blizzard, the Storm That Changed America* might fit in nicely here, too.

- Sing a few poems from *The Gargoyle on the Roof* and ask the kids to name the songs. Then give them some palindromes, oxymorons, or anagrams from the Jon Agee books (Chapter 3).

- From Chapter 5 (American Journeys) talk about the mystique of the "Wild West." Tell about *Bad Guys* by Andrew Glass, and also mention the lesser-known people in *Into a New Country: Eight Remarkable Women of the West* and *My Heroes, My People: African Americans and Native Americans in the West*.

- The animal book that never fails for me is *Exploding Ants: Amazing Facts About How Animals Adapt*. For a gross-out booktalk, pair it with *Cannibal Animals*, another title filled with shocking information. To calm everyone down, I would then discuss *How the Wolf Became the Dog* and *Why the Cat Chose Us*.

- I love biographies, so I would include some of those, possibly *Spellbinder: The Life of Harry Houdini* (Chapter 6), *Through My Eyes* by Ruby Bridges (Chapter 5), or *A Special Fate: Chiune Sugihara: Hero of the Holocaust* (Chapter 4).

- Mention some of the many fascinating books about ancient civilizations (Chapter 4). My new favorite is *Mummies of the Pharaohs: Exploring the Valley of the Kings*. You can also talk about *Secrets of the Mummies: Uncovering the Bodies of Ancient Egyptians* and *Lost Temple of the Aztecs*, both by Shelley Tanaka.
- End with *Wolf Girls* and *The Mary Celeste*, two intriguing unsolved mysteries discussed in Chapter 7.

A NOTE ABOUT US

I am a children's literature consultant and a nationally known speaker. I also write a quarterly column on nonfiction booktalking for *School Library Journal*. I have a Master's of Library Science degree from the University of Minnesota. Although most of my career has been in Minnesota as the supervisor of Youth Services in the Anoka County Library, my first job was working for the Queens Borough Public Library in New York City. I have done hundreds of booktalks on nonfiction, and I am a public speaker on several other topics as well.

Marcia is a book lover and fellow librarian who also has experience in the publishing business. We met in 1992. As we are both fans of children's author Maud Hart Lovelace, we formed what eventually became the Maud Hart Lovelace Society, and Marcia edited and wrote our newsletter. She later left the Minneapolis–St. Paul area to earn her Master's of Library Science degree at the University of North Carolina at Chapel Hill. She has been an elementary school librarian in Bloomington, Indiana, and is currently the media director at Olson Middle School in Bloomington, Minnesota, where she is building up a nonfiction book collection and running a student book club.

We both love children's books and read them for pleasure even when we are not preparing a book. We are fanatics about quality books, and we bring different perspectives to our joint projects—one from a public library, one from a school library.

We hope this book will simplify your life and add a new spark to your booktalking.

Kathleen Baxter
January 2002

CHAPTER —————————— 1

Great Adventures: Disasters, Quests, and Explorers of the Seas

DISASTERS

Just about everyone is fascinated by the story of the *Titanic*, one of the worst sea disasters the world has ever known. The 1997 movie brought the story to a wide audience, and a book about the *Titanic* is always a good way to start off a set of booktalks about famous disasters.

If you like to look at pictures and read true stories about the ship, the things that were on it, the people, and the events that happened during its famous first voyage, take a look at *Titanic* by Simon Adams. You'll find it hard to put down. For example, on page 21, there is a picture of 13 of the ocean liner's stewardesses. Under the photo is this caption: "Out of a crew of 899, there were only 18 stewardesses. Despite the mix of sexes among the passengers, the old superstition about women at sea—and the social attitudes toward women at that time—dictated the White Star Lines' employment policies. But the 'women and children first into the lifeboats' rule ensured that 17 of the stewardesses survived the disaster."

Show the audience a sampling of the colorful pictures and then tell about other disasters they may not know as much about.

You might have heard of Robert Ballard, who discovered the wreckage of the *Titanic*. Read about this and other disasters and mysterious disappearances in *Ghost Liners: Exploring the World's Greatest Lost Ships*.

Did you know that two years after the *Titanic* sank another ship called the *Empress* went down near Canada? This shipwreck killed 1,012 people—8 more than perished on the *Titanic*. And while the *Titanic* took two hours to sink, the *Empress* went under in 14 minutes. It sank quickly partly because passengers had their portholes open, causing the ship to rapidly fill with water when it was struck by another ship. Read about what happened and how the ship looks now. The wreckage of the *Empress* is close enough to the surface that experienced divers can explore it. Wouldn't that be fascinating?

This attractive book is a big crowd pleaser—show any of the pictures as you talk about the shipwrecks.

Treasures of the Spanish Main by Dorothy Hinshaw Patent tells the story of a shipwreck that happened hundreds of years ago and the quest to find its lost treasure. Mel Fisher was a treasure hunter who spent 16 years looking for the sunken treasure of a ship called the *Atocha*. What he found was worth billions of dollars.

In 1622, two years after the Pilgrims landed in Plymouth, Massachusetts, Spain controlled most of South America and all of Mexico. Spaniards had brutally conquered the Native Americans who lived there and were stealing all of the gold, silver, and precious jewels they could find and taking them back to Spain.

One of 28 ships sailing back to Spain, the *Atocha* was caught in a storm off the coast of Florida and sank. Only 5 of the 265 people on board survived.

Of course, the Spaniards tried to recover the wealth, but it was a challenging task. The ship was 55 feet below water, and divers could barely make it all the way down before they ran out of breath. After another storm, the wreck became almost impossible to locate, and the salvage crew finally gave up. The wreck lay undisturbed for more than 300 years, although historians and treasure seekers always knew it was there.

Then Mel Fisher started looking and used every possible research method. The biggest breakthrough came when a friend of his, Eugene Lyon, went to Spain to study old Spanish documents. Fisher told him that if he found anything at all about the *Atocha*, he should pursue it—and Lyon did. He figured out that Fisher was looking in the wrong place. When Fisher started looking again, this time more than 100 miles away from the place where he had started but near the location Lyon had discovered, he found the wreck he was seeking.

This is an amazing story in a book jam-packed with stories and color photographs. Show your audience the photo of the divers on page 36.

Not all shipwrecks end in tragedy. One of the greatest triumphs ever involved a seemingly devastating shipwreck. Jennifer Armstrong tells the story in her book *Shipwreck at the Bottom of the World: The Extraordinary True Story of Shackleton and the* Endurance. Some people consider Sir Ernest Shackleton to be a great hero because of the events this book describes. It is an incredible story and would make a terrific movie.

In 1914 everyone wanted to explore the North Pole and the South Pole. Explorers found backers, raised funds, and formed ideas of how to go about their explorations. Not a novice explorer, Sir Ernest Shackleton outfitted a Norwegian ship, renamed it the *Endurance*, hired what he believed was an excellent crew, and set out for

Antarctica. He had a crew of 27, plus one stowaway who was discovered later. On the ship spirits were high, but nothing that followed occurred as Shackleton had planned.

Caught in the ice, the *Endurance* was crushed and eventually sank, leaving the men without a warm place to stay or enough to eat. How every single one of the crew survived (eating mainly raw penguin and seal meat) and how Shackleton led this expedition makes for one of the finest stories ever told. This group of men accomplished one impossible thing after another. Armstrong uses actual photographs throughout the book. Show the man on page 68 whose beard and moustache are solid ice.

Another good book about Shackleton comes from the National Geographic Society. *Trial by Ice: A Photobiography of Sir Ernest Shackleton* by K. M. Kostyal would be a great choice for pleasure reading or a biography book report. Packed with photographs, it is a gripping story. The picture on page 43 of the sled dogs watching the sinking ship is a great one to show. Can you imagine being outside in Antarctica for more than a year? These explorers lived through one trip, and many signed up to do it again. Shackleton must have been an amazing leader.

If your students get interested in Shackleton's voyage, they can find out more about the polar regions by reading *Polar Exploration: Journeys to the Arctic and Antarctic* by Martyn Bramwell. This DK book is full of illustrations, photographs, and captions and has a fold-out spread all about Shackleton's "Great Escape" (pages 28–31). The last section of the book, "The Scientific Age," tells about the scientific research that goes on at the poles. Antarctica has no native people—but 10,000 scientists operate research stations during the summer. In the winter months, however, fewer than 1,000 people remain. Would you want to live in such a cold and remote place?

The world has survived a lot of disasters, and more are certain to come. In fact, the last third of *Disasters* by Ned Halley predicts the kinds of disasters that may happen to Earth and its people.

Some of these disasters, like the sinking of the *Titanic*, the eruption of Mount Vesuvius, the Exxon *Valdez* oil spill, and the nuclear disaster at Chernobyl, are well known. Others, in many cases much worse disasters, are relatively unknown. For example, the volcanic explosion of Indonesia's Krakatau Island in 1883 killed more than 36,000 people. No one lived on the island, but people on the surrounding islands were killed. Even 3,000 miles away, people could hear the noise of the eruption.

The book covers many other disasters, including ice storms, tornadoes, brush fires, and swarms of locusts. You may recall hearing about these insects in the Bible in the story of Moses and in *On the Banks of Plum Creek* by Laura Ingalls Wilder. Show your audience the locusts on page 22.

It is thrilling to hear stories about people who lived through disasters. Ellen Leroe's book *Disaster! Three Real-Life Stories of Survival* profiles three such stories. Did you know that just two years after the *Titanic* sank, another shipwreck occurred that killed 1,012 people? The ship was the *Empress of Ireland*, which sank in just 14 minutes after being struck by another ship in Canada's St. Lawrence Seaway. (This shipwreck is also profiled in *Ghost Liners*, discussed above.) Seventeen-year-old Tiria from New Zealand was on the ship with her Aunt Winnie. Tiria survived in the water until a rescue ship came, but her aunt did not live through the disaster. Her story is a quick read and will fascinate the same kids who love *Titanic* stories. The other two disasters profiled in this book involve the "airships" that ruled the sky in the early part of the twentieth century. They were dirigibles, or blimps, and they were quite luxurious. Beginning on page 77 is the story of the airship *Italia* that set off on a polar expedition in 1928. The control cabin crashed into an ice pack in the Arctic Ocean, and the rest of the dirigible sailed away. Nine men and a dog were marooned for 48 days in the freezing Arctic. After many failed attempts, they were finally rescued. The six crewmen who blew away with the airship were never found. No one knows where their airship went down or what happened to them.

You can read about another dirigible disaster in Patrick O'Brien's *The* Hindenburg. At that time, the *Hindenburg* was the biggest thing that had ever flown. But it didn't fly for long, and its destruction was terrible.

The *Hindenburg* was a German airship—modern, luxurious, and fast. It could cross the Atlantic Ocean in fewer than three days. The fastest oceangoing ships took five days. It was not the first airship ever built though. They were invented in Germany by Count Zeppelin, who was able to fly for 18 minutes in his dirigible in 1900. By 1911 his dirigibles were regularly flying people around Germany, and during World War I the dirigibles were used to drop bombs on the people of London. This was a new advance in warfare, but it ended with the English developing faster, higher airplanes that machine-gunned and destroyed the dirigibles.

Developed after the war, the *Hindenburg* was the biggest dirigible ever built. It started making regular journeys to Brazil and the United States. It looked as though the future of flight might lie in dirigibles—until the *Hindenburg* exploded in New Jersey on May 6, 1937. Read about this horrible disaster in this colorful book. Show your audience the two-page spread of the *Hindenburg* blowing up.

Marian Calabro gives an account the Donner party's disastrous trip in *The Perilous Journey of the Donner Party*.

Figure 1.1. *The Perilous Journey of the Donner Party* by Marian Calabro.

More than 150 years after this group of pioneers traveled from Illinois to California, people are still intrigued by their horrible fate. Have any of your listeners ever heard of the Donner party? Do they know why the group became so famous?

In 1846 some people wanted to move to California, where they could get free land that was fertile and beautiful. Getting there, however, wasn't always easy. It was a long and difficult journey with mountains that travelers had to cross. There weren't any good roads, and there weren't many maps. However, many people had already traveled to California and Oregon safely, and newcomers could follow the wagon-wheel ruts they had made. They knew about landmarks to watch for along the way and forts to stop at where they could purchase more supplies.

George Donner organized a group of people in Springfield, Illinois, to travel to California, and he thought he had a good idea for getting there. A new book called *The Emigrant's Guide to Oregon and California* by Lanford Warren Hastings told about a shortcut. Hastings didn't claim to have taken this shortcut more than once, but he said it would save hundreds of miles. The Donner party decided to try it.

They could not have made a bigger mistake. First of all, they were a slow group. As they traveled along the trail, other pioneers joined them, but they could not seem to go very fast. Mr. Hastings's book advised travelers to follow a time line and indicated that getting stranded in the mountains after it started snowing would be dangerous. Fights broke out over what the group should do. One fight even ended in one of the group members being killed. Another person, a sick old man, was left to die while the wagon train moved on. The group also had to cross a desert. Although that part of the journey was supposed to take two days, it actually took several, and the group nearly ran out of water. Everything that could go wrong did, or so it seemed.

The travelers ended up stranded in the mountains after it started snowing, and they did not have enough food—not nearly enough. They began to starve, and people began to die. When they died, the other people looked at the dead bodies and saw meat that could save them. They started to eat the dead people. They became cannibals.

Rescues were attempted, but, in the end, of the 90 people originally in the Donner party, 47 survived and 43 died.

Not only does this interesting book tell us what happened on the trip, but it also tells what happened to the survivors, many of them children, and even about some of their descendants today.

On page 83 there is a black-and-white photo of the kind of land that wagon trains had to cross.

Dorothy Hinshaw Patent describes another famous disaster in *Lost City of Pompeii*. One of the worst disasters in history occurred when Mount Vesuvius, a volcano in Italy, erupted almost 2,000 years ago. Amazingly, we can still read an eyewitness account of the eruption as it happened (see page 13).

We know that almost everyone in the cities of Pompeii and Herculaneum died horribly but fairly quickly. Few people knew that the ruins were there until 1710, when a well digger accidentally dug into the theater of Herculaneum. Soon everyone who could get to the area tried to find and take away ancient treasures, but their attempts did not last long because the rock that had covered the cities was too hard to dig through.

By 1748 serious excavations had begun, but many of the treasures that were found were looted. Finally, in 1860 a man named Giuseppe Fiorelli was put in charge of the project, and thanks to him, today we can still view some of the most incredible ruins on Earth.

Dorothy Hinshaw Patent likes history, and this book is loaded with great facts. Here are some examples:

- The skeletons of more than 50 gladiators were found in the amphitheater. Two of those gladiators were chained to a wall.

- Two thousand years ago, many people became slaves when pirates raided the ships they were traveling on—and the poor travelers were sold into slavery.

- People ate lying on their left sides, and a popular dessert was honeyed eggs. To make this dish, eggs were beaten with olive oil, cooked, and served with honey and pepper on top.

- One of the bakeries in Pompeii had 81 loaves of bread in its oven when the volcano erupted.

- "One wall painting in Pompeii shows children working hard, cleaning cloth by trampling it in vats. The job must have been unpleasant, for cloth was stiffened with human urine before being put into the vats with cleansing agents" (page 49).

There are some great pictures. Show the one on page 7 of the dog. It includes a sign, "Cave Canem," which means "beware of the dog." Not everything has changed in the last 2,000 years!

More natural disasters can be found in *Nature's Fury: Eyewitness Reports of Natural Disasters* by Carole G. Vogel. This fascinating book tells the stories of real people who have survived earthquakes, tornadoes, hurricanes, blizzards, drought, fire, and floods. A map of the United States shows where all these disasters occurred—if you live near one of them, of course, you must tell about that particular disaster. If not, mention the Good Friday earthquake in Alaska. Eight-year-old Anne Thomas was swept down a mountain while still in her house. The photograph of Anne's neighborhood on page 23 is dramatic. The blizzard of 1888 that hit New York City is also interesting. About 200 people froze to death in the streets. One man made it all the way home but couldn't get in his front door because of a snowdrift higher than his head. His story is on page 77. Vogel's bibliography at the back of the book is impressive and useful—it lists magazine articles, books, and Web sites with more information about all of the disasters she writes about. This book would be a great complement to a lesson on primary sources because Vogel did so much work to locate and speak with these disaster survivors.

The blizzard of 1888 is described in detail in Jim Murphy's *Blizzard: The Storm That Changed America*. Some people called this storm the "Great White Hurricane." Even today, more than 100 years later, we call it the famous blizzard of 1888. And it was some blizzard.

> A blizzard is defined as any storm where snow is accompanied by temperatures of 20 degrees Fahrenheit or lower, plus winds of at least 35 miles per hour. During the Blizzard of 1888, temperatures often went below zero, and winds were clocked at 75–85 miles per hour. (page 25)

The worst of it was along the eastern seaboard. A storm from the west and one from the south collided there and changed the history of America.

The United States was not expecting a blizzard, so no one was prepared for one. It had been a nice, mild winter, and no one had any warning about what was about to happen. The National Weather Service, which didn't exist yet, got its start largely due to that blizzard. At a New York City weather station, the anemometer, a machine that measures wind velocity, froze stiff, and a brave young sergeant risked his life to fix it.

In New York City, snow, unfortunately, was not the only thing that was blowing around. There were no antilitter laws, so garbage of all sorts was flying around and hitting people.

Trains were stopped or thrown off their tracks. Passengers froze to death trying to walk to safety. Horses, trying to make it through frozen streets piled high with snow, were whipped to death. Poor families were not only cold but also starving. The city had no real snow cleanup department, and what administrators did was sometimes almost stupid. For example, the superintendent of streets and roads instructed workers to clean the streets in one area—but they left an 11-foot-high wall of snow around the streets with no entrances! The streets might be clean, but no one could get to them!

Jim Murphy tells amazing stories of kids and grownups who lived with, fought with, and sometimes died in the blizzard.

Show the picture on page 60 of the tangled wires in the Wall Street area. Laws required all wires to be underground, but no one followed the laws.

Mystery on Everest: A Photobiography of George Mallory by Audrey Salkeld tells about George Mallory's quest for glory and the disastrous results. He is the person who made the famous response to a question about Mount Everest: Why do you want to climb it? "Because it's there" (page 7). Mallory died climbing Mount Everest, and we still don't know whether he made it to the top. He made his attempt in 1924, and his frozen body, in perfect condition on the mountain where he died, was not discovered for almost 75 years.

When Mallory was a boy at a private school in England, one of his teachers invited him to spend his summer vacation climbing in the Alps. He was hooked. From that time on, he loved climbing mountains. He had a lot of adventures—and some close calls—and even fought in World War I, where he had an easier time of it than many.

Mallory had trained himself to endure discomfort and sometimes slept without blankets to get used to being cold. The biggest challenge to any mountain climber anywhere was Mount Everest, the highest mountain in the world. It was the one all climbers wanted to conquer. Surveyors had known since the mid-1800s that Everest was the tallest mountain in the world, but no Europeans or Americans had ever climbed it. Mallory made his first try three years before the attempt that killed him.

Read about his adventures and about the most important clue as to whether he made it to the top: his missing camera. Someday someone will find it! Show your audience the picture of the climbers on page 38. Climbers today would consider the clothes they were wearing then impossible for scaling a mountain.

Mount Everest has challenged many climbers, and you can read about some more of them in *The Top of the World: Climbing Mount Everest* by Steve Jenkins. Many people have tried to climb this mountain, and people who come from other places usually hire Tibetan people called Sherpas to help them. The Sherpas know the mountains and are accustomed to working in them. The first successful international attempt to climb Everest took place in 1953, when Edmund Hillary and Sherpa Tenzing Norgay reached the top.

This book is full of fascinating information. Anyone who wants to climb Everest has to do it very carefully and quite slowly, partly to get used to the lack of oxygen and partly because of the extreme cold. Just to start, climbers must hike 100 miles. And then they must wait, for the mountain can be climbed at only a few times during the year—in the spring and in late summer. At other times, the weather is too dangerous. Climbers have been blown right off the mountain by powerful winds. So people wait in camps for their turn to try to climb to the summit.

Another danger to mountain climbers is avalanches. More people are killed by avalanches than by anything else. And the cold is so severe that climbers can get frost-bitten fingers and toes, which then have to be amputated.

There have been only 1,057 successful attempts to reach the top of Mount Everest, and 161 climbers have died on the mountain. This book, with its beautiful illustrations, will make you want to know more about it. Most of the illustrations are great to show.

QUESTS

Triumph on Everest: A Photobiography of Sir Edmund Hillary by Broughton Coburn is one book about Mount Everest that doesn't belong in the "Disasters" section. Sir Hillary is the first person who successfully reached the peak of the mountain. Tenzing Norgay, a Sherpa who lived in Nepal, accompanied him. One of the biggest challenges the team faced was crossing the Khumbu icefall, with its crevasses, ice pinnacles, avalanches, and chunks of ice bigger than a house. Show the photograph on pages 22 and 23 of this landscape. Also show the photo of Norgay standing at the top of the mountain (page 32). Hillary didn't take any pictures of himself at the peak, saying, "Tenzing is no photographer, and Everest was no place to begin teaching him."

Perhaps the most amazing aspect of Hillary's life is his later devotion to helping the Sherpas by building schools and hospitals and participating in environmental programs to protect their land. Another interesting fact is that Hillary's son Peter also reached the peak of Mount Everest. This book is both an exciting adventure and the inspirational story of a man dedicated to service.

She sells seashells by the seashore.
The shells she sells are seashells I'm sure.
So, if she sells seashells by the seashore,
I'm sure the shells are seashore shells.

Do you know this famous tongue twister? Do you know that it is about a real person? Her name was Mary Anning, and you can read about her quest in Laurence Anholt's *Stone Girl, Bone Girl: The Story of Mary Anning*. Mary, a little girl who loved fossils, lived near the cliffs of Lyme Regis in England. Because the cliffs were made of clay, they were dangerous and crumbly, and Mary's father taught her to look for stones with "pictures" of animals in them. Mary became fascinated by these relics and started collecting them. She didn't even know what they were called until some women saw her collection and told her they were fossils.

When Anning's father died, she and her mother became very poor. Anning thought of selling her fossils, and she kept looking for more. With the help of a little dog, she discovered the biggest fossil ever found up to that time. Read the book to find out what it was and what she did with it. If you want to give away the plot, show the picture near the end of the book of the men carrying the fossil home.

Many scientists have searched for information about dinosaurs. Brian Floca tells about a groundbreaking journey in his book *Dinosaurs at the Ends of the Earth: The Story of the Central Asiatic Expeditions*. In 1922 three American men journeyed into the Gobi Desert in Mongolia searching for fossils. They and their staff crossed the desert in about 20 automobiles. This was an unusual trek, for there were no roads in the desert. Every few weeks a camel caravan would bring them new supplies.

These scientists were successful beyond their wildest dreams. Not only did they uncover dinosaur fossils—more than they had equipment to handle—but they also found a fossilized dinosaur egg, the first proof ever that dinosaurs were hatched, not born.

If you like dinosaurs and paleontology, this is a great book to read. Show your audience the picture of the camel caravan arriving with supplies.

Many fossil hunters have exciting lives, as you will discover when you read *Dragon Bones and Dinosaur Eggs: A Photobiography of Explorer Roy Chapman Andrews* by Ann Bausum. Some people believe that Andrews was the real-life model for Indiana Jones, and it is true that he hated snakes. When you read the quote from him on the front page of the book, you'll get an idea of what his searches for dinosaurs might have been like:

> In the [first] fifteen years [of fieldwork] I can remember just ten times when I had really narrow escapes from death. Two were from drowning in typhoons, one was when our boat was charged by a wounded whale; once my wife and I were nearly eaten by wild dogs, and once we were in great danger from fanatical lama priests; two were close calls when I fell over cliffs, once I was nearly caught by a huge python, and twice I might have been killed by bandits.

This is an exciting book about a man who led a very exciting life and found outstanding dinosaur fossils in the middle of the Gobi Desert. He inspired many other future dinosaur hunters to follow their dreams just as he had done. He started out working as a janitor at the American Museum of Natural History and ended up as its director.

Read his story and show the photo of the cars driving through China and Mongolia on pages 28 and 29.

Cathy Forster, another fossil hunter, has spent her life loving and studying dinosaurs. Find out more about her career in Nic Bishop's *Digging for Bird-Dinosaurs: An Expedition to Madagascar*.

Figure 1.2. *Digging for Bird-Dinosaurs: An Expedition to Madagascar* by Nic Bishop.

Forster is a paleontologist at the State University of New York at Stony Brook. One of the things she is most interested in is the relationship between birds and dinosaurs. Many people think that birds are descended from dinosaurs and that at least some of the dinosaurs were covered with feathers.

This is the story of an expedition Forster made to Madagascar, an island off the coast of East Africa, where she looked for dinosaur fossils—especially bird dinosaur fossils. These are hard to find because they are small and break easily.

Digging up dinosaurs isn't nearly as much fun as it sounds. You have to work in the hot sun all day and sleep in tents at night, and you seldom have baths or interesting food. In fact, almost every evening, Forster has rice and beans for dinner.

Forster made some wonderful discoveries to ship back to her university to be worked on more extensively. Even the way the fossils are shipped without being damaged is interesting. It may take years just to clean all the fossils.

A fascinating book with amazing photographs, this is one you can recommend to any child with an interest in archaeology. Show the photo on page 6 of Forster with the skeleton and ask the kids to guess what kind of skeleton it is (the answer: a penguin).

Do you have students who like adventure? They might not know it, but archaeology could be the career for them. Read about another inquisitive person in Giovanni Caselli's *In Search of Troy: One Man's Quest for Homer's Fabled City*. If you have ever heard of Troy and the Trojan War, you probably know this is a great story. It's the subject of one of the most famous poems ever, the *Iliad* by an ancient Greek poet named Homer. It tells the story of Helen, the most beautiful woman in the world, who ran off or was kidnapped by Paris, a man from the city of Troy. This incident started a terrible war, and many people have heard of the famous Greek warrior Achilles. Many people also know the story of the Trojan horse, which was a huge wooden horse in which soldiers were hiding. The Trojans wheeled the horse into their city, and this was the beginning of the end. That night the soldiers climbed out of the horse and destroyed the city of Troy.

For more than 2,000 years, people have been fascinated by this story. More than 160 years ago, a German boy named Heinrich Schliemann read the story and vowed that he would someday find the city of Troy. Nobody knew where it was anymore, but he was sure he could find it. And he did!

This book tells about Schliemann's quest and shows us many pictures of the search, the archaeological dig, and the treasures he found there. It also tells us that, for almost 50 years after World War II, the treasure was lost. Show the picture of the Trojan horse on page 34.

Many kinds of scientists go on quests. In Donna M. Jackson's *The Wildlife Detectives: How Forensic Scientists Fight Crimes Against Nature*, you will read about a quest to solve a mystery and capture a criminal. Almost everyone has heard of endangered species. They are animals whose numbers are greatly reduced over what they used to be and are in danger of becoming extinct. Often the reason for their decline is that hunters kill them for their body parts.

Jackson tells us that a whale tooth can be sold for $2,000. A tiger skin may fetch $10,000, and an impressive set of elk antlers can bring about $8,000. This book follows the story of Charger, an elk that was killed in Yellowstone Park.

People loved to take pictures of Charger, and it seemed that he liked to show off for them. On the day he was killed, many people had photographed him. (Show your audience the picture of him on page 11, taken the day before he was killed.) The next morning, one of the photographers found his body—with the antlers removed.

Many scientists worked together to find the person who had killed Charger. How they did so and how the criminal was punished makes for interesting reading. Jackson also includes good information about animal poaching around the world.

Pat and Linda Cummings introduce many inspiring adventurers in *Talking with Adventurers: Conversations with Christina M. Allen, Robert Ballard, Michael L. Blakey, Ann Bowles, David Doubilet, Jane Goodall, Dereck & Beverly Joubert, Michael Novacek, Johan Reinhard, Rick C. West, and Juris Zarins*. When a person decides to make a career of scientific investigation, one place they might work is indoors in a laboratory. But that isn't where the people in this book wanted to work. These people wanted to work outdoors, to have adventures, to find out unknown things, to discover. And they did.

You have probably heard of some of these adventurers. Robert Ballard, who found the *Titanic*, is probably the most famous, but he says that finding the *Titanic* is not the achievement he is the proudest of. Instead, he is prouder of discovering hydrothermal vents and also ancient Roman trading ships. Dr. Michael L. Blakey is proudest of his research on an African burial ground in New York City. He discovered that conditions for slaves 200 years ago were so bad that nearly half of the slave children died by the age of 12.

Each adventurer has a great story to share, and the questions the interviewers ask them are the ones we want the answers to. The color pictures are also great fun—see the one on page 81 of Rick C. West eating a cooked tarantula. Would you ever want to be that adventurous?

Another book about daring people is Margo McLoone's *Women Explorers of the World: Isabella Bird Bishop, Florence Dixie, Nellie Bly, Gertrude Bell, Margaret Bourke-White*. Have you ever heard of Nellie Bly? She is probably the most famous woman mentioned here, and she really had an adventure. Nellie was born the thirteenth of 15 children. She didn't have much money, but she was given a wonderful opportunity when she wrote a letter to the editor of the *Pittsburgh Dispatch*. He had said women should stay in the home, and she disagreed. The editor liked her letter so well that he hired her to be a reporter. Nellie Bly was not her real name, but she soon became famous, and in 1889 she went on a trip around the world. There was a book out called *Around the World in Eighty Days*, and the publisher of Bly's paper wanted to see whether a reporter could travel around the world in fewer days than that. Remember, there were no airplanes at that time. Do you think she was able to do it?

Bly is one of five adventurous women described in the book. Read about Isabella Bishop, who traveled across the Himalaya Mountains riding a yak!

Show your audience the photo of Nellie Bly on page 22. That bag in her hand is all the luggage she carried on her trip.

Judith Heide Gilliland tells the story of another adventurous woman in *Steamboat: The Story of Captain Blanche Leathers*. Blanche Douglas grew up on the Mississippi River and loved it. She loved watching the water hiding its secrets, and she enjoyed watching the huge, beautiful steamboats come to her hometown to be loaded with cargo to take downriver to New Orleans.

When Blanche was 21, she met a handsome young steamboat captain named Bowling Leathers. She fell in love immediately and was thrilled that, when she married him, she would actually be living on one of those wonderful riverboats.

But that was not enough for Blanche. She wanted to learn how to navigate the river and get a steamboat captain's license of her own. This book tells how she did it—the first woman ever to do such a thing.

Fun pictures will delight your audience. Show the one of the "graveyard" in the river early in the book.

Many people throughout history have gone on treasure hunts. Peter Lourie's *Lost Treasure of the Inca* tells of a treasure—maybe the greatest one of all time—that still hasn't been found. For more than 400 years it has been missing—hidden somewhere in Ecuador in the Llanganatis Mountains. There are directions as to where to look for it, but no one has been able to interpret those directions and follow them to the treasure—although some people claim that they have. But no one has ever shown anyone else any of the gold, at least not so far. This is what happened.

In the early 1500s the Inca Empire in South America was huge, with more than 12 million people. The Incas believed that everything they owned belonged to their king, the Sun King, who was also a god. The king was named Atahualpa, and in 1532 he had visitors. Those visitors were a Spaniard called Francisco Pizarro and his men, who planned to conquer the Incas and steal their land and gold for Spain. Atahualpa greeted them in peace, but Pizarro captured him, and the Spaniards killed thousands of the Incas. Imprisoned, Atahualpa realized how much the Spaniards loved gold, so he offered to give them big rooms full of it if they would let him go. They agreed. The Incas brought much gold to Pizarro, but the Spaniards melted it down and sent it back to Spain—and killed Atahualpa anyway.

The Spaniards did not know that the biggest gold shipment of all—at least 750 tons—was on its way, being delivered by the king's most trusted general. This general was near the Llanganatis Mountains, where he had grown up, and when he learned about the Spaniards' treachery, he took the treasure into the mountains and hid it. People have been looking for it ever since.

Peter Lourie, an American, tells this story in a fascinating way—and also tells us about his adventures when he went to find the treasure for himself. If you like historical mysteries—and if you think you might be good at solving them—this book is for you. Directions for finding the treasure are included.

Speaking of treasure, *How to Find Lost Treasure in All Fifty States and Canada Too!* by Joan Holub is sure to interest young people who like a good adventure.

Everyone has heard about treasure hunters, but most of us do not know about any lost treasure that might be fairly close to where we live. This book gives you a great place to start. Holub decided to research lost treasure in the United States and Canada and to write a few pages about one well-known story in each state and province. Some of these stories are so famous that a lot of people have heard of them: the Lost Dutchman mine in Arizona, Captain Kidd's buried treasure in Connecticut, Jean Lafitte's pirate booty in Louisiana, and D. B. Cooper's treasure in Washington. But others may surprise you. In Minnesota, for instance, the criminal "Ma" Barker may have hidden a fortune in bank robbery and kidnapping loot. The book provides rough maps and a ton of ideas. Get started by reading about treasure in your own state, and then take a look at others to see whether anything piques your interest. Somebody has to find it someday, right? It might be you!

Marc Aronson's *Sir Walter Ralegh and the Quest for El Dorado* describes still another treasure seeker. In the United States, most often his name is spelled "Raleigh," but Aronson tells us that "Ralegh" is how he himself spelled his name in his adult life.

Figure 1.3. *Sir Walter Ralegh and the Quest for El Dorado* **by Marc Aronson.**

Almost everyone who has ever heard of Sir Walter Ralegh knows at least two things about him: He had something to do with tobacco, and his name is associated with it, and he once laid his cloak over a mud puddle so that Queen Elizabeth I would not get her feet wet.

The first piece of information is true—Sir Walter was involved in growing and popularizing tobacco. The second may be true. And may not be. It is a popular story, but we are not sure it really happened. But if you have never heard of this man or know only these two things about him, you are missing some interesting information.

Sir Walter Ralegh was born relatively poor and definitely unimportant. But he was an ambitious and intelligent man, and 400 years later he is still famous for what he accomplished. As a British citizen, he was one of the major influences in making England a world power. When he was a child, no map of England even included roads. By the time he died, much of the world had been mapped, and his interest in and knowledge of the world helped that to happen.

One way that he was able to gain power and influence was by flirting with the queen. She loved to have men around her who adored her, or at least pretended to, and he was very good at it—until he fathered a child by a lady-in-waiting and the queen threw them both into jail. Ralegh was very good at a lot of things, but he was also extremely talented at getting himself into trouble, and he spent a good portion of his life in jail. In fact, he died by being beheaded for treason.

Ralegh was a fascinating man, and you can spend a few great hours getting to know him.

Modern people also have quests, not always for money, but for the opportunity to live in peace and freedom. We see refugees on television, but most of us haven't experienced this struggle firsthand. *One Boy from Kosovo* by Trish Marx is the story of a refugee, a 12-year-old Albanian boy named Edi, who had to flee his home with his brother, sister, and parents because the family was terrified that Serbians would attack them and destroy their home and maybe even kill them. So they got on a bus that took them away from the fighting and ended up living in a tent city where about 30,000 people lived.

The refugees had to stand in line for food and water several times a day. They slept on cots and had almost no clothing. They had no television or movies.

How would you feel if you had to live in a place like that? Read this excellent book to learn what it's like. Show the picture of the tent city on page 11.

Leaving Vietnam: The Journey of Tuan Ngo, a Boat Boy by Sarah S. Kilborne is a book about refugees for young elementary school students.

Do you know what a boat person is? In the 1970s and the 1980s Americans heard a lot about the boat people, who were willing to do almost anything to escape from the Viet Cong—who were ruling Vietnam—and especially to go to America. This is the true story of one of those people, a boy who escaped with his father. They knew that if they were captured, they would be sent to prison camp, a place where the father had already spent five years eating nothing but rotten potatoes. They left in the middle of the night with 31 other people—only to discover that life on the boat was awful. People were sick and hungry and thirsty, and their tiny, crowded boat was even attacked by pirates, who took all of their valuables. They finally had to sink their own boat in hopes of being saved.

How Tuan Ngo finally got to America—but not without an awful lot of hassle— makes for an exciting story.

Show your audience the picture of Tuan Ngo on page 9.

EXPLORERS OF THE SEAS

Throughout history, sea journeys have seemed like a glamorous life. However, the reality wasn't quite so glamorous, as Jim Murphy reveals in *Gone A-Whaling: The Lure of the Sea and the Hunt for the Great Whale.* Gone a-whaling! It sounds so exciting. Maybe it was something like "Join the Navy and see the world." You could take a job on a whaling ship and travel everywhere, looking for whales and harpooning them when you found them—and come home to impress everyone with all your newfound knowledge and wealth.

That is what boys then thought, and what many of us today still think. But whaling was a hard, boring, filthy, lonely, miserable business, and, as often as not, the poor boys who sailed on whaling ships made little or no money. They ate rotten food, drank bad water, and were not always let off the ship when it landed in a foreign place. They were crowded into tiny spaces with no privacy and very little to do. Each person had so little space that reading matter was passed around to anyone who wanted it, so it quickly became tattered. Fights, which started mainly because everyone was bored, were frequent. Sometimes the sailors were gone from home for three or more years! Most of the boys who had once been eager to go whaling went on only one trip and were ecstatically happy to spend the rest of their lives at home.

Some women, almost always the wives of the whaling ship captains, went whaling, too.

This book describes different types of whales, including "right" whales (so called because they were at first easy to find and catch), blue whales, and sperm whales, which were worth the most money. The process of finding a whale to kill (which took longer and longer as whale hunts made some of the whales almost extinct), the filthy process of cutting it apart, and the fact that some whales fought back, with horrifying results, are all described in detail.

Find out what happened to the crew of the *Essex*, which was destroyed when the whale it was hunting rammed the ship and sank it. (Clue: Think Donner party.)

For a modern view of sea exploration, guide students toward George Sullivan's *To the Bottom of the Sea: The Exploration of Exotic Life, the* Titanic, *and Other Secrets of the Oceans*. "The reality is we know more about Mars than we do about the oceans" (page 15). What a statement! And the person who said it is Sylvia Earle, former chief scientist at the National Oceanographic and Atmospheric Administration. The bottom of the sea is the most unexplored space on planet Earth. But we are finally making a good start at finding out what is there.

The world's first research submarine, called a *bathysphere*, was not made until the 1930s. Before people could really explore the ocean floor, they had to be able to remain underneath the surface for long enough to take a good look around. On their own, human beings cannot dive much more than 30 or 40 feet without severe pain, and very few people can hold their breath for more than a minute or so. The bathysphere was thus a wonderful invention and a great start at finding out what was on the ocean bottom. For many years, scientists believed that no life could survive in such a dark place without any nutrients. They were wrong.

By 1960 scientists had established a record for the deepest dive ever, 6.8 miles down. This record will probably never be broken, for experts know of no deeper spot in the ocean than the one in which the dive took place. And now, thanks to great advances in submarine design and the invention of robot TV cameras and underwater sonar sleds, we are quickly learning much more about the ocean. A sonar sled can produce "detailed images of as much as an acre of the seafloor at a time, a vast improvement over what was previously possible" (page 20). When scientists are searching an area for something, they call it "mowing the lawn"!

And what do they search for? Shipwrecks, among other things. Read about the wreck of the passenger ship *Central America* that happened in 1857. Four hundred twenty-five people died, and the ship was loaded with gold. And Roman ships sank almost 2,000 years ago. And the *Titanic*! Read about "Godzilla," the biggest black smoker in the world. What is a black smoker? It is a hot vent, deep in the ocean. This fascinating book will make you want to know more.

Have you ever wanted to swim with dolphins? Dr. Kathleen Dudzinski, who does it all the time, writes about it in *Meeting Dolphins: My Adventures in the Sea*. Dudzinski is a marine biologist with a passion for dolphins. If you have seen the IMAX movie about dolphins, you have seen her work. She calls dolphins the "ultimate social animals" because they almost always swim in pairs or groups and form friendships that can last a lifetime. Bottlenose dolphins can live for 50 years while Orcas can live to about 80 years. Dolphins are amazing animals, and Dudzinski studies their behavior. She tries to find out whether they have a language and how they communicate with each other. Show the photograph of Dudzinski on page 27 and of the dolphin on pages 54 and 55. Is the dolphin being friendly or is it threatening the photographer?

More underwater adventure can be found in Sylvia A. Earle's *Dive! My Adventures in the Deep Frontier*. Earle fell in love with oceans when she was a little girl spending summer vacations at the New Jersey seashore. When she was 12, her family moved to Florida, where their house was on the Gulf of Mexico. Earle sometimes saw dolphins there.

She longed to see where they and other sea animals lived—under the ocean. She began to do that when she learned to snorkel and then scuba dive, but she wanted to go deeper. All of her life she has wanted to go deeper—and she keeps making her wish come true.

There is a major problem with going deep—"The amount of time you can spend without decompression [which allows the nitrogen in your system to dissipate] decreases the deeper you go. It is possible to spend about an hour 50 feet down without taking time to decompress. At 100 feet it is possible to stay less than half an hour; at 150 feet you have about 10 minutes. Even though the time is short, it is longer than what is possible just holding your breath" (page 31).

But Earle thinks it is well worth the effort to spend time seeing where sea creatures live—and seeing creatures and plants that people never knew exist. She has made astounding discoveries and found life where no one thought that plants or animals could possibly live. And she has now devised a way to go down more than 1,200 feet.

This book is filled with incredible pictures of the ocean and the creatures that live there. There is still much to explore there and much to be discovered. Show the picture of the coral on page 56 or the jellyfish on page 48.

As the previous books prove, men are not the only ones exploring and doing exciting things. Lots of women have adventures and make discoveries, and *Women Explorers of the Oceans: Ann Davison, Eugenie Clark, Sylvia Earle, Naomi James, Tania Aebi* by Margo McLoone tells us about some of them. Look at the picture of Ann Davison on page 8. Davison was the first woman to cross the Atlantic Ocean in a sailboat, all by herself. It was a grueling trip—she could barely walk by the end of it—but she made it.

Sylvia Earle loved the oceans so much that she became a marine biologist. In 1970 she became the leader of Tektite II, an underwater experiment in which five women scientists lived under the sea for two weeks.

It's fun to read about women who have done daring things. Show your audience the photos of Earle and Davison.

Those who serve in the military have sea adventures of a very different kind. For students interested in military vehicles and forces, Capstone Press is a good source of high-interest books. The "Serving Your Country" series has several winning titles. Michael Green's *Air Rescue Teams* tells about an adventurous career on the oceans.

Throughout history, people have gotten into trouble and needed to be rescued. When the *Titanic* sank, no one was close enough initially to do much rescuing. The passengers who scrambled into lifeboats had to wait until another ship arrived several hours later.

In the 1920s the United States Coast Guard began to perform air rescue missions, using airplanes to search for and rescue passengers of wrecked or sunken ships and people whose airplanes had crashed into the ocean. (Think of John F. Kennedy Jr.) In World War II, these teams became especially important, for German submarines sank many ships of the United States and its allies, and much rescue work was needed. Coast Guard air rescue teams rescued more than 1,000 people during World War II.

The United States Air Force also has air rescue teams called pararescue teams, or "PJs." These teams also started during World War II. No women are allowed to become PJs, and the men who are chosen have to go through a tough training program, during which they spend 10 days in the mountains with only basic survival gear. They have to kill and eat small animals. Show the picture of the rescue on page 5.

A second Michael Green book, *U.S. Army Special Operations*, tells about a force that is of great interest to many young readers. To be in the U.S. Army Special Operations Forces (SOF), you have to be special—not only fit, but skilled and intelligent and very well trained. You might know these forces by another name: the Green Berets.

Although the U.S. Army has used specialized forces since its beginning during the American Revolution, the official special forces did not begin until World War II.

Members of the SOF usually travel by helicopter, but they need special equipment to perform their duties. They all need to be able to swim while wearing their clothes and carrying all of their gear. They go through extensive special survival training.

A lot of people think it would be a great thing to be a Green Beret. Do you think it would be fun? Show the audience the picture on page 7.

Another Capstone Press book called *U.S. Navy Special Forces: SEAL Teams* by Michael Burgan tells of more adventures at sea.

Figure 1.4. *U.S. Navy Special Forces: SEAL Teams* **by Michael Burgan.**

SEALs are "specially trained members of the U.S. Navy. They perform high-risk missions that regular navy members are not trained to do." The acronym "SEAL" stands for sea, air, and land. SEALs are experts at working in water, but they also have great expertise on land and in the air. They have another area of expertise as well: They keep their mouths shut and don't talk about their missions.

In World War II, America's enemies often placed mines and barricades along beaches. To try to make landings as safe as possible, we realized we needed experts to prepare the way before our main troops went in. The group that was formed to do this eventually became the SEALs.

Every SEAL is a volunteer, but he has to work very hard to make it through training. No women are allowed. About 7 out of every 10 volunteers drop out because the training is so rigorous.

This book has many excellent photographs (show your audience the ones on pages 16 and 22) as well as some Web sites and addresses to which you can write for information.

BIBLIOGRAPHY

Adams, Simon. *Titanic* (Eyewitness Books). DK, 1999. ISBN 078944724X. 60 p. Grades 4–8.

Anholt, Laurence. *Stone Girl, Bone Girl: The Story of Mary Anning.* Illustrated by Sheila Moxley. Orchard Books, 1999. ISBN 0531301486. Unpaged. Grades 2–4.

Armstrong, Jennifer. *Shipwreck at the Bottom of the World: The Extraordinary True Story of Shackleton and the* Endurance. Crown, 1998. ISBN 0517800136 (trade); 0517800144 (lib. bdg.). 134 p. Grades 5–8.

Aronson, Marc. *Sir Walter Ralegh and the Quest for El Dorado.* Clarion Books, 2000. ISBN 039584827X. 222 p. Grades 5–up.

Ballard, Robert D. *Ghost Liners: Exploring the World's Greatest Lost Ships.* Little, Brown, 1998. ISBN 0316080209. 64 p. Grades 4–7.

Bausum, Ann. *Dragon Bones and Dinosaur Eggs: A Photobiography of Explorer Roy Chapman Andrews.* Photographs from the American Museum of Natural History. National Geographic Society, 2000. ISBN 0792271238. 64 p. Grades 4–7.

Bishop, Nic. *Digging for Bird-Dinosaurs: An Expedition to Madagascar.* Houghton Mifflin, 2000. ISBN 0395960568. 48 p. Grades 4–7.

Bramwell, Martyn. *Polar Exploration: Journeys to the Arctic and Antarctic.* Illustrated by Marje Crosby-Fairall and Ann Winterbotham. DK, 1998. ISBN 0-7894-3421-0. 48 p. Grades 4–7.

Burgan, Michael. *U.S. Navy Special Forces: SEAL Teams* (Warfare and Weapons). Capstone Books, 2000. ISBN 0736803408. 48 p. Grades 4–6.

Calabro, Marian. *The Perilous Journey of the Donner Party.* Clarion Books, 1999. ISBN 0395866103. 192 p. Grades 5–8.

Caselli, Giovanni. *In Search of Troy: One Man's Quest for Homer's Fabled City.* Peter Bedrick Books, 1999. ISBN 0872265420. 44 p. Grades 4–7.

Coburn, Broughton. *Triumph on Everest: A Photobiography of Sir Edmund Hillary.* National Geographic Society, 2000. ISBN 0-7922-7114-9. 64 p. Grades 4–8.

Cummings, Pat, and Linda Cummings, Ph.D. *Talking with Adventurers: Conversations with Christina M. Allen, Robert Ballard, Michael L. Blakey, Ann Bowles, David Doubilet, Jane Goodall, Dereck & Beverly Joubert, Michael Novacek, Johan Reinhard, Rick C. West, and Juris Zarins.* National Geographic Society, 1998. 96 p. ISBN 0792270681. Grades 5–8.

Dudzinski, Kathleen. *Meeting Dolphins: My Adventures in the Sea.* National Geographic Society, 2000. ISBN 0-7922-7129-7. 64 p. Grades 4–8.

Earle, Sylvia A. *Dive! My Adventures in the Deep Frontier.* National Geographic Society, 1999. ISBN 0792271440. 64 p. Grades 4–6.

Floca, Brian. *Dinosaurs at the Ends of the Earth: The Story of the Central Asiatic Expeditions*. Dorling Kindersley, 2000. ISBN 0789425394. Unpaged. Grades K–3.

Gilliland, Judith Heide. *Steamboat: The Story of Captain Blanche Leathers*. Illustrated by Holly Meade. DK, 2000. ISBN 0789425858. Unpaged. Grades 1–3.

Green, Michael. *Air Rescue Teams* (Serving Your Country). Consultant: Senior Airman Gary A. Flossman, Ph.D. Capstone Press, 2000. ISBN 0736804706. 48 p. Grades 4–8.

———. *U.S. Army Special Operations* (Serving Your Country). Consultant: Col. R. A. Jones, retired, U.S. Army SOF. Capstone Press, 2000. ISBN 0736804714. 48 p. Grades 4–8.

Halley, Ned. *Disasters*. Kingfisher, 1999. ISBN 0753452219. 64 p. Grades 4–6.

Holub, Joan. *How to Find Lost Treasure in All Fifty States and Canada Too!* Aladdin, 2000. ISBN 0689826435. 182 p. Grades 4–up.

Jackson, Donna M. *The Wildlife Detectives: How Forensic Scientists Fight Crimes Against Nature*. Photographs by Wendy Shattil and Bob Rozinski. Houghton Mifflin, 2000. ISBN 0395869765. 48 p. Grades 3–7.

Jenkins, Steve. *The Top of the World: Climbing Mount Everest*. Houghton Mifflin, 1999. ISBN 0395942187. Unpaged. Grades 3–5.

Kilborne, Sarah S. *Leaving Vietnam: The Journey of Tuan Ngo, a Boat Boy* (Ready-to-Read). Illustrated by Melissa Sweet. Simon & Schuster Books for Young Readers, 1999. ISBN 0689807988. 48 p. Grades 2–3.

Kostyal, K. M. *Trial by Ice: A Photobiography of Sir Ernest Shackleton*. Published by arrangement with the National Geographic Society. Scholastic, 2000. ISBN 0-439-19922-0. 64 p. Grades 4–8.

Leroe, Ellen. *Disaster! Three Real-Life Stories of Survival*. Hyperion Books for Children, 2000. ISBN 078682474-3. 233 p. Grades 5–8.

Lourie, Peter. *Lost Treasure of the Inca*. Boyds Mills Press, 1999. ISBN 1563977435. 48 p. Grades 4–6.

Marx, Trish. *One Boy from Kosovo*. Photographs by Cindy Karp. HarperCollins, 2000. ISBN 0688177328. 24 p. Grades 4–6.

McLoone, Margo. *Women Explorers of the Oceans: Ann Davison, Eugenie Clark, Sylvia Earle, Naomi James, Tania Aebi*. Capstone Press, 2000. ISBN 0736883122. 48 p. Grades 4–6.

———. *Women Explorers of the World: Isabella Bird Bishop, Florence Dixie, Nellie Bly, Gertrude Bell, Margaret Bourke-White*. Capstone Books, 2000. ISBN 0736803130. 48 p. Grades 4–6.

Murphy, Jim. *Blizzard: The Storm That Changed America*. Scholastic, 2000. ISBN 0590673092. 136 p. Grades 4–8.

———. *Gone A-Whaling: The Lure of the Sea and the Hunt for the Great Whale*. Clarion Books, 1998. ISBN 0395698472. 206 p. Grades 5–8.

O'Brien, Patrick. *The* Hindenburg. Henry Holt, 2000. ISBN 080506415X. Unpaged. Grades 2–4.

Patent, Dorothy Hinshaw. *Lost City of Pompeii* (Frozen in Time). Benchmark Books, 2000. ISBN 0761407855. 64 p. Grades 4–8.

———. *Treasures of the Spanish Main* (Frozen in Time). Benchmark Books, 2000. ISBN 0761407863. 64 p. Grades 5–8.

Salkeld, Audrey. *Mystery on Everest: A Photobiography of George Mallory*. Foreword by Conrad Anker. National Geographic Society, 2000. ISBN 0792272226. 64 p. Grades 4–7.

Sullivan, George. *To the Bottom of the Sea: The Exploration of Exotic Life, the Ti-tanic, and Other Secrets of the Oceans*. Twenty-First Century Books, 1999. ISBN 0761303529 (lib. bdg.). 80 p. Grades 4–6.

Vogel, Carole Garbuny. *Nature's Fury: Eyewitness Reports of Natural Disasters*. Scholastic Reference, 2000. ISBN 0-590-11502-2. 121 p. Grades 5–8.

CHAPTER ————2

The Natural World: Amazing Animals and Fascinating Science

AMAZING LAND ANIMALS

All kids seem to love animals, and many of them have dogs and cats. How did we get from wild cats like tigers to the house pets so many people enjoy? Cat lovers will find lots of interesting tidbits in John Zeaman's *Why the Cat Chose Us*. Did you know that humans started befriending cats because they were such good hunters? Cats liked to live near people because where people lived, rats and mice also lived. And cats eat rats and mice. At some point, people started noticing this, and when people settled down to farm instead of moving around constantly, they realized that cats could guard their grain. It was a win-win situation. The cats guarded the people's food and got their fill of rodents. In 1938, in England, a five-month-old cat named Peter killed 400 rats in four weeks!

But scientists think that cats became pets only about 5,000 years ago, not very long ago in the life of human beings. Egyptians regarded cats as sacred beings and were probably the first to make pets of them. When they died, the Egyptians even mummified them. They did not want anyone else to have cats and managed to keep it that way for a long time. But now people almost everywhere have cats.

The author tells us a lot of great information. Have you ever heard that it is bad luck to have a black cat cross your path? Most of the negative superstitions about cats started in the Middle Ages, when cats became associated with pagan religions and especially with witches. Many people started to hate cats. This turned out not to be a good thing, for when bubonic plague—a terrible disease carried by the fleas on rats—broke out, there were very few cats around to kill the rats.

Read Zeaman's book to find out more about one of our favorite animals. The book is loaded with pictures, and the frontispiece is delightful to show.

Why Do Cats Meow? by Joan Holub is another great choice for cat lovers. Guess what the most popular pet in the United States is? The cat (dogs are second). This book is filled with lots of fun facts about cats. Do you have one? Do you know how much it weighs? Most grown cats weigh between 6 and 18 pounds (although one cat is on record as having weighed 47 pounds). You can weigh yours by holding it while you step on a scale. Then put the cat down and step on the scale again. Subtract your weight now from your weight when you were holding the cat. What is left is what your cat weighs.

Do you know that a mother cat can have more than 20 kittens a year? One cat had 400 kittens in her lifetime.

Cats have whiskers, and these help it figure out whether its body will fit in a place. They also help cats find their way in the dark. Cats sleep about 16 hours a day. Take a look at this interesting book and show the photo on page 17 of the cat hissing.

Calico's Cousins: Cats from Around the World by Phyllis Limbacher Tildes is crammed with lovely illustrations of many breeds of cats. Cat lovers will be enraptured. Manx cats have no tails. Norwegian Forest cats love cold, wet weather. The British Shorthair is descended from cats brought by the Romans to Britain 2,000 years ago. An especially fine picture to show is that of the Turkish Van and the Turkish Angora, both of which enjoy playing in water. But almost any picture you choose will make kids want to read this book.

Although dogs are the second most popular pet in the United States, you will have many dog lovers in your audiences. *How the Wolf Became the Dog* by John Zeaman is a good choice for them. Human beings did not always have dogs to love, and this book tells us how we managed to turn wild wolves into tame dogs.

Scientists believe that human beings first had dogs as pets at least 25,000 years ago. They know that ancient people ate wolves and used their fur for warm clothing. Their theory is that, at some time, people killed a wolf and found a cub—which they took home and raised. They discovered several good things about those cubs, and many of the good characteristics were because they were wolves.

First, wolves live in packs. They depend on each other. When a wolf cub was raised by human beings, it learned to depend on them. Most wolf packs have a leader, and the others obey that leader. Does that remind you of dogs?

Some dogs don't look at all like wolves. The book explains the reason for this, too. People wanted animals that would behave and look certain ways, and to get such animals, they had to breed them. Zeaman provides great information on how people did this.

Kids who have or like dogs will want to try this book. Show just about any photograph, but the one on page 45 is accompanied by some interesting information.

Joan Holub answers a good question in her book, *Why Do Dogs Bark?* Well, they bark because they want to protect their owners. They like to guard your house and yard, and they want to tell you about any strangers in the area. Some of them may even bark just to say hello when you come home.

There is fun, easy-to-read information about dogs in this book. Do you know that when a dog howls, it has usually been alone too long and is looking for its owner? Other dogs might hear the howling and howl back to say hello—or dogs may think music is howling and howl back at it.

Why do dogs bury bones? How well do dogs see? Can they hear better than you do? A dog's sense of smell is more than 100 times more sensitive than a human being's, which is one reason dogs like to sniff you. They can smell you a lot better than they can see you.

When two dogs meet, they decide which one of them is "top dog." Their tails may stick straight out. But when one dog's tail is high up and the other's tail is down, the high-tail dog is the boss. Show the picture on page 33 of a high-tail dog.

Capstone Press has a nice series of high-interest books on individual dog breeds. Remember the Taco Bell dog? Charlotte Wilcox, author of *The Chihuahua*, tells us that Chihuahuas are the smallest dogs in the world. Although there are many theories about their origin, most people think they are native to Mexico, where you can see thousand-year-old stone carvings of dogs that look very similar to modern-day Chihuahuas. They make very good pets, partly because they are so small but also because they do not make big messes. They easily get cold and shiver, so many owners make little sweaters or coats for them.

Look at the great photos in this book—any one of them will really grab kids, especially the cover and the one on page 16.

Charlotte Wilcox also wrote *The Weimaraner*. Weimaraners are known as "Gray Ghosts" because of their gray hair and eyes. They are sleek and slender hunting dogs, and because they have a great sense of smell, some of them are used for detecting drugs.

Figure 2.1. *The Weimaraner* by Charlotte Wilcox.

The story of how Weimaraners came to the United States is fascinating. For years, there was a Weimaraner club in Germany, and only club members could own Weimaraners. An American breeder wanted to breed them in the United States, but the club would sell him only neutered dogs that could not breed. Finally, as World War II was about to break out in Germany, the club sold four unneutered dogs to the American breeder so that he could breed them. They did this because they were afraid that their kennels might be destroyed in the war.

If you have any of William Wegman's books of Weimaraners dressed as people, you'll definitely want to pair them with this title. Great photos entice readers. Show them the one on page 27.

You won't believe what you don't know about wolves until you read *Growing Up Wild: Wolves* by Sandra Markle. Wolves live in a very structured society, and when pups are born, their mothers take good care of them. When their mother is busy hunting, other members of the pack act as baby-sitters.

Newborn wolves are blind and deaf and have no teeth. They have to stay very close to their mother's body for about three weeks. Their mother feeds them milk and, as they get older, partially chewed food that she brings back to them. She also teaches them how to survive in the world. And they need to learn well because only about half of all wolf pups survive past their first year.

Just like any other kind of puppy, wolf pups like to play. They also need to learn to hunt. Because they get so tired from running around, they have to take frequent naps. Show your audience the glorious photos in this book, especially the one of the pup sleeping on page 21 and the mother and her pups on page 11.

For a look at a close relative of the wolf, try Stephen R. Swinburne's *Coyote: North America's Dog*. Exactly how do you pronounce that word "coyote"? Some people say kigh-oh-tee with three syllables, and others say kigh-ote with two. It turns out that both ways are correct.

These beautiful animals are native to North America. If you live in the United States, coyotes are probably closer to you than you might think. Biologists believe that about 5,000 coyotes live in crowded Los Angeles! Coyotes adapt very easily to different environments, and they eat almost anything. They are wonderfully good at catching mice, but they also love many fruits and vegetables—and garbage. Their average weight is about 40 pounds. Wolves can weigh about three times as much as coyotes, but they look the same. Coyotes live for five to seven years and they mate for life, or until one of the pair dies.

This book is filled with great color photos of coyotes. Show your audience the cover and the picture on page 24 of coyotes howling.

To learn more about a wild type of cat, read *Lynx* by Jalma Barrett. Lynx live mostly in Canada, but a few live in the forests in parts of the United States. They like to hide and to live alone, so we do not know as much about them as we do about other wildcats.

An average lynx weighs about 84 pounds—seven or eight times as much as an average house cat. You can tell a lynx from other wildcats because it has long tufts under its chin called muttonchops, and its tail has a black tip. Above all, it has huge paws. Its paws are so huge that a lynx can walk on top of the snow without sinking, almost like it is wearing snowshoes. But just like your cat at home, a lynx purrs when it is happy.

Lynx like to live alone and be alone. A male may let its mate and cubs share its territory, but otherwise it wants every other lynx to stay away. This book is loaded with great photos about this unusual animal. Show your audience the photo of the lynx's huge paws on page 8 and of the cubs on page 16.

Bears are beautiful animals, and almost everyone loves them. *Growl! A Book About Bears* (Hello Reader! Level 3) by Melvin Berger has some great information and wonderful photos of bears.

Did you know that a bear is hungry almost all of the time? Big bears, such as grizzlies, may need as much as 35 pounds of food every day. That's a lot. And bears can smell dead animals—animals they could eat—up to 12 miles away. Their big noses, called snouts, are very good at smelling. They can also smell human beings about one mile away.

They sleep during the winter, but we are no longer sure that they hibernate the way some other animals do. The mothers take very good care of their babies, called cubs. Usually two are born at a time, and they are very tiny, only about a pound each. Their mother has to teach them how to do almost everything. Take a look at this easy-to-read book about a favorite animal. Show the picture of the cubs and their mother up in a tree.

Meerkats by Robyn Weaver describes an animal that is not related to the cat. As a matter of fact, meerkats belong to the mongoose family. Some of you may have heard of the famous mongoose Rikki-Tikki-Tavi, but the most famous meerkat was in the movie *The Lion King*. Do you remember his name? The meerkat in the picture on page 10 is guarding his burrow and watching over the young ones. Probably the neatest picture is on page 18, which shows a meerkat group trying to escape from a predator.

You will learn a lot about rabbits in *Rabbits, Rabbits and More Rabbits!* by Gail Gibbons. Here's an amazing fact: Rabbits have looked pretty much the same for about 65 million years. Wild rabbits live on every continent except Antarctica, and all tame rabbits are descendants of European common rabbits. The smallest full-grown rabbit weighs only about 2 pounds, but the largest may weigh as much as 24 pounds. A male rabbit is called a buck, and a female rabbit is called a doe.

The author tells us how to take good care of pet rabbits and also that we should never ever try to make a pet out of a wild rabbit.

"Most of the time the short fluffy tail of a rabbit has a splash of white on it. When a rabbit senses danger, it will flash the white of its tail as a warning to other rabbits." Show your audience the picture of the rabbit flashing its white tail or the two-page spread showing the difference between rabbits and hares, which are their cousins.

Gail Gibbons tells us a lot about pigs in her colorful book titled *Pigs*. Right away, she lets us know that pigs are not dirty and smelly. Scientists believe that people started taming pigs about 8,000 years ago. They raised them to eat and used their hides to make things. All pigs are descended from wild boars, but today there are about 300 different kinds of pigs. Gibbons shows us pictures of several of those kinds.

Some scientists believe that pigs are smarter than dogs. They are definitely the smartest farm animals and can be trained to do things like retrieve and roll over. When they get hot, they like to roll around in water to moisten their skin so they do not get sick. If nothing else is available, they will wallow in mud but would much rather roll around in clean water. You might be surprised at all of the things you don't know about pigs. Show the picture of the different breeds on the double-page spread.

Note: If I were booktalking this book, I would definitely include the information that my father raised pigs at one time. They were Poland China pigs, which are pictured in the double-page spread just mentioned. One of them weighed 1,350 pounds and was called the "Prince of the West." His picture was in many newspapers. Always personalize your booktalk if at all possible.

A warthog is a very unusual-looking animal. It belongs to the same family as pigs and looks somewhat like them, but a lot different as well. Read more about them in *Warthogs* by Kevin Holmes. Like the meerkat (also in this chapter), the warthog was prominent in the movie *The Lion King*. They are called warthogs because many of them have bumps on their faces that look like warts.

Warthogs live in Africa and weigh about as much as a grown human being—between 130 and 250 pounds. Their eating habits are unusual. They dig up food with their tusks, but they have to hunch down on their knees to do it. In this position they are very vulnerable to attack by predators. Show your audience any of the photos in this colorful book.

Experts estimate that in 1875 there were 50 million of a different animal. And it took only 25 years to kill almost the entire lot. Can your students guess what animal this is? It is the American buffalo, which you can learn about in Ken Robbins's book *Thunder on the Plains: The Story of the American Buffalo*.

Legends say that buffalo herds could be nearly 200 miles long. They came to America over the land bridge that used to span North America and Asia. So did the people that we today call Native Americans or American Indians. Those Native Americans hunted the buffalo and used every part for tools, eating utensils, clothing, and, of course, food. Hunting buffalo was difficult. They are by far the largest animal to run wild in North America. A grown buffalo weighs as much as a car.

This is the story of what they were like, told with sorrow for what used to be but also happiness because the buffalo is not extinct. Today there are approximately 200,000 buffalo, although they no longer roam free.

Show your audience the photo of the man standing on the mound of buffalo skulls. And, if you have visited Yellowstone National Park or the Badlands of South Dakota, tell students about your memory of these majestic animals.

Several attractive books about gorillas have come out in recent years. *Gorillas* by Seymour Simon provides a great introduction to these humanlike creatures. Real gorillas are not very scary. They are not violent, and they do not eat meat, but they sure do remind you a lot of human beings. Simon says gorillas and humans share 98 percent of the same DNA. One big difference is that a gorilla is hairy all over except for its face, chest, palms of its hands, and soles of its feet.

All wild gorillas live in Africa, and there are three types—western and eastern lowland gorillas and, probably the most famous, the mountain gorillas, which Dian Fossey studied. (Read more about her in *Light Shining Through the Mist: A Photobiography of Dian Fossey*, discussed in Chapter 4.)

Gorillas live in family groups of from 2 to 35 animals. The family is led by a silverback, an older gorilla with graying hair. They spend much of their time feeding and eat up to 50 pounds of plants every day. This is a fascinating book with remarkable photographs. Show the one of the mountain gorilla showing its tongue and the one of the threatening, angry gorilla.

You'll learn even more interesting facts in Karen Kane's *Mountain Gorillas*.

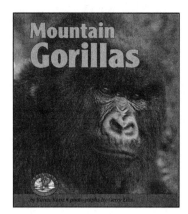

Figure 2.2. *Mountain Gorillas* **by Karen Kane.**

Gorillas are primates, animals that have bodies shaped like human bodies and hands shaped like human hands. Monkeys are primates, too, and so are people. But gorillas do not walk like we do—they walk on all fours.

Mountain gorillas live in a very small area of an African rain forest, where it is damp and hot. They spend most of their time eating, for they are big. A male gorilla can weigh as much as 450 pounds.

There are no mountain gorillas in zoos. If you want to see one, you have to go to Africa and see them in the wild. Because only 600 or so of them are still alive, they are an endangered species, so it might be worth the trip. Show the picture of the baby gorilla riding on its mother's back on page 30.

Gorilla lovers will want to go on and read *Koko-Love! Conversations with a Signing Gorilla* by Dr. Francine Patterson. Koko is the world's first "talking" gorilla, and it is great to find out how she is doing now. Koko and Penny Patterson, a young graduate student, met in 1972, when Koko was one year old. Penny decided she would try to teach Koko how to communicate with people, and she did that wonderfully well. Koko can now "say" more than 1,000 words in American Sign Language, and she can also read some of them. She tells jokes and uses a computer. She has even been known to lie once in a while.

When Koko was five years old, she got a new adopted brother, whose name was Michael. Michael now knows more than 500 words. Michael and Koko are like any brother and sister. They roughhouse, and sometimes Michael calls Koko a stinker!

A third gorilla, Ndume, was brought into the family to become Koko's mate. Read this fun book and learn about the amazing things that are happening in this gorilla family. Show the picture of Michael calling Koko a stinker on page 9.

All animals are interesting, from the largest gorilla to the smallest insect. *Bug Faces* by Darlyne A. Murawski shows us some surprising close-ups of bugs. This book has outstanding photographs and includes some excellent information. For instance, did you know that:

- A daddy longlegs has its eyes on top of its body?

- A cockroach has long feelers called *palps* that pretaste food and keep it from eating something harmful?

- Grasshoppers do not have teeth?

- Only female mosquitoes drink blood?

- Butterflies taste with their feet?

Show the photo of the snout that "can use the two feelers in the middle of its face like windshield wipers to clean its eyes."

Cockroaches by L. Patricia Kite tells us that cockroaches lived on Earth even before the dinosaurs. They haven't changed much, but some people hate them. There are more than 3,500 kinds of cockroaches, and most of them do *not* live near people. But the ones that do can be pests. People think they are dirty, and almost everyone agrees that they are ugly.

Figure 2.3. *Cockroaches* **by L. Patricia Kite.**

The biggest roaches are the size of a small mouse! They like dark places and avoid light as much as possible. Some have four eyes. They breathe through about 20 holes in their exoskeleton, which is a hard shell covering the whole body.

"They eat rotten wood, dead animals, other insects, paper, and glue. They eat computer wires, animal droppings, soap, vegetables, grease, candy, paint, and dog food" (page 22). In fact, they eat just about everything.

Cockroaches are just as interesting as they look. Show the picture of the parts of a cockroach on page 18 and the death's head cockroach on page 8.

Donna Schaffer has written a book about an animal most people know nothing about—mealworms. Because some people raise mealworms to feed their pet birds, fish, and reptiles, you might think they get their name because they make good meals. But, as a matter of fact, they get their name from what they eat. Meal is grain that has been ground into tiny pieces. Yellow mealworms are called grub worms, and people use them as bait for fishing.

Mealworms live only 5 to 10 days out of their pupal shells. *Mealworms* includes not only Web sites but also provides an experiment you can do with mealworms. Good photos to show are on pages 17 and 21.

You can learn a lot about a subject when you ask questions and get good answers. *Did Dinosaurs Live in Your Backyard? Questions and Answers About Dinosaurs* by Melvin and Gilda Berger has both.

Here are some of the fun ones. Do you know any of the answers?

Q Which was the first dinosaur?

A Although no one really knows the answer to this, we do know that Herrerasaurus was among the first. It was six to eight feet tall, walked around on two feet, ate smaller animals, and weighed about 300 pounds.

Q Were all of the Jurassic dinosaurs large?

A No. Although Compsognathus was about the size of a small chicken, it was not cute. It ran fast on two legs with its mouth open, snapping up insects and small animals.

Q What did the biggest dinosaurs eat?

A Plants. Some of them ate as much as *one ton* of food a day.

Q Which dinosaur had the longest neck?

A Mamenchisaurus, found in China, had a neck about 30 feet long—as long as a big bus!

Q Did plant eaters chew their food?

A Some did, but others did not. Some plant eaters swallowed lots of small stones early in their lives. These stones stayed in their stomach and ground up the food they ate.

Q Were there more meat eaters or plant eaters?

A Plant eaters—there were 10 to 20 kinds of plant eaters for every one kind of meat eater.

If you like dinosaurs and would like to know more, take a look at this terrific book.

In *Dinosaurs* by Paul Willis (a Reader's Digest Children's Book), the table of contents asks some questions that will grab your interest right away. Why would a dinosaur have stripes like a tiger? What could dinosaurs do that no animal before them could do? What animals were small and furry and first appeared with the dinosaurs?

Our knowledge of dinosaurs is changing so rapidly that you must seek out the newest books to have even a chance of keeping up. This is a first-rate book to browse through, and the pictures are exceptional. It also provides science fair and craft projects.

Did you know that the word "dinosaur" means "a fearfully great or terrible lizard"? Did you know that a Tyrannosaurus weighed as much as a killer whale but was twice as big? And why do you think the dinosaurs died out? This book explains some of the theories. Which do you believe? Show any of the pictures to your audiences.

Here are a couple of shocking ideas: Many scientists believe that your backyard could well contain a dinosaur! And that you see the descendants of dinosaurs every day. Sound unbelievable? A few years ago they would have had a hard time believing these things, too. But now fossils have been found, and because of the scientists' research, many now feel certain that dinosaurs were the ancestors of birds. Find out more in *Feathered Dinosaurs* by Christopher Sloan.

Dinosaur bones are very similar to those of birds, and this made scientists wonder years ago whether birds and dinosaurs are related. But what really made them stop and wonder was the discovery in China of dinosaur fossils that had feathers on them. What did this mean? How did dinosaurs, almost none of which could fly, turn into birds, almost all of which *can* fly? And what other kinds of clues might help solve the mystery? It turns out that scientists have found lots of clues and are discovering more all of the time.

With huge, colorful pictures, this book tells us about feathered dinosaurs and other dinosaurs and the lives they led. What we know about them is changing almost daily, and the new information is exciting and thought provoking.

Feathered Dinosaurs has so many glorious photographs and illustrations that almost any one of them will work. But try the picture on page 10 of the oviraptor feeding its babies in their nest. And then show the one on page 23 of the modern bird, the cassowary, which looks a lot like its ancestor, the oviraptor. For a great booktalk, pair this with *Digging for Bird-Dinosaurs* found in Chapter 1.

REPTILES AND AMPHIBIANS

Lots of people like snakes, and lots of people can't stand them, but kids will have fun reading about them in Dorothy Hinshaw Patent's *Slinky Scaly Slithery Snakes*. We should come to terms with snakes because they are everywhere except on some islands and near the North and the South Poles. And many kinds of snakes can help people. Some snakes are very dangerous to people as well as to other animals. The most dangerous cobras spit venom at the eyes of their enemies.

Show the picture of the eastern hog-nosed snake on page 13 and read this quote: "When threatened, it lifts and flattens its neck, and hisses. If the enemy comes closer, the snake strikes at it with its mouth closed. If that doesn't work, the snake violently twists its body about, vomits, and defecates. Then it rolls over on its back and lies completely still, its tongue hanging from its open mouth as if it were dead. When the enemy leaves, the snake turns over and crawls off."

Constrictors, such as boas and pythons, kill by wrapping themselves around their prey and squeezing it so hard that it cannot breathe and its blood can't flow. It dies fairly quickly. Show the picture on page 24 of the snake eating a crocodile or alligator in stages. You'll learn a lot with this fun book.

Most great animal nonfiction books feature outstanding photography, and *The Red-Eyed Tree Frog* by Joy Cowley is no exception. Astounding photographs fill this beautiful, but very simple, book.

The red-eyed tree frog lives in the rain forest in Central America. The photographs show the frog's efforts to find something to eat—and to not be eaten in the process. This is a quick booktalk, but flipping through the book will sell it instantly to an eager audience. Show the two-page spread of the frog finding and eating a moth—or any photograph. They are all extraordinary.

The frog fans in your audience will also enjoy *Flashy Fantastic Rainforest Frogs* by Dorothy Hinshaw Patent. Many of the animals that live in tropical rain forests are very unusual to our North American eyes. Perhaps some of the most unusual are the frogs, frogs that can have bright pink bellies or red stripes and can be orange or blue. Some are as big as kittens.

Frogs live everywhere in the rain forest. Some of them never leave the trees; others never leave the ground. Some of those on the ground—the large "horned frogs"—just sit and wait for other animals to wander by. They even eat mice and small rats.

An especially interesting frog is the poison dart frog, whose skin contains bitter-tasting chemicals. "Native hunters in Colombia roll the tips of their blowgun darts onto the skin of certain poison dart frogs. The hunters use it to kill game, but they must be very careful. The skin of one small frog can contain enough poison to kill more than a hundred people" (page 15).

This book describes many of the different types of frogs—even one kind that hatches directly out of its egg without first becoming a tadpole. Filled with colorful illustrations, *Flashy Fantastic Rainforest Frogs* is a fun read. Flip through the book to show a variety of the illustrations.

Some kids love amphibians, and *Chameleons Are Cool* by Martin Jenkins describes one fascinating kind. Chameleons are really neat, but they don't make great pets—most of them get sick and die if you try to make a pet of them. They do not just look grumpy because the corner of their mouths turn down—they really are grumpy and sometimes get into fights with other chameleons.

One of the many unusual things about chameleons—most of which come from Madagascar—is that their eyes move separately from each other—not like our eyes, which move together. One eye can look in one direction, and the other in a different direction.

In his book, *All About Turtles*, Jim Arnosky shows us in three two-page spreads how big an alligator snapping turtle can be. Pretty big! (Show your audience.)

We still do not know everything there is to know about turtles, for instance, whether they can hear. They have no teeth and no ears that we can see, and maybe they sense vibrations in the ground. But they have sharp eyesight and can see things far away.

This book tells you a lot about turtles. As it says, turtles are like other reptiles in that they need to warm themselves up by sitting in a sunny spot and cool themselves off by finding shade or going underwater. Reptiles are not like us. Our bodies do many things to regulate our temperature and make us comfortable.

The more than 200 species of turtles fall into three groups: freshwater, saltwater, and land dwelling.

Did you know that the top of a turtle's shell is called a *carapace* and the bottom is called a *plastron*? Show the picture of the carapace and the plastron. Read this book to learn about a fascinating animal.

For a beautiful combination of text and photographs, don't miss *Interrupted Journey: Saving Endangered Sea Turtles* by Kathryn Lasky. Did you know that sea turtles are one of the most solitary animals in the world? In their entire lives they never interact with their parents, brothers, or sisters. The species is threatened by humans because, although these turtles live in the sea, they must lay their eggs on land.

Fifty years ago, 40,000 female turtles would swim ashore at a beach in Mexico at certain times of the year to lay their eggs. By the 1970s fewer than 1,000 turtles were coming to the beach. Since then, due to much human effort, the population has grown to more than 3,000. Show some of the pictures from the last four two-page spreads to show people helping out the mothers and baby turtles. This book will make you want to be a turtle rescuer.

Crocodiles and Alligators by Seymour Simon has a picture of a gharial on the first page opposite the text. Gharials are the only other animal closely related to alligators, caimans, and crocodiles. The gharial has long, thin jaws, and that is where it got its name. These animals spend most of their time in the water, where they can attack anything that gets too close. They use their powerful jaws to rip apart whatever they catch—but their jaws are much better at snapping shut than at popping open. Some people can even hold a gharial's jaws together using just their hands.

These animals were even around at the time of the dinosaurs, but no one yet knows why they didn't die out when the dinosaurs did. Some of the crocodiles that lived then were as much as 50 feet in length, about the length of a large trailer truck. The biggest ones today are about 19 feet long, still pretty impressive. This book is full of excellent photos. See what you can learn about these remarkable animals.

BIRDS AND ANIMALS OF THE AIR

Bizarre Birds by Doug Wechsler starts out by telling us the one thing all birds have in common and no other animal has. Can you guess? Not beaks, not scaly legs, not wings. Feathers.

People have long wanted to look like the most spectacular birds. All over the world, people use feathers to decorate themselves. People wear feathers in their hats. In Hawaii, royalty wore capes made entirely of feathers. Can you think of other people who wore feathers?

The cover shows a Royal Flycatcher with its crest fanned out—a spectacular sight. The book is full of fascinating facts about birds. Honeyguides love to eat beeswax, and we still do not know how they digest it. Sheathbills eat seal droppings. Macaws eat clay. Grebes eat their own feathers—for a good reason. The small feathers stay in their stomachs to protect the stomach lining from sharp items.

Another chapter describes nests. The common murre's nest is "merely a single egg, placed on a small ledge on a sea cliff. Because the murre's egg is long and skinny at one end, it rolls in circles when pushed so it does not fall off the cliff" (page 34).

Full of color photos, this book is really fun to read. Show your audience the front and back covers and the picture of the murres and their nest on page 32.

Everybody likes penguins, but not many of us ever get to see them in their real home, Antarctica and the Southern Hemisphere. *Penguin* by Rebecca Stefoff has terrific photographs and tells us how penguins live. Did you know that they have baby-sitters? One adult penguin baby-sits all of the chicks so that other adult penguins can go fishing.

A penguin chick is covered with soft, thick, downy feathers. When it grows up, these come off to reveal the sleek feathers of an adult—the kind we usually think of when we think of penguins.

Penguins mate for life and can identify their mate in a crowd of a thousand. This book offers a great chance to learn more about them.

Lots of people would like to swim with dolphins—but how would you like to live with penguins? Sophie Webb did just that and has written about the experience in *My Season with Penguins: An Antarctic Journal*. She had traveled in many different countries, "painting, drawing and studying birds." She had dreamed of going to Antarctica and suddenly got the opportunity when she was asked to join a project studying Adelie penguins. She would be in Antarctica for two months, December and January. She would live in a tent and go to the bathroom outside. December and January are summer in Antarctica, but even so, it can get very cold indeed.

Webb watched the penguins and drew hundreds of pictures of them. She caught and banded them and put transmitters on some so that researchers could learn where they went and how far they traveled. She almost never got to take a bath and says she smelled like a penguin, which is not a good thing.

She watched penguin chicks hatching, growing up enough to take care of themselves, and then leaving. She saw penguins stealing from each other and watched predators, such as seals and big birds, capture and eat some of them, especially chicks.

She had a wonderful time, and this book tells all about it. Show the picture on page 23 of the penguin with the radio transmitter attached to its back.

Do you want to know even more about this interesting bird? Then open a copy of *Penguins!* by Gail Gibbons.

Do you know that there are 17 different kinds of penguins? Gibbons's book presents pictures of all of them. The tallest one, the emperor penguin, is about four feet tall, and the shortest one, the little blue penguin, is only about a foot tall. Not all penguins look the same; there are actually big differences among them. They all live in the Southern Hemisphere, although not only in Antarctica.

Penguins are great swimmers and divers, but they cannot fly at all. Read about the colonies they live in and what they do to keep warm when the weather gets really, really cold—as low as 60 degrees below zero Fahrenheit. Show the first picture of the different kinds of penguins.

Unbeatable Beaks by Stephen R. Swinburne is a very short but stunning book. Swinburne tells us he loves birds and especially all of the different kinds of bird beaks. Have you ever thought about this? Take a look at the colorful illustrations of the different kinds of birds and beaks. As the author says, "The neatest thing besides two feet, without question, is a beak." After you look through the book and discover some of the many things birds use their beaks for, take a look at the pictures on the last two pages and see whether you can match the bird with its beak.

Ducks! by Gail Gibbons is for very young readers. Ducks are waterbirds and are called waterfowl. All waterfowl have webbed feet and waterproof feathers. There are about 150 kinds of waterfowl—can you think of how many kinds you might have seen? They live on every continent except Antarctica.

Figure 2.4. *Ducks!* by Gail Gibbons.

Dabbling ducks eat food close to the surface of the water, such as plants, seeds, insects, and small animals such as worms and snails. Diving ducks, on the other hand, often dive 10 to 25 feet below the surface. As you might guess, they eat fish as well as water plants, clams, and snails.

This book is full of excellent information about a bird that most of us love to watch. Show the picture of the mother duck and her ducklings on the second-to-the-last page.

The title *Ducks Don't Get Wet* by Augusta Goldin says it all. Stunning new illustrations highlight this third revision of a Let's Read and Find Out science book. Because of their oil glands, ducks do not get wet. They smear oil over their feathers from a gland near their tail, and that makes them waterproof. There is a science experiment at the end of the book.

Teachers who do units on bats will love *Bats! Strange and Wonderful* by Laurence Pringle. Packed with fascinating bat facts and detailed illustrations by Meryl Henderson, it is both educational and fun. You may not have known that almost 1,000 kinds of bats exist, but only 44 of those species live in North America. Did you know that megabats weigh up to four pounds? (That's half the size of a cat.) Or that microbats can weigh less than a U.S. penny? All of the bats in North America are microbats, and they make good neighbors because they eat insects such as mosquitoes. Page 18 has nice illustrations and an explanation of vampire bats. Pair this book with the fiction book *Stellaluna* by Janell Cannon and a nonfiction book with photographs of bats for an unbeatable booktalk or lesson on this misunderstood species of mammal.

Gail Gibbons provides more information in her book called *Bats*. Even though bats have been around for 50 million years, they have not changed much. Their fossils indicate that they still look about the same as they did in prehistoric times.

Bats eat lots and lots of insects. The ones that live in Bracken Cave near San Antonio, Texas, eat about 250 tons of insects a night. In this way bats help people, but people do not always help bats out. Because people don't like them, they may destroy their homes, and pesticides can kill them. Many bats are now endangered, but people are beginning to realize how important they are. Now some people are building bat houses to provide shelter for them.

Find out how bats are born and where they live. The smallest bat weighs only one-fourteenth of an ounce. The biggest bat has a wingspan of five feet! Show the picture of the fishing bat.

ANIMALS OF THE WATER

High-quality books about animals of the sea are becoming more available. *Sea Critters* by Sylvia A. Earle gives a good introduction. "Nearly all of Earth's water—97 percent—is ocean. It's an ocean filled with life! Sea critters abound, making every spoonful a kind of living soup. Of the more than 30 great divisions of animal life, most can be found in the sea" (page 4).

That's pretty amazing, and so are the photographs in this beautiful book, which describes some of the extraordinary creatures that live in our oceans. Start with the sponge, a creature full of holes. Some sponges, like the one in the picture on page 6, are big enough to sit in! These animals have no brains, but they have been around for more than 500 million years.

Sea worms sometimes have several hearts, and there are many kinds of them. Take a look at the spectacular Christmas tree worm on page 11. Share this fact with your audience: Most of the animals in the ocean are smaller than your thumb, but the giant squid is larger than a school bus! End your booktalk by showing the beautiful picture of the sea lily on page 23.

Gail Gibbons takes us right down to the bottom of the ocean in *Exploring the Deep, Dark Sea*. But the bottom of the ocean is not the same everywhere. In fact, we are not even sure how different it is because scientists have explored only about 2 percent of the ocean floor so far. Gibbons tells us we know more about the surface of the moon than we do about our oceans. We know that the oceans are vast—more than three-fourths of the Earth's surface is covered by them. And the deepest parts of the ocean go almost six miles down.

This book describes the journey of a submersible, a "small … diving vessel that can measure, videotape, and collect samples of water, plants and animals found on the ocean." This submersible drops about 100 feet per minute. The first part of the ocean it reaches is the sunlight zone, where most of the marine plants and animals live. Then it descends into the twilight zone—really! This area, about 450 to 3,300 feet down, is too dark and cold for plants to grow, and at 1,500 feet, the submersible needs to turn on its light. Many of the sea creatures here are bioluminescent—they give off their own light. You can see a flashlight fish from 100 feet away. Finally, the submersible reaches the dark zone, more than 3,300 feet down. Incredible creatures live here, and you can read about them in this fascinating book. You can also find out what zone is even lower than the dark zone.

The picture of the squid in the twilight zone is good to show, but almost any of the pictures will work for a booktalk.

Learn more about the bioluminescent sea creatures in Gail Gibbons's book by reading *The Winking, Blinking Sea: All About Bioluminescence* by Mary Batten. This book is full of astonishing photographs of ocean animals that make their own light from chemicals inside their bodies, and they use that light to help them survive. "Some flash a special signal that tells who they are. Some glow with color to attract mates. Some use their lights to scare enemies. Some use their lights to find food. Some hide in glittering bursts of miniature fireworks."

You can hardly believe your eyes as you gaze at these photos. Take a look at the deep sea worm or the fire worm. Astounding stuff.

Another fascinating aspect of marine life is the coral reef. Coral reefs are among the most beautiful things on our planet. Mary M. Cerullo tells us how they were formed and what kinds of plants and animals live there in *Coral Reef: A City That Never Sleeps*. In coral reefs, "weirdly shaped 'plants' and 'shrubs' are actually the skeletons of millions of sea animals" (page 2). Corals come in many different types and colors, and the "chief architect" is the coral polyp, which is about as big as a pea. It lives inside a circular stone house that it creates and that remains even after the animal inside it is dead. As more and more corals build upon the skeletons or stone houses, the reef is formed.

Cerullo tells us that the coral reef is like a city in many ways, partly because it is so crowded. It is hard to find a home in a coral reef because so many creatures live there. What helps is the fact that creatures share the same space. One animal leaves its space during the day while a nocturnal animal moves in—and vice versa. They maintain different schedules. Think of submarines in which the sailors share the same bunks, which they can do because they are on duty at different times.

The animals that live in the coral reef are beautiful and very colorful. Scientists are not yet sure why they are so colorful, but they have some theories. In addition, the animals relate to each other in many ways—cleaner fish clean inside the mouths of larger fish, although they sometimes get eaten in the process.

One of the most amazing is the parrot fish. "[It] has a mouth made for munching. It is a most useful tool because it recycles the reef. This fish's teeth have fused together into a strong scraper that knocks off chunks of coral. The parrot fish feeds on the algae that grows on the dead coral or the zooxanthellae in living coral. These coral scrapings are ground up by a second set of teeth in the parrot fish's throat and passed out the other end, creating coral sand for tropical beaches. A study in Bermuda concluded that for every acre of coral reef, one ton of coral skeletons was converted into sand each year, primarily through the feeding habits of parrot fishes" (page 27).

Unfortunately, human beings are not doing good things for the coral reefs. Take a look at this wonderful book with its marvelous photos and learn about these incredible structures.

Show your audience the photo of the parrot fish's teeth on page 27 or of the lion-fish on page 33 or almost any of these photos.

Sylvia A. Earle, who wrote *Hello, Fish! Visiting the Coral Reef*, is a famous ocean explorer, and here she describes some of the fish she sees when she explores coral reefs around the world. Coral reefs are made up of billions of skeletons of tiny animals called corals. The fish that live there are both strange and beautiful.

Take a look at the stargazer, a very unusual camouflaged fish; the brown goby, who lives in an empty worm tube; and the frogfish, which looks a lot like a frog. This is easy to read but is also full of interesting information.

A simpler book on the same topic is Madeleine Dunphy's *Here Is the Coral Reef*. Its stunning illustrations and a cumulative verse painlessly teach kids about the ecosystem of a coral reef. Show them a few pictures to pique their interest during a talk on the sea and its creatures. The second-to-the-last one of the shark and the eel is especially enticing.

Very early readers and ESL students will enjoy two simple books filled with eye-catching photographs. Flip through *Sea Anemones* and *Sea Urchins*, both by Lola M. Schaefer, showing your audience the photos, the vocabulary lists, and the Web sites. These are simple but beautiful introductions to the subject.

Karen Wallace writes about a marine animal that will amaze you in *Gentle Giant Octopus*. The beautiful pictures are tantalizing. Octopuses use their tentacles to sense things—just like we use our fingers. They can do many things we cannot: "Usually, the Giant octopus is reddish brown, but when it's hunting or hiding, it can change to become very dark or very pale within seconds" (page 16). Do you know what an octopus does when attacked? And did you know that a mother octopus can lay as many as 60,000 eggs—but other animals love to eat baby octopuses, so only two out of three live to become adults? Great pictures are fun to show.

Have you or anyone in your audience ever gone whale watching? Did you see a whale? Whales, Faith McNulty tells us in *How Whales Walked into the Sea*, are strange animals. And she tells us why. If you know a lot about science, what she says may not be new to you, but for a lot of us, this will be surprising information.

We now know that 50 million years ago the ancestors of whales were furry, four-legged animals that lived on land. The oceans were warmer, shallower, and wider than they are today. These animals, called Mesonychids, would wade into the water to eat. Over the years they learned to swim—and some of them swam better than others. The better swimmers had broad feet like paddles, and after thousands of years all of the Mesonychids that swam far into the ocean developed broad feet.

The story of the evolution of the whales goes on with excellent pictures of their development over millions of years. The Mesonychids developed into the Ambulocetus, the walking whale, which evolved into the Rodhocetus, a whale that was barely able to walk, and so on. Today, whales have arm, wrist, and finger bones—but these are inside their flippers! All that is left of the fur of the Mesonychid is the whiskers on the whale's upper lip or chin. Tiny leg bones are hidden in the whale's body. Who knows what will happen next! Almost all of these fascinating illustrations are good to show, but try the one of the Ambulocetus.

When most of us think of big animals, we think of whales or elephants or maybe a rhinoceros. But we most likely do not think about the animals discussed in *Freshwater Giants: Hippopotamus, River Dolphins, and Manatees* by Phyllis J. Perry. Most freshwater fish and animals, including the beaver, the otter, and the muskrat, are quite small. But the subjects of this book are quite big.

Average hippos are 12 to 14 feet long, and when mature, an adult male weighs about 7,050 pounds. They live in slow-moving water—they don't like fast-moving currents. They can stay underwater for five minutes at a time. All of the wild hippos now live in Africa, but their existence is precarious. A baby hippo has about a 45 percent chance of being killed in its first year, usually by lions, leopards, and hyenas.

There are only a few river dolphins left in the world. They have unusual names—the susu and bhulan live in and around India, the baiji is found in the Yangtze River in China, and the tucuxi and boto live in South America. Did you even know there are dolphins who live in rivers?

Finally, there are the manatees, who spend their whole lives in water. They live in Africa, South America, and around the Caribbean. These are the only freshwater giants who live in the wild in the United States, and many are in Florida. The adult manatee weighs more than 1,500 pounds. Manatees are intriguing animals, and they are in danger from their greatest enemy—humans. Read about them and find out what we can do to help. Show the picture of the hippo underwater on page 16 and the river dolphin (boto) on page 32.

With its unusually busy graphic design, *The Truth About Great White Sharks* by Mary M. Cerullo will probably appeal enormously to some kids while it turns others off. The facts, however, are great fun to read.

Almost everyone knows at least one thing about the great white shark, which is a very scary animal. When the movie *Jaws* came out, many people refused to go swimming in the ocean because they were afraid a great white shark might eat them.

Scientists now believe that great white sharks bite people only accidentally—and they usually take only one bite and then swim away. Of course, if they bite off part of your body, that isn't good. There is a picture on page 37 of Rodney Fox, who was bitten by a shark and lived to tell about it. He had to have 462 stitches in his chest, arm, and hand. Now Fox studies great white sharks.

The truth is that we do not know much about great white sharks but are learning more all the time. Because the sharks are dangerous to humans and live mostly in deep, unexplored areas of the ocean, we have not been able to learn as much about them as we would like. Today people study them by staying in "shark cages," which can be lowered into the water but prevent them from being tasted by the shark.

This is an amazing animal, and you will enjoy reading about it. Show the fold-out picture of the shark on pages 23 and 24.

A much less threatening animal that spends its time in the water is the beaver. Most of us know that beavers are very good at cutting down trees and building dams. Glen Rounds tells us even more in *Beaver*, a book that is easy and fun to read. Did you know that beavers are very clumsy on dry land but are powerful swimmers who do a lot of their work underwater? They like to live in deep ponds, and, if there are no deep ponds nearby, they make their own by building dams. When they swim in these ponds, their enemies cannot catch them.

Beavers are interesting animals to know about. Take a look at this neat book. Show the picture of the beaver building a dam.

Building Beavers by Kathleen Martin-James also gives good information about beavers. Fine photos illustrate this simple book for the youngest readers.

A beaver's house is called a lodge, and beavers love to build lodges. They are vegetarians, so they do not eat meat. Their teeth are long and sharp, and they can cut down trees with them very easily. Beavers are great underwater swimmers and use their tails to help them swim and to balance on land as well as to slap other animals that are trying to catch them. Learn more about these fascinating, beautiful animals. Show the picture on page 17 of the beaver lifting its tail to slap a predator.

ANIMAL BEHAVIOR

Some of the best animal books of recent years deal with animal behaviors—how they eat, sleep, move around, take a bath, mate, and die. These books make great booktalks because you can throw out startling facts and leave your audience begging for more.

Exploding Ants: Amazing Facts About How Animals Adapt by Joanne Settel is filled with curious facts about animals, some you might have heard of and some not so familiar. The color photographs make the information even more enticing. Were you aware that some frogs can drop their eyes into their throats when they are eating something that is alive and fighting? A frog can use its front feet to cram in a live rat, for instance, but its eyes are loose, and when it is time for the final swallow, the eyeballs help push the food in.

Or take the deep-sea anglerfish. The male is only two inches long, but the minute he leaves his egg, he finds a two-to-four-foot-long mate to attach himself to. His mouth permanently attaches itself to the female's skin (show the picture on page 35), and his eyes and digestive tract break down because he does not need them any longer.

A swallowtail butterfly larva looks like a bird dropping. This is a great disguise, for no predator wants to eat a bird dropping. Cuckoos lay their eggs in the nests of other kinds of birds. The cuckoo's baby hatches first and pushes the other eggs out. The poor mother bird has a baby almost as big as she is—and soon bigger—and does not know what happened. Bringing that cuckoo baby enough food tires her out.

Some ants are living honey jars. Their bodies expand and become huge globes full of honey, and Australian Aborigines consider them a great treat. They pop them in their mouths and eat them like candy!

Some birds balloon. Some ants explode. Tiny tongue worms live in the nose of a dog. The animal world is full of astonishing things, and this book will whet your appetite for more.

Splash! Splash! Animal Baths by April Pulley Sayre makes a nice booktalk for young children because of the vivid photographs. The photo of the pig in the mud will be popular, as will the one of the lioness licking her paws. Students may not have heard of oxpeckers, which the book shows picking ticks off of a giraffe. The photo of the shrimp crawling into the moray eel's mouth is also interesting—this shrimp is an "animal dentist" that picks and eats food off of the eel's teeth! Team this book up with individual books about the animals mentioned, and you'll have a great booktalk for early readers.

Where Are the Night Animals? by Mary Ann Fraser is another book for young readers. A very simple text describes the life of nocturnal creatures. Some animals are, like most of us, awake during the daytime, but others are awake all night long. What do they do? What kinds of animals stay up all night? Can you think of any?

"Animals that are more active at night are called nocturnal. They have adapted to life in the dark. We never see most of these animals. They are hiding during the day when we are awake" (page 15). Read this interesting book to find out what night animals do in the dark. Show almost any of the beautiful pictures. The double spread of the opossum and her babies on pages 8 and 9 is especially appealing.

Learn about interesting uses for ears by reading *Animal Ears* by Lisa Trumbauer. Ears enable people to hear. They also do that for animals, but they do other things as well. Look at the picture of the elephants on pages 4 and 5. Elephants use their huge ears to fan themselves. Animals also use their ears to help them cool off. You will learn some new things about ears.

Follow the preceding book with *Animals Eating: How Animals Chomp, Chew, Slurp and Swallow* by Pamela Hickman, which provides a wealth of fascinating animal facts. Show the two-page spread on pages 8 and 9 and read some of the "If you were a crocodile" tidbits. Did you know crocodiles carry stones in their stomach to grind food and keep them below the water's surface? Or that they can go for six months without eating? Another fun picture is found on page 17. Why is a giraffe's tongue black? According to the text it is covered by a natural sunscreen. Snakes are always fun to read about, and on pages 26 and 27 you will find a description of how pythons and anaconda can eat animals much larger than themselves. After eating a big meal (such as a deer or a human), the snake may not need to eat again for a year.

Speaking of eating habits, find out lots more in *Animals Eat the Weirdest Things* by Diane Swanson. To us, it is absolutely amazing what animals eat. But, as the author points out, we people have eaten some mighty strange things, too. She even includes a recipe for cooking a tarantula—which some people do!

Animals eat, among other things, blood, vomit, dung, rotting flesh and bones, boats, books, and blankets. Some animals eat their own skin. Salamanders frequently eat the skin they have just shed. A good source of food for many animals is other animals who have died. Some animals, such as hyenas, eat almost every part of a carcass.

Show your audience the picture on the front cover of a beaver eating an oar. Part of the appeal for the beaver is that the oar is soaked in sweat.

Follow the preceding book with another one along the same lines—*Cannibal Animals: Animals That Eat Their Own Kind* by Anthony D. Fredericks. Biologists estimate that there are more than 1,300 kinds of cannibal animals—animals that eat their own kind. With great, colorful photographs, Fredericks tells us that animals eat each other for three main reasons:

1. Eating your neighbor is quick and easy and provides a good food source.

2. You can eliminate your future competitors for other food in the area.

3. You can control your population. Sometimes there are too many animals for the available food. Animals can thin out their numbers this way.

How animals eat each other can surprise you. Black widow spiders and praying mantis females eat their mates. Praying mantises sometimes bite the head off the male while they are mating. Sand tiger sharks eat each other inside their mother's womb. Some midges (small insects) have eggs inside their bodies that develop into larvae. Those larvae feed on their mother—from the inside out. After a time, they kill her and get out. Some animals kill and eat their own babies, including guppies, some gerbils, and certain brown bears as well as others. Horned frogs sometimes attack each other. Sometimes a frog attacks a bigger frog and tries to swallow it—but it will not fit in its throat. Frequently both frogs die.

And, of course, we have all heard of cases in which human beings killed and ate each other. (*The Perilous Journey of the Donner Party* from Chapter 1 might be appropriate at this point in the booktalk.) Show almost any of the color photos in this book, although the ones of the black widow spider and the praying mantis are particularly good.

The fascinating facts just keep on coming in Jack Myers's book *On the Trail of the Komodo Dragon and Other Explorations of Science in Action* (Scientists Probe 11 Animal Mysteries). Do you think that horses sleep standing up? Many people do, but this is not so. Horses sleep either in a kneeling position or else lying on their sides. Jack Myers, who has a science column in *Highlights for Children*, gives us 11 chapters answering this and other questions about animals and their behavior.

Try to figure out how cats can fall so well—and why human beings are not very good at falling from tall places without getting hurt. Learn how much energy hummingbirds need just to exist—and how they get it. How do we know that cheetahs are the world's fastest animals? Why do snakes flick their tongues? Learn the answers to these questions and more from this fun book. Show your audience the cover and the picture of the cat skydiving on page 14.

FASCINATING SCIENCE

Weather is generally a hot topic with young readers. Marilyn Singer gives a global view of it in *On the Same Day in March: A Tour of the World's Weather*.

What kind of weather is it today where you live? If you went halfway around the word, what do you think *that* weather would be like? And if you went halfway *down* the world, what kind of weather do you think *that* would be like?

This fun book shows what the weather is like around the world on a single day in March—and the variety will surprise you! Our planet is a very big place with many different kinds of weather. Take a look at this interesting book. Show almost any of the two-page spreads.

Many people are afraid of lightning and thunder. We have no reason to be scared of thunder, but we have excellent reasons to be frightened of lightning. *Flash, Crash, Rumble, and Roll* by Franklyn M. Branley explains how thunder and lightning happen and gives some tips that tell us when dangerous lightning might be very close and what safety measures we can take so that we do not get hurt.

On pages 10 and 11 is a picture of a plane avoiding a dark thundercloud. "The rushing air could turn a plane upside down. It could even rip off the wings." Read this book for some great information.

Here's another interesting weather fact: Pink snow has fallen. Jennifer Dussling tells us how it happens in *Pink Snow and Other Weird Weather*. She tells us that all snow is made in clouds, and sometimes red soil and dust are picked up by strong winds and blown into snow clouds. When snow forms around that red soil, it is pink!

You have probably heard other stories of weird weather, and here we learn some more. In France in 1833 toads fell down with the rain one day. Tornadoes do very strange things—in one house in Ohio, everything was broken except three things: a mirror, a case of eggs, and a box of Christmas tree ornaments! The Empire State Building is struck by lightning about 40 times a year, and one man, a park ranger named Roy Sullivan, has been struck by lightning 7 times. This is a fun book to read. Learn the reasons these things happen. Show the picture of Roy Sullivan on page 31.

More extreme weather is explained in *Wild Weather: Blizzards!* by Lorraine Jean Hopping. Exactly what turns a snowstorm into a blizzard? For starters, blizzards are not just bad snowstorms. They are also bad windstorms, with winds that blow 35 miles an hour or more. The snow blows so fast and so far that sometimes everything looks white, and people cannot even see things very close to them. Some people have frozen to death very near to the door of their house.

This book not only educates us about blizzards; it also tells us some true stories. In Buffalo, New York, in 1977, the snow was so deep that deer walked right out of the zoo. They just walked over the top of the fences that had held them in. In Nebraska, in 1888, a teacher in a small school that was made of sod (bricks of earth) was terrified when her schoolhouse started blowing apart because of the blizzard. She tied all 13 of her students together with twine, and, in a big group, they managed to walk to a small shack where they stayed during the blizzard. In 1982 a rock climber in New Hampshire was caught in a blizzard on Mount Washington, which has recorded the highest winds on Earth. By the time he was found, his legs were frozen and had to be amputated. But Hugh Herr, the climber, still goes climbing—with his artificial legs.

Show your audience the picture of the Nebraska schoolteacher on pages 8 and 9 and of Hugh Herr on page 23. You could easily pair this book with *Nature's Fury: Eyewitness Reports of Natural Disasters* and *Blizzard: The Storm That Changed America*, both found in Chapter 1.

Laurence Pringle, a highly respected science writer, writes about our natural world in *The Environmental Movement: From Its Roots to the Challenges of a New Century*. This book isn't just for assignments, although it would do that very well, too.

If you are interested in saving the Earth, this is a great book to read. It starts out with a quotation from the Bible: "Be fertile and increase, fill the earth and subdue it and have dominion of the fish of the sea and over the fowl of the air and over every living thing that creepeth upon the earth" (page 10). Following that is a quotation from Rabbi James Prosnit, made in 1990: "We have dominated the earth and subdued the fish of the sea and the results are terrifying" (page 10).

Only in the last 100 years or so have people started to take seriously our uses of the Earth's resources. Earth Day did not start until 1970. People who want to preserve our environment have had a hard time convincing others that their point of view is valid.

This book is full of interesting information, such as the fact that sometimes businesses create a group to support their interests but give it an "environmental" name. This is called *greenscamming*. One such group was called Keep America Beautiful, Inc., but its purpose was to oppose recycling laws.

Read the information about growing cacao trees, whose seeds are the basis for chocolate.

Pair this book with *Easter Island: Giant Stone Statues Tell of a Rich and Tragic Past* (Chapter 4) by Caroline Arnold for a sobering look at what can happen to a place when its resources are used up.

Kids who care about saving the Earth will also want to read *Global Warming: The Threat of Earth's Changing Climate*, also by Laurence Pringle. This attractive, colorful book will be welcomed by science teachers looking for detailed, yet easy-to-read information. The world's temperatures vary greatly over time. In fact, scientists think we are due for an inevitable ice age in 10,000 years or so. What we are doing to the Earth is leading us toward global disaster. Read this book to find out what is happening and what we can do to stop global warming.

Read about a time when the Earth's climate changed drastically in *Asteroid Impact* by Douglas Henderson. What he describes could happen again. It has happened many times already, but most of the comets and asteroids that hit the Earth are very small and have not caused much damage. The asteroid that struck what is now the Yucatán peninsula in present-day Mexico, however, caused an enormous amount of damage and, in the process, killed off all of the dinosaurs—about 65 billion years ago. The crater it created is more than 110 miles across!

Henderson tells us in detail what happens when a fast-traveling object hits another object. The bigger the objects that collide, the greater the damage. Scientists estimate that the asteroid that hit Earth was probably six miles across. The collision caused an explosion much greater than any atom bomb could produce. It was so huge that it covered almost the entire world with dust, heating it up so much that it killed nearly all life, and then cooling it off.

If you like dinosaurs and are interested in current theories about their disappearance, this book, with its glorious illustrations, is for you. Show the audience almost any of the pictures, but the one on page 11 of the asteroid approaching the Earth is striking, as is the one on page 18 of the asteroid actually hitting the Earth.

Incredibly popular Bill Nye the Science Guy presents 12 impressive experiments and fun information about the four oceans in *Bill Nye the Science Guy's Big Blue Ocean*. Nye points out right away that sailing the "Seven Seas," a phrase we still hear, is an outdated one, coined before people had explored the whole world. Can you name all four oceans? Do you know that exploring outer space is easier in some ways than exploring our oceans? That we have exactly the same water in our oceans as was on Earth 4 billion years ago? Maybe Cleopatra once drank the water you are drinking today.

Figure 2.5. *Bill Nye the Science Guy's Big Blue Ocean* **by Bill Nye with Ian G. Saunders.**

This user-friendly, colorful book presents a great deal of fun information. Show the cover and flip through it so your audience can enjoy some of the pictures.

Let's-Read-and-Find-Out Science books from HarperCollins are great for introducing science topics to primary students. *Sounds All Around* by Wendy Pfeffer is one of these books and is about a topic everyone can relate to.

Have you ever thought about the different sounds you can make? You can make sounds with your mouth, your hands, and your feet, for starters. What are some of these sounds?

Sounds are made from vibrations. Vibrations create waves, and when these waves reach our ears, tiny bones in our ears vibrate, and we hear these vibrations as sounds. A long time ago, people used drums to send sound messages to people in other places. We still use sounds to send messages—a fire siren tells us to get out of the way, a knock asks whether anyone is at home, and clapping your hands tells people they have done a good job.

This book is full of interesting information about sounds. It even tells us how we measure sounds and includes some experiments for kids to do. Show the picture on page 4 of the kids making sounds.

Another good science introduction for young readers is Stephen R. Swinburne's *Guess Whose Shadow?* Everybody has a shadow. Can you see yours right now? Have you ever really looked at it? Does it sometimes change size? Are there times when you can see it really well and times it's not there at all? This book is full of pictures of people and things and their shadows. You can play guessing games with them. Take a look.

Do you know what the biggest shadow of all is? It is night! Show your audience the great photo on the first page.

Also by Stephen R. Swinburne is *Lots and Lots of Zebra Stripes: Patterns in Nature.* Like *Out of Sight: Pictures of Hidden Worlds* (Chapter 7), this book makes for a great guessing game. Excellent photos in this beautiful book are fun to look at. After you look at them you'll see the world outside in a new way.

What are patterns? Look at the pictures and see whether you can name more things that have patterns like the ones in the pictures. Show the children some of the full-page pictures to whet their appetites for more.

Gloria Skurzynski has written a couple of science books for upper-elementary-aged students. Being able to float in the air because you don't weigh anything sounds like fun, and that is what you will learn about when you read *Zero Gravity*. Gravity pulls us toward the Earth and holds us there, but astronauts who are orbiting the Earth do not experience gravity because the centrifugal force of their rotations frees them from gravity's pull.

The orbiting astronauts weigh nothing. They can float their food into their mouths, and they don't need a bed to sleep on because they float on air that is more comfortable (and fits them better) than any mattress. They have to be strapped to a board so they do not float—but their arms float and they resemble ghosts. They don't need chairs because they naturally fall into a semisitting position. If they have long hair, it sticks out in all directions.

This is a fascinating book about a fun subject. Show the picture on page 22 of the man floating the candy into his mouth.

On Time: From Seasons to Split Seconds, also by Gloria Skurzynski, makes the concept of time come alive with clear explanations and color pictures. Skurzynski explains seasons, years, months, weeks, days, hours, and seconds and the reasons humans have become such devoted timekeepers. The aerial views of Stonehenge on page 10 and the Aztec sun stone on pages 16 and 17 are attention grabbing, and a good story to retell is found on page 22. Did you know that Christopher Columbus was stranded for many months on the island we now call Haiti? The natives there brought him and his crew food for a while, but they soon refused to supply the crew any longer. Because Columbus knew about the motions of the sun, moon, and stars, he was able to devise a plan to trick the natives. He threatened to ask his god to take away the moon if they didn't bring food again. The natives didn't believe him, but as Columbus predicted, the moon began to disappear. Of course, he had known an eclipse was going to occur, and he timed it with his hourglass (much like the miniature kind found in many board games today).

Some words you might want to mention are found on page 32. Did you know that a picosecond is a trillionth of a second and that a femtosecond is a thousandth of a picosecond? With a little encouragement, young scientific minds should find this book very interesting.

Do Stars Have Points? Questions and Answers About Stars and Planets by Melvin and Gilda Berger answers questions that you probably didn't even realize you wanted to ask. For instance, how many stars do you think we can see on a clear night? The answer is, with the naked eye, about 3,000. But with a telescope, millions. We have no idea how many stars there are, but astronomers believe there are at least 200 billion billion.

Here's another one: How long would it take a car going 60 miles an hour to reach the sun? It would take 177 years. But light moves so rapidly that it takes only eight minutes for light from the sun to reach us.

Have you ever wondered about the North Star? It is very important because it is almost straight up over the North Pole. From the Northern Hemisphere, it looks as though it does not move. Because of its fixed position relative to us, sailors have used it to find their way.

The tilt of the Earth causes the seasons to change. The United States and Canada have spring and summer when the Northern Hemisphere leans toward the sun due to the Earth's tilting. In our fall and winter, the Earth tilts away from the sun. The exact opposite occurs in the Southern Hemisphere.

We do not feel the Earth moving because everything on it is moving with us at exactly the same time.

The Bergers' book ends with a list of a few of the questions astronomers ask. Maybe someday you can find out the answers to these (all on page 47):

- How big is the universe?
- Are there planets orbiting other stars in space?
- Can humans live on Mars?
- Is there intelligent life anywhere else in the universe?

The science that involves what goes on in our own bodies can be as fascinating as outer space, as *Big Head!* by Dr. Pete Rowan proves. What miraculous things are right there inside your head? For starters, there are about 100 billion brain cells, and each of them is connected in hundreds of ways to other nerve cells. One of the things we have learned about them is that all of our thinking is done by means of electricity and chemicals.

Big Head! has excellent illustrations of the things inside your head. One of the many facts it explains is this one: Smell is the most emotive of the senses. If you smell something familiar, you can instantly remember where you smelled it before.

The book has numerous overlays that will attract kids' attention. And although the print is small, this book is so well designed that simply showing kids the cover and flipping through it will capture an audience for you.

Learn even more about the human brain in *Hmm? The Most Interesting Book You'll Ever Read About Memory* by Diane Swanson. Read the great "fast facts" on page 10. Did you know that all the neurons in your brain would reach to the moon and back if strung end to end? Or that your brain can send and receive millions of signals in a single second? Many pages have a "You Try It" section with fun activities. Try the one on page 17 with your audience. Ask a volunteer to write down a seven-digit number and then have another volunteer remember it. Then have the second volunteer transfer it to long-term memory by saying it and writing it out. At the end of your booktalk go back to the volunteer and see whether that student remembers the number.

If so, the student's brain has sprouted new *dendrites*. Both teachers and students will find this book fascinating.

Younger students will enjoy learning answers to some of life's perplexing questions in *Why I Sneeze, Shiver, Hiccup and Yawn* by Melvin Berger. Have you ever wondered why, all of a sudden, you sneeze? Or get the hiccups? Both of these things surprise us sometimes—a sneeze that just happens and hiccups that embarrass you.

These are reflexes, reactions that happen very quickly and are very hard to stop. Yawning and shivering are also reflexes that involve your nervous system—which has two parts, the nerves and the spinal cord and brain.

"Nerves are like telephone wires. They carry messages back and forth. The brain and spinal cord are like the main office of the telephone company. All of the messages must go through there" (page 9).

This book gives lots of great examples, such as the fact that when we get burned, we often move away from the heat source before we are even aware that it is burning us. Reflexes are automatic, fascinating things, and this book tells us about them. Show the picture of the girl hiding and sneezing on page 4.

Science is a wonderful thing when it is truly useful. Do you ever get bored when you are waiting for your food to be served? Especially when you are in a restaurant? Well, *While You're Waiting for the Food to Come: A Tabletop Science Activity Book: Experiments and Tricks That Can Be Done at a Restaurant, the Dining Room Table, or Wherever Food Is Served* by Eric Muller takes care of that problem. While you are waiting, maybe you can work on your school science fair project with the ideas in this book.

The experiment on pages 4 and 5 called "In Bad Taste" is a fun one. Do you think that your tongue is the only part of your body that really tastes things? Try this experiment and find out whether that is true.

Try looking through the top of a salt shaker and see what happens. You may be surprised (this experiment is on pages 34 and 35). With the experiment on pages 24 and 25 you can even dumbfound people by figuring out which way a bottle top will land before you even spin it. And pages 48 and 49 tell you how to make your own homemade lava lamp. All of this is just a start—try these the next time you have to wait for your food.

Speaking of food—most of us love it and could learn a lot from *Food Rules! The Stuff You Munch, Its Crunch, Its Punch, and Why You Sometimes Lose Your Lunch* by Bill Haduch. This funny, thought-provoking book is jam-packed with great information. It starts out with a few interesting facts about food on page 3, including the following:

> If you lump it all together, you spend more than 15 full days a year doing nothing but eating.
>
> If you *dump* it all together, you spend almost four full days a year doing nothing but going to the bathroom.
>
> Every year, you eat about 170 grocery bags of food.
>
> Fewer than half of the world's people use a fork, knife, and spoon to eat. The rest use chopsticks, just a knife, or just their hands.

One important thing we should all know is that the hypothalamus is what makes us hungry. This small area in our brain regulates our bodies in many different ways, and one of those is to tell us we want to eat.

This is great stuff, and as we read, we discover even more. Do you know that a sumo wrestler may eat as much as 20 pounds of meat in one day? Or that Lewis and Clark traded their medicine for Native Americans' dogs—and then they ate the dogs, which really disgusted the Native Americans?

And do you know that 80 percent of the world's people happily eat bugs? Only those in the United States, Europe, Canada, and the polar regions do not like this idea. Your friends will be delighted with your stories as you read this book.

BIBLIOGRAPHY

Arnosky, Jim. *All About Turtles*. Written and illustrated by Jim Arnosky. Scholastic, 2000. ISBN 0590481495. Unpaged. Grades 1–3.

Barrett, Jalma. *Lynx* (Wildcats of North America). Photographs by Larry Allan. Blackbirch Press, 1999. ISBN 1567112595 (lib. bdg., alk. paper). 24 p. Grades 3–5.

Batten, Mary. *The Winking, Blinking Sea: All About Bioluminescence*. Millbrook Press, 2000. ISBN 0761315500. Unpaged. Grades 3–5.

Berger, Melvin. *Growl! A Book About Bears* (Hello Reader! Level 3). Scholastic, Cartwheel Books, 1998. ISBN 0590632663. Unpaged. Grades 1–2.

————. *Why I Sneeze, Shiver, Hiccup and Yawn* (Let's-Read-and-Find-Out Science, Stage 2). Illustrated by Paul Meisel. HarperCollins, 2000. ISBN 0060281448. 33 p. Grades 1–3.

Berger, Melvin, and Gilda Berger. *Did Dinosaurs Live in Your Backyard? Questions and Answers About Dinosaurs*. Illustrated by Alan Male. Scholastic Reference, 1998. ISBN 0590130781 (plb.); 0439085683 (pbk.). 48 p. Grades 4–6.

————. *Do Stars Have Points? Questions and Answers About Stars and Planets*. Illustrated by Vincent Di Fate. Scholastic Reference, 1998. ISBN 0590130803 (plb.); 0439085705 (pbk.). 48 p. Grades 4–6.

Branley, Franklyn M. *Flash, Crash, Rumble, and Roll* (Let's-Read-and-Find-Out Science, Stage 2). Illustrated by True Kelley. HarperCollins, 1964, 1985, 1999 (revised edition, newly illustrated). ISBN 0060278587; 0060278595 (lib. bdg.); 0064451798 (pbk.). 32 p. Grades 2–3.

Cerullo, Mary M. *Coral Reef: A City That Never Sleeps*. Photographs by Jeffrey L. Rotman. Cobblehill Books/Dutton, 1996. ISBN 0525651934. 58 p. Grades 4–8.

————. *The Truth About Great White Sharks*. Photographs by Jeffrey L. Rottman. Illustrated by Michael Wertz. Chronicle Books, 2000. ISBN 0811824675. 48 p. Grades 4–8.

Cowley, Joy. *The Red-Eyed Tree Frog*. Illustrated with photographs by Nic Bishop. Scholastic, 1999. ISBN 0590871757. Unpaged. Grades pre-K–2.

Dunphy, Madeleine. *Here Is the Coral Reef.* Illustrated by Tom Leonard. Hyperion Books for Children, 1998. ISBN 0786821353 (lib. bdg.). Unpaged. Grades K–2.

Dussling, Jennifer. *Pink Snow and Other Weird Weather* (All Aboard Reading Level 2). Illustrated by Hedi Petach. Grosset & Dunlap, 1998. ISBN 0448418878 (gb.); 0448418584 (pbk.). 48 p. Grades 1–3.

Earle, Sylvia A. *Hello, Fish! Visiting the Coral Reef.* Photographs by Wolcott Henry. National Geographic Society, 1999. ISBN 0792271033. Unpaged. Grades 2–4.

———. *Sea Critters.* Photographs by Wolcott Henry. National Geographic Society, 2000. ISBN 0792271815. 32 p. Grades 1–4.

Fraser, Mary Ann. *Where Are the Night Animals?* (Let's-Read-and-Find-Out Science, Stage 1). HarperCollins, 1999. ISBN 0060277173; 0060277181 (lib. bdg.); 0064451763 (pbk.). 32 p. Grades 1–3.

Fredericks, Anthony D. *Cannibal Animals: Animals That Eat Their Own Kind.* Franklin Watts, 1999. ISBN 0531117014 (lib. bdg.); 0531164209 (pbk.). 64 p. Grades 3–5.

Gibbons, Gail. *Bats.* Holiday House, 1999. ISBN 0823414574. Unpaged. Grades 1–3.

———. *Ducks!* Holiday House, 2001. ISBN 0823415678. Unpaged. Grades 1–3.

———. *Exploring the Deep, Dark Sea.* Little, Brown, 1999. ISBN 0516309451. Unpaged. Grades 1–4.

———. *Penguins!* Holiday House, 1998. ISBN 0823413888. Unpaged. Grades 1–3.

———. *Pigs.* Holiday House, 1999. ISBN 0823414418. Unpaged. Grades 1–3.

———. *Rabbits, Rabbits and More Rabbits!* Holiday House, 2000. ISBN 0823414868. Unpaged. Grades 1–3.

Goldin, Augusta. *Ducks Don't Get Wet.* Illustrated by Helen K. Davie. HarperCollins, 1999. ISBN 006027882X. 32 p. Grades K–3.

Haduch, Bill. *Food Rules! The Stuff You Munch, Its Crunch, Its Punch, and Why You Sometimes Lose Your Lunch.* Illustrated by Rick Stromoski. Dutton, 2001. ISBN 0525464190. 106 p. Grades 4–8.

Henderson, Douglas. *Asteroid Impact.* Dial Books for Young Readers, 2000. ISBN 0803725000. 40 p. Grades 4–7.

Hickman, Pamela. *Animals Eating: How Animals Chomp, Chew, Slurp and Swallow.* Illustrated by Pat Stephens. Kids Can Press, 2001. ISBN 1-55074-577-8. 40 p. Grades 2–4.

Holmes, Kevin. *Warthogs.* Bridgestone Books, an imprint of Capstone Press, 1999. ISBN 0736800670. 24 p. Grades 2–4.

Holub, Joan. *Why Do Cats Meow?* Illustrated by Anna DiVito. Dial Books for Young Readers, 2001. ISBN 0803725035. 48 p. Grades 1–3.

———. *Why Do Dogs Bark?* Illustrated by Anna DiVito. Dial Books for Young Readers, 2001. ISBN 0803725043. 48 p. Grades 2–3.

Hopping, Lorraine Jean. *Wild Weather: Blizzards!* Illustrated by Jody Wheeler. Scholastic, 1998. ISBN 0590397303 (pbk.). Unpaged. Grades 2–3.

Jenkins, Martin. *Chameleons Are Cool.* Illustrated by Sue Shields. Candlewick Press, 1997, 1998. ISBN 0763601446. 30 p. Grades 1–3.

Kane, Karen. *Mountain Gorillas.* Photographs by Gerry Ellis. Lerner, 2001. ISBN 0822530406. 48 p. Grades 2–4.

Kite, L. Patricia. *Cockroaches.* Lerner, 2001. ISBN 0822530465. 48 p. Grades 3–5.

Lasky, Kathryn. *Interrupted Journey: Saving Endangered Sea Turtles.* Photographs by Christopher G. Knight. Candlewick Press, 2001. ISBN 0-7636-0635-9. Unpaged. Grades 2–5.

Markle, Sandra. *Growing Up Wild: Wolves.* Atheneum Books for Young Readers, 2001. ISBN 0689818866. 32 p. Grades 2–4.

Martin-James, Kathleen. *Building Beavers* (Pull-Ahead Books). Lerner, 2000. ISBN 0822536285. 32 p. Grades K–3.

McNulty, Faith. *How Whales Walked into the Sea.* Illustrated by Ted Rand. Scholastic, 1999. ISBN 0590898302. Unpaged. Grades 2–5.

Muller, Eric. *While You're Waiting for the Food to Come: A Tabletop Science Activity Book: Experiments and Tricks That Can Be Done at a Restaurant, the Dining Room Table, or Wherever Food Is Served.* Illustrated by Eldon Doty. Orchard Books, 1999. ISBN 0531301990 (trade); 0531071448 (pbk.). 83 p. Grades 4–6.

Murawski, Darlyne A. *Bug Faces.* National Geographic Society, 2000. ISBN 0792275578. Unpaged. Grades 1–4.

Myers, Jack. *On the Trail of the Komodo Dragon and Other Explorations of Science in Action.* Illustrated by John Rice. Boyds Mills Press, 1999. ISBN 1563977613. 63 p. Grades 4–6.

Nye, Bill. *Bill Nye the Science Guy's Big Blue Ocean.* With additional writing by Ian G. Saunders. Illustrated by John Dykes. Hyperion Books for Children, 1999. ISBN 0786842210 (trade); 0786850639 (lib. ed.). 48 p. Grades 3–5.

Patent, Dorothy Hinshaw. *Flashy Fantastic Rainforest Frogs.* Illustrated by Kendahl Jan Jubb. Walker, 1997. ISBN 0802786154. 32 p. Grades 2–4.

———. *Slinky Scaly Slithery Snakes.* Illustrated by Kendahl Jan Jubb. Walker, 2000. ISBN 0802787436. 32 p. Grades 2–4.

Patterson, Dr. Francine. *Koko-Love! Conversations with a Signing Gorilla.* Photographs by Dr. Ronald H. Cohn. Dutton Children's Books, 1999. ISBN 0525463194. 32 p. Grades 3–6.

Perry, Phyllis J. *Freshwater Giants: Hippopotamus, River Dolphins, and Manatees.* Franklin Watts, 1999. ISBN 0531116816 (lib. bdg.); 0531164241 (pbk.). 64 p. Grades 3–5.

Pfeffer, Wendy. *Sounds All Around* (Let's-Read-and-Find-Out Science, Stage l). Illustrated by Holly Keller. HarperCollins, 1999. ISBN 0060277122. 32 p. Grades 1–3.

Pringle, Laurence. *Bats! Strange and Wonderful*. Illustrated by Meryl Henderson. Boyds Mills Press, 2000. ISBN 1-56397-327-8. 32 p. Grades K–3.

———. *The Environmental Movement: From Its Roots to the Challenges of a New Century*. HarperCollins, 2000. ISBN 0688156266. 144 p. Grades 4–8.

———. *Global Warming: The Threat of Earth's Changing Climate*. SeaStar Books, 2001. ISBN 1-58717-009-4. 48 p. Grades 5–8.

Robbins, Ken. *Thunder on the Plains: The Story of the American Buffalo*. Atheneum Books for Young Readers, 2001. ISBN 0689830254. Unpaged. Grades 2–4.

Rounds, Glen. *Beaver*. Holiday House, 1999. ISBN 082341440X. Unpaged. Grades 1–3.

Rowan, Dr. Pete. *Big Head!* Illustrated by John Temperton. Alfred A. Knopf, 1998. ISBN 0679890181. 44 p. Grades 5–up.

Sayre, April Pulley. *Splish! Splash! Animal Baths*. Millbrook Press, 2000. ISBN 0-7613-1821-6. Unpaged. Grades K–2.

Schaefer, Lola M. *Sea Anemones*. Consulting editor: Gail Saunders-Smith, Ph.D. Consultant: Jody Byrum, science writer, SeaWorld Education Department. Pebble Books, an imprint of Capstone Press, 1999. ISBN 0736802487. 24 p. Grades 1–2.

———. *Sea Urchins*. Consulting editor: Gail Saunders-Smith, Ph.D. Consultant: Jody Byrum, science writer, SeaWorld Education Department. Pebble Books, an imprint of Capstone Press, 1999. ISBN 0736802517. 24 p. Grades 1–2.

Schaffer, Donna. *Mealworms*. Bridgestone Books, an imprint of Capstone Press, 1999. ISBN 0736802096. 24 p. Grades 2–4.

Settel, Joanne, Ph.D. *Exploding Ants: Amazing Facts About How Animals Adapt*. Atheneum Books for Young Readers, 1999. ISBN 0689817395. 40 p. Grades 4–6.

Simon, Seymour. *Crocodiles and Alligators*. HarperCollins, 1999. ISBN 0060274735; 0060274743 (lib. bdg.). Unpaged. Grades 3–6.

———. *Gorillas*. HarperCollins, 2000. ISBN 0060230363. Unpaged. Grades 3–5.

Singer, Marilyn. *On the Same Day in March: A Tour of the World's Weather*. Illustrated by Frane Lessac. HarperCollins, 2000. ISBN 0060281871. Unpaged. Grades 1–3.

Skurzynski, Gloria. *On Time: From Seasons to Split Seconds*. National Geographic Society, 2000. ISBN 0-7922-7503-9. 41 p. Grades 3–7.

———. *Zero Gravity*. Simon & Schuster Books for Young Readers, 1994. ISBN 0027829251. 32 p. Grades 4–6.

Sloan, Christopher. *Feathered Dinosaurs*. Introduction by Dr. Philip J. Currie. National Geographic Society, 2000. ISBN 0792272196. 64 p. Grades 4–7.

Stefoff, Rebecca. *Penguin* (Living Things). Benchmark Books, 1998. ISBN 0761404465 (lib. bdg.). 32 p. Grades 1–3.

Swanson, Diane. *Animals Eat the Weirdest Things*. Illustrated by Terry Smith. Henry Holt, 1998. ISBN 080505846X. 64 p. Grades 4–6.

———. *Hmm? The Most Interesting Book You'll Ever Read About Memory* (Mysterious You). Illustrated by Rose Cowles. Kids Can Press, 2001. ISBN 1-55074-595-6; 1-55074-597-2 (pbk.). 40 p. Grades 4–7.

Swinburne, Stephen R. *Coyote: North America's Dog*. Boyds Mills Press, 1999. ISBN 1563977656. 32 p. Grades 4–6.

———. *Guess Whose Shadow?* Boyds Mills Press, 1999. ISBN 1563977249. 32 p. Grades 1–2.

———. *Lots and Lots of Zebra Stripes: Patterns in Nature*. Boyds Mills Press, 1998. ISBN 1563977079. 32 p. Grades pre-K–2.

———. *Unbeatable Beaks*. Illustrated by Joan Paley. Henry Holt, 1999. ISBN 0805048022. Unpaged. Grades 1–3.

Tildes, Phyllis Limbacher. *Calico's Cousins: Cats from Around the World*. Charlesbridge, 1999. ISBN 0881066846 (reinforced); 0881066494 (pbk.). Unpaged. Grades 1–3.

Trumbauer, Lisa. *Animal Ears*. Yellow Umbrella Books, 2001. ISBN 0736807233. 17 p. Grades 1–3.

Wallace, Karen. *Gentle Giant Octopus*. Illustrated by Mike Bostock. Candlewick Press, 1998. ISBN 076360318X. 30 p. Grades 1–3.

Weaver, Robyn. *Meerkats*. Bridgestone Books, an imprint of Capstone Press, 1999. ISBN 0736800662. 24 p. Grades 2–4.

Webb, Sophie. *My Season with Penguins: An Antarctic Journal*. Houghton Mifflin, 2000. ISBN 0395922917. 48 p. Grades 4–up.

Wechsler, Doug. *Bizarre Birds*. Photographs by the author and VIREO. Boyds Mills Press, 1999. ISBN 1563977605. 48 p. Grades 4–6.

Wilcox, Charlotte. *The Chihuahua*. Capstone Press, 1999. ISBN 0736801588. 48 p. Grades 4–up.

———. *The Weimaraner*. Capstone Press, 1999. ISBN 0736801634. 48 p. Grades 4–up.

Willis, Paul. *Dinosaurs* (Reader's Digest Pathfinders). Reader's Digest Children's Books, 1999. ISBN 1575842882; 1575842963 (lib. bdg.). 64 p. Grades 4–7.

Zeaman, John. *How the Wolf Became the Dog* (Before They Were Pets). Franklin Watts, 1998. ISBN 0531114597 (lib. bdg.); 053115906X (pbk.). 64 p. Grades 4–6.

———. *Why the Cat Chose Us* (Before They Were Pets). Franklin Watts, 1998. ISBN 0531114589 (lib. bdg.); 0531159051 (pbk.). 64 p. Grades 4–6.

CHAPTER ————————— 3

Playing with Words: Poetry, Wordplay, and Notable Writers

POETRY

It may surprise adults to know that kids enjoy poems—and not just funny ones. Some of the books in this section are humorous, but they encourage kids to branch out and read other poems that might be sad or serious or thought provoking. When booktalking, use poems to break up the booktalk, add humor or wordplay, or tie in with a nonfiction book on a similar topic. In the following sections you will find poems about dinosaurs, bugs, pets, and other animals—use these when booktalking the books in Chapter 2. Booktalking poetry is easy—just read a poem or two and you're done. In the annotations that follow we have pointed out some of the best poems for reading aloud and drawing attention to these fine books.

Kids love poems about school, especially if they're funny. Just about any choice in *The Bug in Teacher's Coffee and Other School Poems* (An I Can Read Book) by Kalli Dakos would be a good one. This book is easy to read and will make you laugh. It is a great booktalk filler.

Read aloud "Flying Around the Classroom" on page 20 and "I'm the Teacher's Cookie" on page 33.

Weird Pet Poems compiled by Dilys Evans is crammed with fun poems. While showing the picture of the exuberant kid on pages 8 and 9, read aloud the poem "Hooray! Hooray!" which is about anticipating getting a new pet. Try "Nothing on a Bulldog's Face" on page 11 and "The Porcupine" on page 14.

Little Dog Poems by Kristine O'Connell George provides you with very short, simple, delightfully illustrated poems that make great booktalk fillers. Read almost any one of them and you will find an audience for the book. A particular favorite is the first poem, "Cold Nose, Reflection, Enemy." It would not take long to read all the poems. Pick your favorites and read them aloud.

Love Letters by Arnold Adoff is perfect for Valentine's Day but could also be used any time of the year. Teachers will appreciate it for the creative writing ideas it generates and the thinking it inspires. Each poem is a message from a student to a secret admirer, friend, enemy, mom, dog, cat, or other significant being. Read some of the poems and have students discuss who "wrote" them. What is he or she like? Why did he or she write the poem? Do you think the object of affection in the poem ever got to read it? Colorful and enticing, this book leads naturally to creative-writing projects in which students write their own love poems to their dogs, cats, friends, or teachers. Read the poems called "Dear Playground Snow Girl" and "Dear Playground Snow Boy" for a good sense of these love letters.

Flicker Flash by Joan Bransfield Graham is a good choice for young elementary school readers. Brightly colored graphics illustrate this book of small poems about light. Try reading two or three of them aloud to break up a booktalk session. "Sun," "Match," and "Refrigerator Light" are all good choices.

There is a bit of a plot to *The Last-Place Sports Poems of Jeremy Bloom: A Collection of Poems About Winning, Losing, and Being a Good Sport (Sometimes)* by Gordon and Bernice Korman. After being a D-minus poet in sixth grade, Jeremy is convinced by his teacher to sign up for her poetry workshop. He writes about his year in sports, including football, soccer, hockey, basketball, and baseball. The Kormans are a mother-son team, and Gordon has written many humorous books for upper-elementary and middle school students. These poems are lighthearted and easy to read. A fun one to read out loud is "Time to Quit" on pages 79 and 80.

Wild Country: Outdoor Poems for Young People by David L. Harrison contains poems written for upper-elementary students. Some of these poems about the outdoors are absolutely delightful and brighten up a booktalk. Read aloud "The Eaglet" on page 9:

Soon he must leave.
Soon he'll be ready,
But today the world still looks too big,
The future uncertain.
Not quite ready,
He sits on the family nest and waits for food.

Or pair "Tundra Discoveries" with this poem on page 24, "Musk-Oxen":

Shaggy beasts with the wind in your wool, you graze the tundra
unafraid, unchanged since who knows when.
When wolves come, sniffing your babies, they find you shoulder to shoulder,
long faces like death masks, horns like swords curved at your sides, granite
skullcaps lowered to slam wolves and break bones.
You look disagreeable, formidable, dangerous.
Who wants to taste your babies that much?

Anyone who has ever loved a dinosaur (read the dedication) is going to chuckle at William Wise's poems and may even learn a little by reading *Dinosaurs Forever*. The pictures are silly and fun, and the first page provides a pronunciation guide for those of us who are unsure of the correct way to pronounce dinosaur names.

Read the poems "Dinosaur Colors" or "The Tyrant King" and show their illustrations. And, of course, pair this with other dinosaur books (see Chapter 2) for an even better booktalk.

My America: A Poetry Atlas of the United States is a beautiful book of 50 poems grouped by geographic region and that includes basic information about each state. The poems were selected by Lee Bennett Hopkins. Not every state has a poem about it specifically, but there are poems for each region of the United States. Pick a poem that goes with your area of the country, and if you want to amuse everyone, you might read "Wisconsin in Feb-B-RR-uary" on page 34.

The Songs of Birds: Stories and Poems from Many Cultures is a compilation of poems collected and retold by Hugh Lupton. Regardless of whether you consider yourself a bird lover, this book has some fine stories and poems from all around the world to interest you. Find out how the mosquito lost its tongue in "The Swallow and the Snake" from Palestine. Or how a raven ate an entire whale all by itself in "The Raven and the Whale," an Inuit story. The story of how birds stole fire from the moon is told in an Aboriginal tale, "The Pigeon, the Sparrow-Hawk and the Theft of Fire." Flip through the book to show the audience the spectacular illustrations, and then show them the one of the vulture dance on pages 34 and 35.

If you are booktalking a nonfiction book about insects, be sure to include a poem from *Insect Soup: Bug Poems* by Barry Louis Polisar. He presents several short but very funny poems about bugs in this neat collection. Read aloud "Here Is the Fly."

Here is the spot where the fly touched down.
She paused too long, that's clear.
Swat went the swatter. Zap! It got her.
Now all that's left is a smear.

Jack Prelutsky, a master of funny poems for children, writes poems that kids can sing to music. Take a look at his books and see whether you can tell which songs might work. Kids love to sing these poems.

Here are some that work for the poems in his 1999 collection, *The Gargoyle on the Roof*:

"I'm Not Open for an Hour" "I've Been Working on the Railroad"
"Lament of a Lonely Troll" "Battle Hymn of the Republic"
"Mother Gargoye's Lullaby" "Auld Lang Syne"
"Plaint of the Headless Horseman" "What Shall We Do with
 a Drunken Sailor"

"I'm Bugaboo the Bogeyman" "Onward, Christian Soldiers"
"A Vampire Speaks of Grooming" "Deck the Halls"
"I Am Running Through a Tunnel" "Clementine"
"Song of the Baby Gargoyles" "Yellow Rose of Texas"
"My Sister Is a Werewolf " "Bonnie Blue Flag"
"Basilisk Brag" "Johnny Has Gone for a Soldier"
"I'm Gobbleup the Goblin" "Give My Regards to Broadway"
"Beneath a Bridge" "America the Beautiful"
"Guffin and Giffin" "The Daring Young Man on the
 Flying Trapeze"

"A Vampire Speaks of Circuses" "McNamara's Band"
"Gremlins" "Oh, Susanna"
"A Werewolf of Distinction" "When Johnny Comes Marching
 Home"

"The Gargoyle on the Roof" "Amazing Grace"

For a fun look at food, try *Yummy! Eating Through a Day*, with poems selected by Lee Bennet Hopkins. Read one or two of these poems from a delightful, simple, colorful anthology of poems about food. Try "Morning Smells" by Karen O'Donnell Taylor on pages 4 and 5 or "Ketchup" on page 11.

If you have ever gone camping or wished you could, *Toasting Marshmallows: Camping Poems* by Kristine O'Connell George is the book for you. How do you like your marshmallows toasted: fast and black or slow and golden?

Figure 3.1. *Toasting Marshmallows: Camping Poems* by Kristine O'Connell George.

Read the title poem on page 22 or "Two Voices in a Tent" on page 24.

Do you know what a concrete poem is? It is not like the poems most people are used to seeing. Concrete poems consist of a word or words arranged into particular shapes, and those shapes affect the meaning of the poem and add to what the words are saying. Take a look at the poems in *A Poke in the I: A Collection of Concrete Poems* edited by Paul B. Janeczko.

Read and show your audience "A Weak Poem (To Be Read Lying Down)" by Roger McGough on page 4 and "Popsicle" by Joan Bransfield Graham on page 17.

This book could easily be a springboard to students writing their own concrete poems—be sure to show it to teachers.

More Spice than Sugar: Poems About Feisty Females, a poetry collection compiled by Lillian Morrison, will be welcomed by teachers as well as young readers. Each of these poems celebrates a feisty woman—some famous and some just average. The author says in the preface that she identifies with "female sports figures, women aviators, explorers, and . . . all adventurous, talented women in the arts, in science, in the struggle for human rights, in just plain living."

These poems would be an excellent supplement for a history lesson on famous women such as Fannie Lou Hamer, Rosa Parks, Harriet Tubman, Clara Barton, Joan of Arc, and Molly Pitcher. Also included are poems about sports and famous athletes, including Wilma Rudolph and Joan Benoit. Try booktalking a biography of Harriet Tubman (Chapter 5) and reading the Eloise Greenfield poem on page 59 that begins "Harriet Tubman didn't take no stuff, Wasn't scared of nothing neither, Didn't come into this world to be no slave, And wasn't going to stay one either."

Take a break from your regular booktalk to read a poem or two from *Shoe Magic* by Nikki Grimes, a delightful large and colorful book. Read "The Shoe Rack" on page 5 or "Brandi's Baby Shoes" on page 18, and be sure to show the pictures.

Also by Nikki Grimes is *A Pocketful of Poems*, and what a fun and beautiful poetry book this is. Tiana tells us about her life and interests in the illustrations, with a poem describing them on one page and a haiku poem on the other.

"Haiku," says the author, "is a poetry of brushstrokes. The entire poem is made up of just seventeen little syllables. And yet, with those, a poet can create a sort of painting in miniature. That's what I like about it" (page 31). You might want to try writing some haiku yourself.

Show the illustration and read the poem "Homer" on pages 20 and 21.

FUN WITH WORDS

Charlotte Foltz Jones has great fun with *Eat Your Words: A Fascinating Look at the Language of Food*. This delightful book tells where the names of some of our foods come from. Have you ever wondered why "buffalo wings" are called that? They certainly aren't made from buffaloes. But guess what? Someone in Buffalo, New York, invented them, and that is how they got their name. The name "sardine" came from the island of Sardinia, where sardines were once canned—but there is no fish called a sardine. The most common fish that become sardines are pilchard and young herrings. But to become a sardine, a fish has to be packed in a can. A peanut is neither a pea nor a nut. It is a legume, or a bean.

Did you know that prehistoric people used toothpicks? Americans use about 30 billion a year! Most are made in Maine from birch trees. One tree produces about 4 million toothpicks.

On pages 14 and 15, read aloud some of the "Laws of the Food Police," not all of which may still be enforced.

- In Joliet, Illinois, it is against the law to put cake in a cookie jar.
- Banana peels can't be tossed on the streets in Waco, Texas.
- A Memphis, Tennessee, law prohibits the sale of bologna on Sunday.
- In California, it is illegal to peel an orange in a hotel room.
- It's a crime in Idaho to give your sweetheart a box of candy weighing less than 50 pounds.
- Iowa state law makes it illegal to have a rotten egg in your possession.
- In Greene, New York, it is illegal to eat peanuts and walk backward on the sidewalk while a concert is playing.

Be sure you read the laws that pertain to your own state.

Jon Agee's latest book of palindromes is called *Sit on a Potato Pan, Otis! More Palindromes*. A palindrome is a word or phrase that reads exactly the same forward and backward. Thinking of new ones is a test of creativity, but Agee is good at it. Upper-elementary and middle-school-aged students will get a kick out of these captivating examples of wordplay.

Figure 3.2. *Sit on a Potato Pan, Otis! More Palindromes* **by Jon Agee.**

The book is a collection of cartoons illustrating original (to Agee and a few others, to whom he gives credit) palindromes. Here's an example: An overweight man runs from a prison while one guard tells another "We lost a fatso, Lew." Or, a farmer and his wife, viewing a gaggle of skyward-looking geese comment, "Do geese see God?"

Fun and funny. Readers will want to make up some of their own. You might want to write one of these palindromes on the board and have your audience guess what is unique about the phrase before you tell them what a palindrome is.

Even more fun with words can be found in Agee's *Who Ordered the Jumbo Shrimp? And Other Oxymorons*. This delightful and hilarious book of cartoons illustrates oxymorons ("an expression or figure of speech that combines contradictory or incongruous words"). Show the kids the "light heavyweight," the "sharp curves," and "He's turned up missing." This is unpaged, but you will be laughing as you flip through the pages.

A third winning title from Jon Agee is *Elvis Lives and Other Anagrams*. Just like the other Agee books, it combines wordplay with clever cartoons. If you are booktalking using PowerPoint, scan in some of the anagrams to show to your audience. Some favorites include "Halitosis: Lois Has It," "Funeral: Real Fun," and "School Cafeteria: Hot Cereal Fiasco."

Younger students frequently request books of jokes and riddles. *Riddle-Lightful: Oodles of Little Riddle Poems* by J. Patrick Lewis will intrigue and delight an audience. Try the first one, a fun and easy starter, and then ask them to guess the one that starts "I chase you into bed but you won't let me stay. . ." Be sure to share the illustrations!

More riddle poems can be found in Charles Ghigna's *Riddle Rhymes*. A couple of the riddle rhymes in this fun book will change the rhythm of any booktalk and make it more appealing. Each left-hand page has a riddle poem, and each right-hand page reveals the answer. "Your Secret Companion" is fun, as is "The Invisible Friend," but the most appropriate one for a booktalk is "Undercover Friend," about—what else?—a book. Be sure to show the audience the illustration after they guess the answer.

You can find yet another set of rhyming riddles in *ABC Animal Riddles* by Susan Joyce. This is a delightful alphabet book filled with good poetic clues as well as pictorial ones and information about the number of letters in the word we are looking for. Reading any of the poems aloud will no doubt start a great guessing game with your audience. At the end of the book are ideas for using the book in the classroom.

Many authors have used alphabet books to convey fun and valuable information. One example is Kathy Darling's *ABC Dogs*. The irresistible color photos that fill this treasury will charm your audience. Not only is there an alphabet of dogs, but for each dog, information is placed in a sketch of a bone about the size (large, medium, or small) and color of the breed and describes the job the dog was bred to do. For instance, a Jack Russell terrier's job is to dig. An Irish water spaniel loves to retrieve things from the water. A Queensland heeler herds cattle, and a West Highland white terrier chases mice. Show the audience both the front and back covers and the sheepdog on the other side of the title page.

More alphabetical animals can be found in Terri DeGezelle's *Birds A to Z*. This fun book is filled with nuggets of information for beginning readers. Did you know that the bird called the albatross, pictured on page 2, can sleep while it flies? Or that the reason a woodpecker, on page 24, drills or pecks holes in wood is to pull out bugs with its long sticky tongue? Or that the wingspan of a trumpeter swan can be up to eight feet wide?

At the end of the book are some fun activities to try. How often can you flap your arms up and down in 10 seconds? A hummingbird can beat its wings 700 times in that much time!

Terri DeGezelle continues the theme in *Bugs A to Z*. Bugs are fascinating and sometimes a little scary. We all know about bedbugs, and we joke about them, but have you ever seen one? Look at the picture on page 3. "Bedbugs can live for months without food. When they do eat, they take a bite from birds, dogs and even people." Not good!

Page two has a photo of an aphid being milked by ants for its honeydew.

There is much more interesting information, including that about the moving leaf bug on page 14—it looks almost exactly like a leaf. Page 28 lists some interesting Web sites, for instance, the Yuckiest Bug Site at www.yucky.com.

Another alphabet book for young children is Don L. Curry's *My ABCs*. This is a very simple, attractive, ABC book for beginning readers. It presents just enough information to make a reader feel quite accomplished at the end. Did you know that turtles, for instance, can live for more than 200 years?

At the end of the book are some activities, Web sites, and more information about the animals and objects pictured in the ABC photos.

AN AUTHOR'S LIFE

Upper-elementary school students have probably not read Shakespeare, but they have certainly heard of him. It is never too early to get them interested in great literature, and Aliki makes it easy in *William Shakespeare and the Globe*. This is an absolutely lovely, joyful book written in five acts. The first four tell the story of William Shakespeare and the Globe, the theater in which many of his plays were performed. The last act tells us about Sam Wanamaker, an American boy who dreamed of rebuilding the Globe so that Shakespeare's plays could be performed as they were 400 years ago.

Shakespeare is a mysterious man. We do not know much about his life, but we know a great deal about him from what he wrote. He grew up in Stratford, married young, and went by himself to work in London, which was a big city even then. Its queen, Elizabeth I, loved plays, and Shakespeare wrote the greatest ones ever. Aliki includes much information even on the sides and bottoms of the pages. It may astonish you to read, on pages 46 and 47, some of the words and phrases that Shakespeare made up and that we use all of the time today. Try "upstairs," "downstairs," "successful," "well behaved," "alligator," "knock knock," and "puke" for starters.

Loaded with excellent color illustrations, this book will make you want to know more. Show your audience the illustration of the queen on page 16.

Students interested in Shakespeare will naturally want to know more about the Globe Theatre. Andrew Langley writes about it in *Shakespeare's Theatre*—appropriate for upper-elementary and middle school students. The most famous writer in the English language, if not the world, is William Shakespeare, who is best known for the plays he wrote, such as *Hamlet, Romeo and Juliet, A Midsummer Night's Dream*, and *Macbeth*.

The kinds of plays Shakespeare wrote were influenced by the type of theater in which they were performed. Four hundred years ago, theaters were built almost round, with the middle open to the outside. If it rained, the audience and the actors got rained on, too. These theaters were made of wood, so they caught fire very easily. Most of Shakespeare's works were performed at the Globe, which burned in 1613.

An American actor, Sam Wanamaker, wanted to build a new Globe Theatre as close as possible to the original. *Shakespeare's Theatre* is the story of how he made his dream come true. If you like history, archaeology, building, or theater, this book will interest you. Show your audience the photo of the play on page 35.

Moving a few hundred years into the future, *Laura's Album: A Remembrance Scrapbook of Laura Ingalls Wilder* compiled by William Anderson gives us insight into the life of a beloved American author and pioneer. Many girls (and women) will want to buy this title the minute they see it. Although many of the photos are familiar to longtime fans of the series, some are new, and almost all will be new to most readers. This appealingly designed book compares Laura's life to her books, chronologically, and has many black-and-white and color illustrations. Hold up some of the pictures to entice fans. Of course, recommend that students read the *Little House on the Prairie* books if they haven't already.

Elizabeth MacLeod writes about another beloved children's author in *Lucy Maud Montgomery: A Writer's Life*. Fans of the *Anne of Green Gables* books will want to read this book and look at the photographs of Lucy Maud Montgomery, the Canadian author whose books are famous around the world. Can you believe that Montgomery's manuscript for *Anne of Green Gables* was rejected by the first five publishers she sent it to? When this happened, Montgomery gave up on it and tucked it away in an old hatbox. Months later she got it out and sent it to one more publisher. This one accepted it, and Maud finally fulfilled her lifelong dream of becoming a successful writer. Luckily for her she chose to receive a royalty for each book she sold rather than a onetime payment of $500. Within several years she was making as much money as the prime minister of Canada. Fans of Anne will pore over this attractive book, and some new readers might even get interested in Montgomery's classic books.

Students who enjoy reading will find interesting facts in *Who Were They Really? The True Stories Behind Famous Characters* by Susan Beth Pfeffer. Sometimes authors write stories about people or things they know. And sometimes they change the names of the people they describe. In this book, Susan Pfeffer tells us about some famous books in which the characters were based on real-life people or things.

You probably know that Laura Ingalls was a real pioneer girl, but did you know that the "Lost Boys" in the Peter Pan story were based on real boys? Or that Paddington Bear was a real teddy bear that made Michael Bond want to write about him? Or that Jo March and the other "little women" were based on Louisa May Alcott and her sisters? A lot of kids do not know that there was a real Christopher Robin and that anyone can see his toys, including the real Winnie-the-Pooh. Read the book to find out where they are. Show the picture of those toys on page 54.

Even though it is mainly about the Mississippi River, *Mark Twain and the Queens of the Mississippi* by Cheryl Harness also tells about the life of one of America's most beloved authors. This brief but beautiful history of the Mississippi River is filled with little-known facts. Almost half of the groundwater in the continental United States feeds into the Mississippi. Take a look at the map on the pages 2 and 3 and see whether your area is one that does. The map of how the rivers flow into each other is intriguing.

Harness describes the types of boats that floated on the river for centuries and then takes us to 1831, when a new kind of boat appeared—the steamboat. This was a major invention, for now boats could travel the river in both directions without rowing, towing, or pushing poles. Going up the river against the currents had always been difficult, but now it became quite easy.

One boy who lived on the river was Sam Clemens, who loved to watch the steamboats come to his hometown—Hannibal, Missouri. When he was 21 years old, Clemens decided to make his childhood dream of being a steamboat pilot on the Mississippi come true. He had to learn every one of the 1,300 miles between St. Louis and New Orleans—every bend and island and bank—by heart, and he loved it.

This mix of river and Clemens history makes for an intriguing booktalk. To entice the children, show them the pictures of the steamboats.

Pick and Shovel Poet: The Journeys of Pascal d'Angelo by Jim Murphy tells about a poet who is less well known, but his story is interesting and ties in well with American history units on immigration.

If you go to the museum on Ellis Island, you may see a quote from an Italian immigrant. Paraphrased, it says: "I was told that in America the streets were paved with gold. But when I came to America, I found that not only were the streets *not* paved with gold, but that they were not paved—and I was expected to pave them!"

Pascal d'Angelo, a teenager growing up in Italy in 1910, heard about the gold. He and his father sailed on an immigrant ship to America, sure that they would find a better existence there than the one they had endured in Italy. America promised higher salaries and opportunity, they believed. Both father and son would need to send money home to support the rest of the family, but, all in all, immigration seemed an excellent decision.

They did not know how Italian immigrants were hated at the time, and they didn't know that most opportunities for work were poorly paid and involved backbreaking physical labor. But they found out all too quickly. Low pay and shabby housing were only a few of the problems they faced.

Pascal wanted more, however, even when his father decided to give up and go back to Italy. He learned to read and write English and decided he wanted to become a poet more than anything else—a real, published poet. This story of immigrant life and how Pascal realized his dream is a fascinating one.

It is hard to find a middle school student who has not read *Hatchet* by Gary Paulsen. This book has so fascinated young readers that Paulsen felt compelled to write several sequels and now a companion book called *Guts: The True Stories Behind Hatchet and the Brian Books*.

In *Hatchet*, Brian survives a plane crash, animal attacks, and near starvation. Paulsen himself has survived these things and more and tells of the experiences he drew on in writing this book. Paulsen has seen several plane crashes and their aftermath. When he was seven years old he saw a passenger plane ditch in the Pacific. The plane split in two and people spilled out into the water. He watched as sharks instantly attacked them, even as they were being hauled in by rescue boats. Paulsen has also been in several near-crashes in a Cessna 406 bush plane, the same aircraft that Brian crashes in (these descriptions begin on page 11).

The appeal of this book is the "guts"—the foods that Paulsen has eaten to stay alive. He has eaten everything that Brian eats, including raw turtle eggs. However, that is the one food that he just couldn't keep down. Hearing about his experiences will easily sell this book. Start reading the last paragraph on page 132, which begins, "I have eaten some strange things in my life: raw meat, eyeballs, guts." Read to the end of the chapter. This is a must-read for kids who love Brian's adventures, one that you will love sharing with reluctant readers.

BIBLIOGRAPHY

Adoff, Arnold. *Love Letters*. Illustrated by Lisa Desimini. Blue Sky Press, 1997. ISBN 0-590-48478-8. Unpaged. Grades 1–5.

Agee, Jon. *Elvis Lives and Other Anagrams*. Collected and illustrated by Jon Agee. Farrar, Straus & Giroux, 2000. ISBN 0-374-32127-2. Unpaged. Grades 4–up.

———. *Sit on a Potato Pan, Otis! More Palindromes*. Farrar, Straus & Giroux, 1999. ISBN 0374318085. Unpaged. Grades 4–up.

————. *Who Ordered the Jumbo Shrimp? And Other Oxymorons*. Michael Di Capua Books, HarperCollins, 1998. ISBN 0062051598. 80 p. Grades 4–up.

Aliki. *William Shakespeare and the Globe*. HarperCollins, 1999. ISBN 006027820X; 0060278218 (lib. bdg.). 48 p. Grades 3–5.

Anderson, William (compiler). *Laura's Album: A Remembrance Scrapbook of Laura Ingalls Wilder*. HarperCollins, 1998. ISBN 0060278420. 80 p. Grades 4–up.

Curry, Don L. *My ABCs*. Gail Saunders-Smith, Ph.D., Consultant. A+ Books, Capstone Curriculum, 2000. ISBN 0736870407 (hc); 0736870482 (pbk.). 32 p. Grades K–2.

Dakos, Kalli. *The Bug in Teacher's Coffee and Other School Poems* (An I Can Read Book). Pictures by Mike Reed. HarperCollins, 1999. ISBN 0060279400 (lib.bdg.). 43 p. Grades 1–3

Darling, Kathy. *ABC Dogs*. Photographs by Tara Darling. Walker, 1997. ISBN 0802786340 (hc.); 0802786359 (reinforced). Unpaged. Grades 1–3.

DeGezelle, Terri. *Birds A to Z*. Consultant: Ilze Balodis, Institute for Field Ornithology, University of Maine at Machias. A+ Books, Capstone Curriculum, 2000. ISBN 0736870385. 32 p. Grades K–2.

————. *Bugs A to Z*. Mark O'Brien, Consultant, collections coordinator, Museum of Zoology, Division of Insects, University of Michigan, Ann Arbor. A+ Books, Capstone Curriculum, 2000. ISBN 0736870369. 32 p. Grades K–2.

Evans, Dilys (compiler). *Weird Pet Poems*. Illustrated by Jacqueline Rogers. Simon & Schuster Books for Young Readers, 1997. ISBN 0689807341. 38 p. Grades K–4.

George, Kristine O'Connell. *Little Dog Poems*. Illustrated by June Otani. Clarion Books, 1999. ISBN 0395822661. 40 p. Grades K–3.

————. *Toasting Marshmallows: Camping Poems*. Illustrated by Kate Kiesler. Clarion Books, 2001. ISBN 061804597X. Unpaged. Grades 1–4.

Ghigna, Charles. *Riddle Rhymes*. Illustrated by Julia Gorton. Hyperion Books for Children, 1995. ISBN 1562824791 (trade); 1562824805 (lib. bdg.). Unpaged. Grades K–2.

Graham, Joan Bransfield. *Flicker Flash*. Illustrated by Nancy Davis. Houghton Mifflin, 1999. ISBN 039590501X. Unpaged. Grades K–2.

Grimes, Nikki. *A Pocketful of Poems*. Illustrated by Javaka Steptoe. Clarion Books, 2001. ISBN 0395938686. 32 p. Grades 2–4.

————. *Shoe Magic*. Illustrated by Terry Widener. Orchard Books, 2000. ISBN 0531322861. 32 p. Grades 1–5.

Harness, Cheryl. *Mark Twain and the Queens of the Mississippi*. Simon & Schuster Books for Young Readers, 1998. ISBN 0689815425. Unpaged. Grades 3–5.

Harrison, David L. *Wild Country: Outdoor Poems for Young People*. Wordsong/Boyds Mills Press, 1999. ISBN 1563977842. 48 p. Grades 4–6.

Hopkins, Lee Bennett (compiler). *My America: A Poetry Atlas of the United States*. Illustrated by Stephen Alcorn. Simon & Schuster Books for Young Readers, 2000. ISBN 0689812477. 83 p. Grades 3–up.

———— (compiler). *Yummy! Eating Through a Day*. Illustrated by Renee Flower. Simon & Schuster Books for Young Readers, 2000. ISBN 068981755X. 32 p. Grades 2–4.

Janeczko, Paul B. (editor). *A Poke in the I: A Collection of Concrete Poems*. Illustrated by Chris Raschka. Candlewick Press, 2001. ISBN 0763606618. 32 p. Grades 2–5.

Jones, Charlotte Foltz. *Eat Your Words: A Fascinating Look at the Language of Food*. Illustrated by John O'Brien. Delacorte Press, 1999. ISBN 0385325754. 87 p. Grades 4–6.

Joyce, Susan. *ABC Animal Riddles*. Illustrated by Doug DuBosque. Peel Productions, 1999. ISBN 0939217511. Unpaged. Grades 1–3.

Korman, Gordon, and Bernice Korman. *The Last-Place Sports Poems of Jeremy Bloom: A Collection of Poems About Winning, Losing, and Being a Good Sport (Sometimes)*. Scholastic, 1996. ISBN 0-329-15103-7. 92 p. Grades 4–7.

Langley, Andrew. *Shakespeare's Theatre*. Paintings by June Everett. Oxford University Press, 1999. ISBN 0199105650 (hc.); 0199105669 (pbk.). 48 p. Grades 5–8.

Lewis, J. Patrick. *Riddle-Lightful: Oodles of Little Riddle Poems*. Illustrated by Debbie Tilley. Alfred A. Knopf, 1998. ISBN 0679887601 (trade); 0679887606 (lib. bdg.). Unpaged. Grades 1–5.

Lupton, Hugh (compiler). *The Songs of Birds: Stories and Poems from Many Cultures*. Illustrated by Steve Palin. Barefoot Books, 2000. ISBN 1841480452. 80 p. Grades 4–8.

MacLeod, Elizabeth. *Lucy Maud Montgomery: A Writer's Life*. Kids Can Press, 2001. ISBN 1-55074-487-9. 32 p. Grades 3–6.

Morrison, Lillian (compiler). *More Spice than Sugar: Poems About Feisty Females*. Illustrated by Ann Boyajian. Houghton Mifflin, 2001. ISBN 0-618-06892-9. 80 p. Grades 4–8.

Murphy, Jim. *Pick and Shovel Poet: The Journeys of Pascal d'Angelo*. Clarion Books, 2000. ISBN 0395776104. 162 p. Grades 5–8.

Paulsen, Gary. *Guts: The True Stories Behind Hatchet and the Brian Books*. Delacorte Press, 2001. ISBN 0-385-32650-5. 148 p. Grades 5–8.

Pfeffer, Susan Beth. *Who Were They Really? The True Stories Behind Famous Characters*. Millbrook Press, 1999. ISBN 0761304053. 72 p. Grades 4–6.

Polisar, Barry Louis. *Insect Soup: Bug Poems*. Illustrated by David Clark. Rainbow Morning Music, 1999. ISBN 0938663224. Unpaged. Grades 1–4.

Prelutsky, Jack. *The Gargoyle on the Roof*. Greenwillow Books, 1999. ISBN 0688165532 (lib. bdg.). 40 p. Grades 2–6.

Wise, William. *Dinosaurs Forever*. Pictures by Lynn Munsinger. Dial Books for Young Readers, 2000. ISBN 0803721145. Unpaged. Grades 1–4.

CHAPTER —— 4

Travel the Globe: People, Places, and Historical Events from Around the World

A WORLD OF WONDERS

For an overview of many fascinating places, you can't beat *The World of Architectural Wonders* by Mike Corbishley. From Stonehenge to the Hoover Dam you can learn how and why these great sites were built. Color photographs and drawings enhance the stories of these structures. To make your booktalk even more interesting, pair this book with others in this chapter about the Roman Colosseum or Machu Picchu. This book includes some lesser known architectural wonders, including the tomb of the Emperor Ch'in, Mesa Verde, Great Zimbabwe, and the city of Petra. The photo of the Great Wall of China on page 17 is stunning.

For even more detail about some of the world's most fascinating places, try Russell Ash's *Great Wonders of the World*. This is a DK book, so it has wonderful illustrations and photographs, making it easy to booktalk. It begins with the "seven wonders of the world," of which only one is still standing. Do you know which one? (Answer: the Great Pyramid.) Using descriptions and his knowledge of the ruins, Ash tells about each wonder and then mentions other similar ones. For example, after the description of the Hanging Gardens of Babylon, there is a page devoted to other "wonders of entertainment," including the Colosseum, Walt Disney World, the Sydney Olympic stadium, and Shakespeare's Globe Theatre. The Colossus of Rhodes on pages 30 and 31 is great to show. According to legend, when a tiny flaw was found in the statue, the sculptor killed himself.

Did you know that the Great Wall of China was not considered one of the seven wonders? That is because it was unknown to the original compilers of the list. And did you know that no one could have visited all seven wonders? This is because they did not exist all at the same time. Both children and adults will enjoy this excellent book, which is great for browsing in a classroom or library.

One hundred years ago the world seemed bigger than it does today because airplanes had not yet been invented. Traveling took a long time, but one incredible construction made the world seem a good deal smaller. This was the Panama Canal. On page 6 of Elizabeth Mann's *The Panama Canal* you'll see a map of North and South America. These two continents are connected by a very narrow strip of land called the Isthmus of Panama. When the Europeans first came to the Americas, they wanted to be able to cross from the Atlantic to the Pacific Ocean via the isthmus. If they couldn't, they had to sail completely around the continent of South America, a dangerous trip that took weeks.

The French were the first to consider building a canal there, but they failed because everything that could go wrong did. They lost not only hundreds of millions of dollars but also nearly 20,000 workers to disease. There was a single-track railroad on the isthmus, built by an American in 1855 primarily to help gold seekers get to California more quickly. But the treasure hunters paid a lot to ride on it.

Theodore Roosevelt was convinced that a canal could be built even though he knew the French had failed in their attempt. His plan and the incredible things the U.S. government did to carry it out make a riveting story. The biggest problem American doctors faced was the diseases that were spread by mosquito bites. Dr. Gorgas, who was in charge, devised a screened enclosure that prevented mosquitoes from biting people. The illustration on page 14 shows a man with yellow fever sleeping in one of these enclosures.

Show your audience the map on page 6 and the fold-out picture of the locks system on page 20.

In Search of the Spirit: The Living National Treasures of Japan by Sheila Hamanaka is an unusual book about people who create extraordinary things.

Because Japan was separated from other countries by an ocean, the Japanese people developed many unique arts and crafts. After Japan was defeated in World War II, many of these items started disappearing. The country decided to honor the elders who had devoted their lives to the traditional crafts and performing arts. "Today over one hundred men and women have been given the special title of Bearers of Important Intangible Cultural Assets.... They are popularly called Living National Treasures (page 5)." These craftspeople have spent their lives perfecting their art and have become masters at what they do.

Hamanaka profiles six of these masters: a Yuzen dyer who makes hand-painted kimonos, a bamboo weaver, a Bunraku puppet master, a sword maker, a Noh actor, and a potter. Just a quick glance at the beautiful photographs will convince you of their skill. Take a look at the lovely kimono on page 6, the pot on page 42, and the amazing sword on pages 28 and 29, which has been folded over to have over 1 million layers! Also look at the puppeteer and the actor. After the information on each Living National Treasure comes a section on how these people practice their art or craft. This is an incredible book.

THE ANCIENT WORLD

A Street Through Time: A 12,000 Year Walk Through History by Anne Millard is very enjoyable—and while you are having fun you will learn a lot, too. It starts with a colorful two-page scene of a settlement of Stone Age people along a riverbank. Then it leaps forward through the centuries, showing the same place at different times , and ends up in the modern world. The pictures are grand, and you'll find things to look for all the way through the book. Henry Hyde, we learn at the beginning, is a modern time traveler who gets to see the place in all of the scenes. Can you find him? At the end of the book is a series of other things to look for.

Show your audience any of the two-page spreads. A delightful book for grades 4 and up.

A similar theme occurs in *1,000 Years Ago on Planet Earth* by Sneed B. Collard, III. What was happening all over the planet 1,000 years ago? There is a fascinating list on the first page, including the following information:

- About 250 million people lived on Earth (now there are 6 billion).
- Forests covered between 45 and 60 percent of the Earth's surface.
- Only about half of the world's civilizations had developed a written language.
- Slavery existed on every inhabited continent except Australia.
- People burned wood for light and heat.
- Wars were common.
- Every continent except Antarctica had already been settled.

Read through the book to discover astonishing information about people all over the world. For instance, 1,000 years ago the Chinese had books, whereas in Europe, paper was not even available. A fun multicultural look at another time, this book also includes a list of Web sites.

One fascinating aspect of ancient times is Egyptian mummies. Everyone knows something about them, but there is a lot to be learned from Shelley Tanaka's *Secrets of the Mummies: Uncovering the Bodies of Ancient Egyptians*. Did you know that European tourists in the 1800s sometimes took Egyptian mummies home as souvenirs? They would then invite friends over to view the unwrapping. Although this must have been exciting, fortunately that practice has stopped, and mummies are now being preserved so we can learn more about the ancient Egyptians who made them.

Show your audience the photographs on page 34. This is the mummy of Nakht—a teenage boy. He was wrapped up with his internal organs intact. Scientists have learned that he had a tapeworm growing in his intestines and that he might have died of malaria. Also share the story of Djed, a court musician with terrible teeth. She had a cavity that spread infection throughout her body and poisoned her. Using CAT scans, scientists have reconstructed a picture of what she probably looked like (page 41).

Two photographs with great audience appeal are found on pages 12 and 45.

Many people think that all of the great Egyptian pharaohs were buried in pyramids, but that is not true. *Mummies of the Pharaohs: Exploring the Valley of the Kings* by Melvin and Gilda Berger tells about another site in Egypt where mummies and treasure have been found. More than 3,000 years ago Egyptians constructed tombs in the Valley of the Kings to house their pharaohs' bodies. Egyptians believed that the dead needed their earthly goods in the afterlife, so they filled the tombs with jewels, statues, and household items.

Most people have heard of King Tut. He was buried in the Valley of the Kings, and the discovery of his tomb by Howard Carter and Lord Carnavon is a great story. For five years they searched to no avail. Finally, in the sixth year a young worker kicked some rocks away and hit something hard and sharp. Soon they found a stairway to a tomb. In exploring the tomb's chambers they found great riches and even more mysteries.

Why was King Tut buried so quickly? And why does his skull look like he was killed by a blow to the head? Many mysteries remain about the pharaohs and ancient Egypt, and reading about them will make you want to know more. What, for instance, happened to the mummy of King Akhenaton? Why did it disappear? King Akhenaton made a lot of changes in Egypt. Maybe he made some enemies, too.

The glorious pictures in this book will entice your readers. Be sure to at least show your audience King Tut's skull with the wound in it on page 24. And on page 25 show King Tut's mummified head and his toes capped with gold. You can't read this book without wanting to visit the Valley of the Kings for yourself.

In addition to mummies, ancient Egyptians are famous for their unique form of writing. Find out how scholars cracked their code by reading *The Mystery of the Hieroglyphs: The Story of the Rosetta Stone and the Race to Decipher Egyptian Hieroglyphs* by Carol Donoughue.

Have you ever seen a sign in a language you do not understand? If there is no translation, you can get very confused wondering what the sign says, especially if you think it is telling you to do something.

For hundreds of years, scholars and archaeologists felt very confused because they did not understand a lot about ancient Egypt. They could see that there was writing on the mummies, the obelisks, the art, the pyramids, and the Sphinx, but no one could figure out what the writing said because no one could speak or write ancient Egyptian. Then they found a clue. But it turned out they needed a lot more than just a clue.

In 1799 French soldiers found a stone in a place called Rashid, or Rosetta, near where the Nile River flows into the Mediterranean Sea. This big, flat, broken stone was very unusual because there were three kinds of writing on it. Only one of the kinds made sense to anyone at that time—it was the writing on the bottom third of the stone, which was ancient Greek and which many scholars could read. They soon realized that perhaps all three parts of the stone said the same thing but in different languages and that, if they could only decipher the writing, they might be able to read everything the ancient Egyptians had written.

But the scholars did not know that they were basing their guesses on faulty information. It took them more than 30 years to solve the mystery of the Rosetta stone, and this book tells us how they did it, how we can read some things in hieroglyphs, the ancient Egyptian script, and how we can write our own names in hieroglyphs. If you like to solve puzzles, this book is for you.

Ancient Rome was a fascinating civilization as well. Your audience may have heard of the gladiators, and that may spark their interest in *The Roman Colosseum* by Elizabeth Mann.

One of the most famous buildings ever is the Roman Colosseum. It officially opened almost 2,000 years ago, in A.D. 80, and you can still visit it today.

The Roman people loved to be entertained, and their favorite sorts of entertainment were quite cruel. They loved to come to the Colosseum, where tickets were free, and enter one of the 80 entrances to sit in the 50,000 seats. There they watched gladiators kill each other, or animals kill gladiators, or anybody or anything kill each other.

This interesting book describes how the Colosseum was built, using concrete, which was a new invention at the time. It is filled with colorful photographs and illustrations that show what it was like when gladiators were the heroes of Rome.

Show your audience the illustration on page 21 that depicts slaves walking inside a wheel, just like a wheel your gerbil might walk around in, which is part of a machine that lifts huge stones.

Knights by Philip Steele describes another fascinating aspect of life in the past. In English, the word "knight" originally meant "servant," but in other languages it meant "horseman." Most knights were good horsemen, and the invention that enabled them to ride well came from China. Do you know what it was? It was the stirrup. With a stirrup, a rider was steadied on the horse so he could fight yet not worry about falling off.

This colorful book is loaded with illustrations that show how knights lived. You might wonder where they got their armor. The finest armor was made in only a few cities.

Do you know the names of any real people who were knights? How about Richard the Lionhearted, King of England? How about El Cid? Or William Wallace, whom some called "Braveheart"? Maybe you have heard of fictitious knights from stories, characters like Sir Lancelot, Sir Galahad, St. George, and Don Quixote. We also learn about knights from other cultures. Unbelievably, the Polish cavalry rode on horseback and carried their swords to meet the Nazi invasion of 1939. Needless to say, they did not fare well against the invaders' tanks and airplanes.

Show your audience the picture of El Cid on page 42, the Teutonic knight on page 14, or the knights buying armor on page 19.

If you can't get enough of knights, read *In the Time of Knights: The Real-Life Story of History's Greatest Knights* by Shelley Tanaka. It tells the story of William Marshal, one of the most remarkable knights ever to carry a sword. Born in 1146, Marshal worked his way up to knighthood and had many adventures, honors, and romances. This intriguing book will make you want to read more. Some good pictures to show are on page 11 (Marshal being knighted), page 20 (jousting), and pages 44 and 45 (Pembroke Castle in Wales).

The Viking News by Rachel Wright is one of a delightful series of titles about life in other times. It's great fun to take a look through, and it could help you out with your report. Why do you suppose the Vikings were renowned for their ships? What made their vessels so powerful?

Do you know where the word "berserk" comes from? A berserk was a Viking warrior who put on a bearskin cloak before a battle. In this way, he believed he would take on the strength of a bear. Then, with this mind-set, the warrior fought like he was berserk. One warrior fought so furiously that he fell down and died—without even being wounded.

This book has fun pictures to look at and fascinating tidbits of information. Look at the picture of the ship burial on page 19. Many Viking warriors were buried in their ships.

Lost Temple of the Aztecs by Shelley Tanaka delves into ancient civilizations on the other side of the world. In 1978 archaeologists discovered what they had been seeking for years. Right in the center of Mexico City, buried under parking lots and stores, was the Great Temple of the Aztecs.

Aztecs! Moctezuma! Almost everyone has heard of them. The Aztecs were a cultured, intelligent, advanced society of native Americans whose empire was huge and powerful. Their city, Tenochtitlán, was built on an island in the middle of a lake, and even the man who led its destroyers said it was the most beautiful city in the world.

Moctezuma was king of the Aztecs, and a sad and tragic king he was. When he first heard accounts of the strange white men with short hair that had come in ships from far away, he thought that the leader of these men must be the Aztec god Quetzalcoatl. The year was 1519, and the strange-looking newcomers were not gods. They were ordinary Spaniards, under the leadership of the cruel and greedy Cortés, and they overwhelmed the Aztecs, stealing their gold, killing their king, and destroying their empire. In addition, they spread smallpox—a disease that killed thousands.

This book tells the compelling story of the end of the Aztec Empire. Illustrated with photographs and artwork, it is highly readable. Show your audience the illustrations of the Aztecs welcoming their conquerors with gifts (page 13), of the meeting of Moctezuma and Cortés (page 23), and of Moctezuma showing Cortés his city (page 25). The Aztecs were a cruel society, but so were their conquerors.

Kids might also like to see the photo on page 4 of the consultant to this book, Professor Eduardo Matos Moctezuma, a descendant of King Moctezuma and the archaeologist who supervised the excavation of the Great Temple.

Machu Picchu by Elizabeth Mann tells of an incredible ancient site also in the Western Hemisphere. It is one of the most beautiful places imaginable, and for centuries hardly anyone knew it existed. Built in a spectacular location, it is hard to get to and full of mystery. What is it? Machu Picchu—the city in the clouds. It was built by the Inkas under the leadership of their emperor, Pachacuti, more than 400 years ago. When this remarkable South American city was discovered by the outside world in 1911, it appeared much as it was around the year 1532, when the Spaniards invaded. Because of the dense overgrowth that covered it, the city was basically unchanged. The Spaniards never found it so they never got a chance to destroy it.

The Inkas had no written language, and the conquering Spaniards destroyed much of their civilization, so today we do not know much about them. This book tells the story of these incredible people and their history, as we know it, and about how they managed to build such a magnificent city. Show the picture on page 13 of the messenger, called a "chaski." "Chaskis, running in relays at top speed, could carry a message 250 miles in one day. They ate and slept in roadside rest stops while they waited for the next message" (page 12).

Have you ever heard of the famous statues on Easter Island? If you have, did you wonder where they came from and how they got there? Well, for a long time it was a mystery, but it really isn't any more. Caroline Arnold tells about this interesting ancient site in *Easter Island: Giant Stone Statues Tell of a Rich and Tragic Past.*

Easter Island got its name because a ship captain landed there in 1722 on Easter Sunday and named the island after that day. He didn't care that the people who lived on the island already had another name for their home.

But even 300 years ago, it wasn't much of a home anymore. The island is in the middle of the Pacific Ocean and is more than 1,000 miles away from other inhabited islands. Scientists and archaeologists estimate that by the time it got its new name, people had lived there for more than 1,300 years—and they had used up almost all of its resources. There was not much to eat or drink or make things from.

This book gives you a completely different look at Easter Island. Show the pictures of the huge statues that still stand there and have fascinated people for centuries. Then read the book and find out what happens when people do not get along and when they waste the wonderful things they find on Earth.

The picture on the cover is great (white coral was used to make the statue's eyes). Also show the one on page 25.

GEOGRAPHY

If you know kids who are interested in maps, then *Mapping the World* by Sylvia A. Johnson is a sure winner. In researching her book on foods from the United States, Johnson looked at several old maps and became interested in the subject. This book is the result.

When astronauts first circled the Earth, they said it looked just like the maps they had seen. Maps have come a long way since the earliest ones. For many centuries, maps didn't look at all like a view from outer space looks. The first one pictured in this colorful book was made in Babylonia about 2,500 years ago. You would hardly guess that this crude representation is a map—but it is, and it shows all that anyone in Babylonia was really interested in.

Ptolemy, a Greek who lived in northern Africa 650 years later, laid the groundwork for maps that look a lot more like the world as we know it. But he guessed at a lot of things. Monks in the Middle Ages made maps that centered on religion, and pilgrims in those times made maps that showed only how to get from one place to another—with churches and castles as the main landmarks. Show the kids the map on page 11.

Mapmaking has improved dramatically through the centuries, although the best map may actually be a globe, not a flat map. The Earth is not flat (and according to *Mapping the World*, most educated people have known that for a long time). Flat reproductions of the Earth do not present a realistic image.

Puzzle Maps U.S.A. by Nancy L. Clouse provides a way for young children to learn the names and shapes of the 50 states. The author starts by asking kids to describe what their own state looks like. ("Michigan looks like a mitten with a scarf." "Louisiana looks like an armchair with a fringe"; page 11.) After looking at the map, try to identify the mixed-up states in the pictures in the rest of the book. This makes a great game that will have you looking hard for your own state in every picture! Be sure to show the kids an illustration or two of their own state.

Do you like cities? If you do, read *City of Angels: In and Around Los Angeles* by Julie Jaskol and Brian Lewis. If you are a kid who lives in Los Angeles, you can feel important because this book is dedicated to the children who live there. If you don't, you can still feel lucky because this fun book will give you information about a beautiful, unusual city. Big, colorful pictures show what life is like in this city, named originally after the Queen (Mary) of the Angels in 1781. People from all over the world now live there, and we see a picture of the New Year's parade in Chinatown, of Little Tokyo, of Hispanic Americans on Olvera Street, of the Watts towers and the ancient La Brea tar pits, of glamorous Hollywood, the farmers' market, and the Angel Flight, which is the shortest railway in the world. Show the audience the picture on page 31 of the Angel Flight, which extends only 350 feet.

The third longest river in the United States is the Rio Grande, which for 1,000 of its 1,885 miles creates the border between Texas and Mexico. The Rio Grande is unusual, for it is fairly shallow and frequently very narrow. It can dry up and almost disappear in places. Find out more about this geographical wonder in *Rio Grande: From the Rocky Mountains to the Gulf of Mexico* by Peter Lourie.

Lourie wanted to see what the Rio Grande River was really like, and, to do that, he began in southern Colorado, in the Rocky Mountains, where the river begins. The first town on the Rio Grande is Creede, Colorado, which was once a famous mining town. Possibly the most famous person to live there was Bob Ford, the "dirty little coward who shot Mr. Howard." Tie this book in with *Bad Guys* by Andrew Glass (Chapter 5), who explains who both of those people were. Bob Ford shot and killed Jesse James, the famous outlaw, for the reward. Later, in Creede, he was gunned down in his own saloon.

The river then meanders into New Mexico, near the pueblos, where the early Native Americans lived. Their descendants are still there, and Lourie attended a corn festival there. He did not take photos, for the people in the pueblos have had so many things taken from them by outsiders that they ask tourists not to take photos.

Lourie ended up in Texas, where thousands of Mexicans and other illegal immigrants try to cross the Rio Grande into the United States every day. In Mexico, these people may make 75 cents a day, and even though they know life can be hard here, many want to try it anyway. In one place along the border, called the "Rock Slide," the river becomes too narrow for even a raft to fit in it.

Loaded with color photos, this is an excellent introduction to a fascinating area. Show the photo of the "Rock Slide" on page 37.

Lourie writes about another famous river in *Mississippi River: A Journey down the Father of Waters*. Mark Twain loved the Mississippi River. "He said the river was like a book with new stories to tell every day" (page 46). And Lourie, who also loves rivers, tells us the story of his canoe journey all the way down this one.

The Mississippi River starts in Lake Itasca, in northern Minnesota. At its source, you can easily walk across it without getting your feet wet. If you have been there and walked across the river, be sure to tell your audience about your experience.

The river, however, grows quickly, and by the time it reaches Minneapolis, locks are needed to raise and lower the level of the water to let boats through.

The Mississippi is a treacherous river, and Lourie understood this. By 1867 there were at least 133 sunken hulks in the stretch from Saint Louis, Missouri, to Cairo, Illinois. River men called it "the graveyard."

Two places that impressed Lourie greatly were just north of Saint Louis, where the longest river in the United States, the Missouri, joins the Mississippi and changes its color (show your audience the aerial photo of the two). Then, farther down, the Ohio joins the Mississippi at Fort Defiance in Cairo, Illinois. "With the Ohio's water, the newly invigorated Mississippi becomes a mass of bubbling liquid like a small, angry sea. I was now afraid to paddle in the center of this river. From here onward I vowed to hug the shore, where I would feel safer, out of the torrent and away from the tows" (page 31). If you have ever been to Fort Defiance and seen this, you will know *exactly* what he means.

Lourie had many adventures, which he describes in this fun book. Another good photo to show is the one of Lake Itasca on page 8.

WILDLIFE OF THE WORLD

It's always good to start a booktalk with an attention-getter such as the following information from *The Man-Eating Tigers of Sundarbans* by Sy Montgomery:

In Sundarbans (pronounced SHUN dar bun), an area shared by India and Bangladesh, men go out to fish or cut wood in or near a tiger preserve. Suddenly, with no warning, a tiger jumps on someone's neck, kills him, and hauls his body away. Sometimes the other men never even see the tiger. This happens a lot.

These are the man-eating tigers, and the truth is they do usually eat only men, not women or children. The reason for this may be that the men invade the tigers' territory, and the women and children do not. But why would a tiger attack a man? Isn't it dangerous?

Jim Corbett, a famous tiger hunter early in the 1900s, said that all of the man-eating tigers he had ever encountered were sick, wounded, or old. Attacking other animals who can defend themselves takes more energy than the tiger has. Attacking people is quite simple, especially if the people are looking away from the tiger and unarmed.

Tigers are an endangered species. In 1900 there were about 70,000 tigers and eight subspecies of tigers in Asia. Today there are only about 7,000 tigers remaining. Three of the subspecies—the Bali tiger, the Caspian tiger, and the Javan tiger—are extinct. The tigers who live in the Sundarbans are one of the largest groups anywhere.

This is a very unusual area—part ocean, part river, part trees—with all three parts frequently mixed up with each other. The uniqueness of the area may make the tigers more likely to attack humans. The book includes surprising stories about tiger attacks and a lot of terrific photographs. Take a look at the picture of the tiger on page 16.

South American Animals by Caroline Arnold has excellent photos of some of the many animals that live in South America, the fourth-largest continent in the world. Show the kids the picture of the sloth, an animal found only in Central and South America. This animal moves so slowly that other animals sometimes do not even notice it. Sloths spend a great deal of time hanging upside down from trees and can turn their heads almost completely around. Does anyone know what the word "slothful" means?

Another animal found only in Central and South America, as well as in the southern United States, is the armadillo. Show the kids this picture and ask whether they have ever seen one. Also show the picture of the caiman, a relative of the alligator who looks a little different. This is a fun and interesting book.

Most of us think of the area in South America around the Amazon River whenever we hear the words "rain forest." Would you believe that the United States also has a rain forest? It is not a tropical rain forest, but a temperate rain forest. And you can go there yourself if you travel to the Olympic Peninsula along the coast of Washington.

Virginia Wright-Frierson went there to make a scrapbook of all of the things she saw; *A North American Rain Forest Scrapbook* is the result. She took binoculars and a magnifying glass to look at things both close up and far away. Some of the plants she saw had nifty names like inside-out flower, pimpled kidney, licorice fern, devil's matchstick, and—her favorite—fairy barf.

She also saw some very unusual trees—ones that look as though they are on stilts. When a dead tree, called a snag, falls over, seeds land in it and start to grow. When the dead tree, now a "nurse" tree, finally rots, the trees that have grown on top of it look like they are on stilts!

Virginia saw other amazing things, including a giant banana slug as long as her foot. That slug looks like a snail without a shell. Show your audience the picture of the banana slug and of the trees that look as though they are on stilts.

Learn even more about this temperate rain forest in *Journey Through the Northern Rainforest* by Karen Pandell. The trees there are very tall, but they are narrow at the top so that light and water can get through. Obviously, water is a very important part of the rain forest. All sorts of water-catchers exist there and trap water.

Salmon need rain forests. They are born there and then leave to spend one to five years in the ocean. Amazingly, each fish returns to the stream in the rain forest where it hatched. There they spawn: A female salmon lays eggs that a male fertilizes. Each year there is a "salmon run," which means that the fish return in great numbers. Some of them have to swim upstream, over obstacles and barriers, to return to their homes. It is an amazing phenomenon.

Many of our temperate rain forests are being destroyed just as the tropical rain forests are. Read about what happens when the old-growth trees are cut down. It is not a pretty story. Show your audience the beautiful picture of the trees on the first two-page spread and of the salmon running (back cover).

Light Shining Through the Mist: A Photobiography of Dian Fossey by Tom L. Matthews takes readers to the forests of Africa to learn about a very courageous scientist. Dian Fossey, who became world famous for her work with animals, had only one pet when she was a child—a goldfish. She wrote, "I cried for a week" when that goldfish died.

Fossey grew up in San Francisco, went to college, worked as an occupational therapist, and dreamed, above all, of traveling to Africa. She saved her money but had to borrow a lot in order to travel to Kenya and Tanzania, where she made a side trip to the Virunga Mountains. She had read a book by George Schaller about mountain gorillas and wanted to see some. Little did she know that those gorillas would become the center of her life.

Fossey somehow managed to contact the famous anthropologist Louis Leakey and three years later met him again when he was on a lecture tour of the United States. Dr. Leakey acquired funding that enabled Fossey to live in the Virunga Mountains and study gorillas for three years.

Fossey befriended and protected the gorillas and learned things about them that no one had known before. She hated the poachers, who killed gorillas and cut them apart to sell their hands for ashtrays and their heads for decorations. She also clashed with the people who stole baby gorillas for zoos, not caring how many adults they killed in the process. But Fossey found danger in the jungle—enemies who would one day kill her. Show the photos of Fossey as a child on page 8 and of her with the gorillas on pages 6 and 34.

Gorilla Walk by Ted and Betsy Lewin describes one of the most unusual zoos you will ever hear about. Actually, it isn't really a zoo at all; it is an enclosed and protected area where people pay to enter and see the animals. But getting to this zoo is a challenge.

The animals in this special place are the mountain gorillas in Africa's Virunga mountain range. Westerners did not know these animals existed until 1905, when a German army officer killed one and brought it back for others to see. They were hard to find but were desirable trophies, and people killed several to make ashtrays out of their hands and to mount their heads. By 1925 the government of the country in which they resided (now Rwanda) created Africa's first national park, designed to protect them. Today only about 600 of these gorillas are still alive.

Ted and Betsy Lewin, authors of numerous children's books, wanted to see these gorillas. You have to walk up horribly hot, slippery, steep hills to get to the impenetrable forest where the gorillas live, and you have to pay $150 a day to do it. This book describes two days in which the Lewins went on a memorable walk to see gorillas in the wild, face-to-face. On the first day they climbed for about five hours without adequate water just to get to where the gorillas were.

One interesting thing about this park and these gorillas is that people have spent much time getting them used to human beings. This takes a great deal of time and patience and has a negative effect: Other gorillas shun gorillas who tolerate human beings. Crammed with interesting information and great illustrations, this is a fun book to read.

Deserts by Susan H. Gray introduces kids to some very dry areas of the world. What do you think a desert is like? Dry? Sandy? Hotter than anyone would ever want to be? This book tells us that there are lots of different kinds of deserts, but one thing they all have in common is that they get fewer than 10 inches of rain a year, and water evaporates very quickly in them.

Not all of the deserts are sandy, and not all of them are hot. One cold desert, the Great Basin, is in the United States. The Mojave Desert, on the other hand, has Death Valley, which has gotten up to 134 degrees Fahrenheit. That, of course, was during the day. At night, it may freeze.

The largest desert in the world is the Sahara in Africa, and it is almost as big as the entire United States. Much of the center of Australia is desert as well.

Can you name the four deserts in the United States?

For more great information on deserts and the plants and animals that live in them, read this book.

Show the picture of the chuckwalla on page 38. "When it gets scared, a chuckwalla rushes into a crack in a nearby rock. It breathes in air and swells up. It becomes so tightly packed in the crack that nothing can pull it out" (page 37).

When you booktalk *Tundra Discoveries* by Ginger Wadsworth, you will shift to a cold part of the world. Few people have ever been in the tundra, which circles the Arctic Ocean all around the North Pole. Just below the surface of the Earth a thick layer of soil, called permafrost, is always frozen. There are no trees on the tundra. During the short summers and the long winters, the animals that dwell there are very active.

Take a look at this neat book. On the left-hand page of each two-page spread is a picture of an animal and some information about it. On the right-hand side is another picture, this time of a scene in the tundra, asking questions about the animal you just learned about. It's a fun way to pick up interesting information.

Did you know, for instance, that a polar bear has feet as big as dinner plates? Or that musk oxen stand in a circle to protect their young when they are threatened? Show the audience the picture of the musk ox.

WAR-TORN EUROPE AND THE HOLOCAUST

In 1933 a man named Adolf Hitler became the head of the German government. You may know that Hitler did not think much of people who were not white and Christian. In fact, he preferred people to be blonde, blue-eyed, and "Aryan." He hated gypsies, people with mental illnesses, people of mixed race, and, above all, the Jews.

You probably know what happened to the Jewish people during World War II, when Hitler implemented the unbelievable Holocaust that killed almost 6 million people. *The Nazi Olympics: Berlin 1936* by Susan D. Bachrach takes place before the war, when the Nazi government, led by Hitler, sponsored the 1936 Olympic games in Berlin. By then, Hitler was already starting to treat the Jews very badly, and this book describes how and what he did.

There are loads of photos of actual people and events of the time and also stories of many of the great Jewish, black, and non-Aryan athletes who proved over and over that they could outperform Hitler's team. Not only is this fascinating book a good introduction to the Holocaust, but it also includes information about how Americans treated minority groups (unfortunately, not always well). Show the double-page spread of the audience giving the Nazi salute on pages 72 and 73.

Thanks to My Mother by Schoschana Rabinovici is a terrifying true account of a Holocaust survivor. Susie Weksler, not yet nine years old, saw her father for the last time in June 1941. She never knew exactly what happened to him, although she believes he was shot shortly after that. Her Jewish family, living in Vilnius, Lithuania, was about to experience four years of pure hell.

This Holocaust memoir bears a resemblance to the circles in Dante's *Inferno*. At each step of the journey from her affluent, sheltered, comfortable home to the final death march from a concentration camp in the dead of winter, you believe that things could not possibly get any worse, and yet, without fail, they did. New, impossible horrors arose at every step. But Susie's fierce, stubborn, creative mother managed to ensure the survival of them both.

The Germans took over Vilnius in June 1941 and commandeered the Wekslers' apartment. The soldiers instructed them to leave all of their furniture and kitchen utensils behind. Susie and her family went to live with her grandfather in his spacious home, but almost all of her relatives were there, too, and the situation quickly became crowded and uncomfortable. These conditions were palatial, however, compared to the accommodations in the ghetto. There was not nearly enough space for all the Jews who were relocated, and food shortages became a horrible problem. Regular "actions" reduced the population, for the police would come in and remove as many as 5,000 people in a single day. No one knew for sure what happened to them.

Eventually a group of people constructed an underground "malina," in which they could hide out of sight. The day before the next "action" dozens crawled into it in spite of their claustrophobia and the lack of food and air. One father, in attempting to quiet his screaming baby, smothered it.

The ghetto was liquidated in June 1943, and in a nightmarish scene, Susie and her mother were able to "keep to the right," thus ensuring their survival at least to get out of Vilnius. They were taken in crammed boxcars to Kaiserwald, a work camp where more friends and family died and where Susie worked with caustic acid in a battery "factory," and starvation was a fact of life. Her very youth was a constant source of terror because anyone as young as she should not be alive.

Eventually she and her mother were taken in unbelievable squalor and horror to Stutthoff, near Gdansk, Poland, which was more of an extermination camp. The climax of the book comes on a night in January 1945, when all of the wet, starving women, fresh out of the showers, were made to stand stark naked for hours in below-zero weather. To fall or freeze was to die, and those who survived began a death march. Only the Russian invasion ultimately liberated the prisoners, who tried without success to go back to their old home in Vilnius. Susie eventually ended up in Israel.

This is a fine memoir, but the stuff of nightmares. Recommend it to mature readers of middle school age or older. Included are some poems that Susie wrote while in the camps.

Another recommended Holocaust book for middle-schoolers is *Darkness over Denmark: The Danish Resistance and the Rescue of the Jews* by Ellen Levine. This is a great tie-in for students who have read the Newbery-winning fiction book *Number the Stars* by Lois Lowry.

On April 9, 1940, Nazis invaded Denmark. People had a hard time believing such a thing could happen. The Danes and the Nazis had agreed not to go to war with each other, and Denmark wanted no part of the war. But Denmark was right on the German border, and the Nazis wanted to control it so they would be in charge of access to their own land and for the good farm products Denmark could provide. So they invaded, and Denmark did its best to fight back.

Perhaps the most extraordinary occurrence at this time was Denmark's insistence on protecting its own Jews. Jews were horribly persecuted in Germany and other countries the Nazis invaded, but the Danes insisted that such a thing would not happen in Denmark. Although everywhere else Jews were forced to wear six-pointed yellow stars that said "Jude" (Jew), this never occurred in Denmark. In fact, Jews in Denmark, even under the Nazi occupation, were at first treated pretty much the same as everyone else.

Under Danish law Jews had the same rights as other citizens of Denmark, and they had had those rights for more than 100 years. This in itself was very unusual. In most of Europe, Jewish people did not have equal rights with the citizens of the countries they lived in.

Ellen Levine tells the story of what Danish citizens, male and female, grownups and kids, did to try to defeat the Nazis. You won't forget this one.

Show the picture on page 114 of the RAF bombers flying very low over Shell House, the Gestapo headquarters. The RAF had been instructed to bomb the base in front of the building and set it on fire. Even though 32 Danish prisoners were held in the top story, the Danes felt the building had to be destroyed because it had records of many people who had been involved in the resistance movement. The Danes knew the attack was coming and managed to help 26 of those prisoners escape during the fire. They scared off the German firemen by telling them there were explosives in the fire.

Read another survival story in *Surviving Hitler: A Boy in the Nazi Death Camps* by Andrea Warren. In the summer of 1939, when Jack Mandelbaum was 12 years old, everything in his life changed. That was the year the Nazis invaded Poland, and Jack was not only Polish but also Jewish. His father decided it would be best if his family went to stay with *his* father, 300 miles away. He put them on a train and told them he would send their things and money later.

Neither ever arrived. Jack's father had told him he was now the man of the family, and he took that responsibility seriously. As he watched the Nazis arrive in the town where he now lived, he knew he would try to stay with his family and support them no matter what happened.

But as Jack found out time and again, he had little control over his life in the next six years. He was imprisoned by the Nazis, lived in filthy, horrible camps, was infested with lice, and was given flavored water for food—water often flavored with dirt and rotten vegetables. Jack said, "You never saw grass in a concentration camp, because the prisoners ate it" (page 90). In the end, he was the only one of his immediate family to survive.

This is a compelling story about a boy who was determined to survive—and who succeeded. If you are interested in the Holocaust or wonder how you might have acted if you had been caught up in it, this is a great book for you.

Fireflies in the Dark: The Story of Friedl Dicker-Brandeis and the Children of Terezin by Susan Goldman Rubin tells about an inspiring woman who rose above the awful conditions she faced in a concentration camp.

Friedl Dicker-Brandeis was Jewish, and when Hitler's Nazi troops invaded her home in Czechoslovakia in 1939, she lost both her rights and her privileges. She and her husband first gave up their large apartment in Prague to move to a storeroom in a house in the country. Later they moved to a store shed and then to a small, unheated attic room. But in December 1942 all the Jews in their town were transported to a concentration camp the Czechs called Terezin and the Germans called Theresienstadt.

Each person was allowed to bring about 110 pounds of luggage, and Dicker-Brandeis did something extraordinary with her 110 pounds. She packed her suitcases with art supplies with which she could teach children to create art.

The people in Terezin lived in terror of being transported to other, even worse, places such as Auschwitz—from which no one ever seemed to return.

But Dicker-Brandeis had a mission in life—to teach art. This book tells how she did that and about the children she taught. In addition, it is filled with pictures of dozens of works her students created, most of whom were to die in the concentration camps before the war was over. Rubin interviewed some of those taught by Dicker-Brandeis who did not die.

A Special Fate: Chiune Sugihara: Hero of the Holocaust by Alison Leslie Gold tells another inspiring story, this time of a man who risked his life to save the Jews in Lithuania.

Millions of people died in the Nazi Holocaust during World War II. The majority of them were Jewish. The Nazis hated Jews and blamed them for everything. Some people did as much as they could to help the Jews, but a tiny few did a lot. One of those people was Chiune Sugihara, a Japanese man who was the Japanese consul in Lithuania.

He was representing a country that was on Germany's side during the war, yet he did everything he possibly could to save the lives of the people the Nazis hated the most.

What Sugihara did was to write visas. A visa permits a person to leave one country and go to another, and without one, most Jews faced almost certain death. Sugihara wrote about 6,000 visas, all of them against the express orders of his government. But, because of these visas, many, many people escaped—and lived.

Not only does Gold tell us how Sugihara decided to do something that ended up costing him his career, but she also tells us the incredible stories of two Jewish children whose lives Sugihara deeply affected. This is a tremendous story, and the book has some fine photographs of Mr. Sugihara and his family.

Sugihara also plays a major role in *One More Border: The True Story of One Family's Escape from War-Torn Europe*, written by William Kaplan with Shelley Tanaka. Use this book to introduce Sugihara to elementary-school-aged audiences.

In 1939 Igor Kaplan, his little sister, and his mother and father had to leave their home and move into a hotel. The Nazis were coming, and the Nazis hated Jewish people—and the Kaplans were Jewish. How to escape?

The Kaplans lived in Lithuania, where a wonderful man, Mr. Sugihara, worked in the Japanese embassy and disobeyed his government to issue visas to the Jews so they could leave their country. Mr. Kaplan, almost through good luck, got visas for himself and the two children, but Mrs. Kaplan had to take her chances. The family took the train first to Moscow and then all the way across Siberia on the Trans-Siberian railroad. When they arrived at the last stop, Vladivostok, Mrs. Kaplan had to get a visa—and how could she?

This true story is written by Igor's son. It has fine color illustrations and an excellent collection of vintage photographs detailing the horrors of wartime Europe.

Although not about the Holocaust, *Attack on Pearl Harbor: The True Story of the Day America Entered World War II* by Shelley Tanaka is a book that is too good to miss. The hit movie *Pearl Harbor* created interest in this topic, and Tanaka makes it come alive with the fascinating true stories of a Japanese submarine pilot, a U.S. seaman, and children living in Hawaii.

George DeLong, a 19-year-old sailor (photo on page 13), was aboard the USS *Oklahoma* when the Japanese attack began. His ship was struck and turned over, trapping him and several others in their sleeping quarters. It was like being in a coffin under the sea. Unlike many others, these men were lucky. They survived for 32 hours before being rescued.

Tanaka tells another compelling story about Japanese ensign Kazuo Sakamaki, a pilot of a midget submarine (pictured on page 10). His mission was to sneak into Pearl Harbor and torpedo the ships at close range. He knew he would probably not survive the attack. However, Sakamaki's submarine malfunctioned, he hit a coral reef, and gas and smoke filled the sub and made him pass out. He ended up trying to blow up his own submarine, but even this failed. Sakamaki washed up on the beach and became America's first Japanese prisoner of war.

This book is full of photographs and facts about different aspects of the attack on Pearl Harbor. Once you pick it up you won't be able to stop reading.

Fighting for Honor: Japanese Americans and World War II by Michael L. Cooper is one more World War II book that deals with the plight of Asian Americans after the attack on Pearl Harbor.

President Franklin Roosevelt said, "The principle on which this country was founded and by which it has always been governed is that Americanism is not, and never was, a matter of race or ancestry. A good American is one who is loyal to this country and to our creed of liberty and democracy" (quoted on the page preceding the table of contents).

For Americans who were not white, however, the reality was different. It was unbelievably different for Americans of Japanese ancestry during World War II. In 1941 Japan had attacked America at Pearl Harbor, and afterward, anyone who looked Asian, which, of course, included Korean Americans and Chinese Americans, faced a hard road ahead. Young Oak Kim, a Korean American, tried to enlist in the army but was refused. A few months later, when he was drafted, he was told he could not go into combat by an officer who said, "Wake up. You've got the wrong shape eyes. You've got the wrong skin. Everything is wrong. You can't be a soldier. People like you aren't soldiers" (page 50).

But Asian Americans proved their loyalty to the United States and their astounding courage in battle again and again as the war went on. Young men whose families had been sent to horrible camps built in desolate places around the country showed the world what they were made of. This is an astounding story of injustice and great bravery. Show the audience the poster on page 5.

BIBLIOGRAPHY

Arnold, Caroline. *Easter Island: Giant Stone Statues Tell of a Rich and Tragic Past.* Text and photographs by Caroline Arnold. Clarion Books, 2000. ISBN 0395876095. 48 p. Grades 4–8.

———. *South American Animals.* Morrow Junior Books, 1999. ISBN 0688155642 (trade); 0688155650 (lib. bdg.). Unpaged. Grades 1–4.

Ash, Russell. *Great Wonders of the World.* Illustrated by Richard Bonson. Dorling Kindersley, 2000. ISBN 0-7894-6505-1. 64 p. Grades 4–up.

Bachrach, Susan D. *The Nazi Olympics: Berlin 1936.* United States Holocaust Memorial Museum. Little, Brown, 2000. ISBN 0316070866 (hc.); 0316070874 (pbk.). 132 p. Grades 4–6.

Berger, Melvin, and Gilda Berger. *Mummies of the Pharaohs: Exploring the Valley of the Kings.* National Geographic Society, 2001. ISBN 0-7922-2773-4. 64 p. Grades 4–8.

Clouse, Nancy L. *Puzzle Maps U.S.A.* Henry Holt, 1990. ISBN 0805011439. 32 p. Grades 1–3.

Collard, Sneed B., III. *1,000 Years Ago on Planet Earth.* Illustrated by Jonathan Hunt. Houghton Mifflin, 1999. ISBN 0395908663. Unpaged. Grades 4–6.

Cooper, Michael L. *Fighting for Honor: Japanese Americans and World War II.* Clarion Books, 2000. ISBN 0395913756. 118 p. Grades 5–8.

Corbishley, Mike. *The World of Architectural Wonders.* Peter Bedrick Books, 1996. ISBN 0-87226-279-0. 45 p. Grades 3–6.

Donoughue, Carol. *The Mystery of the Hieroglyphs: The Story of the Rosetta Stone and the Race to Decipher Egyptian Hieroglyphs.* Oxford University Press, 1999. ISBN 0195215532 (lib. ed.); 0195215540 (trade). 48 p. Grades 5–9.

Gold, Alison Leslie. *A Special Fate: Chiune Sugihara: Hero of the Holocaust.* Scholastic, 2000. ISBN 0590395254. 176 p. Grades 5–8.

Gray, Susan H. *Deserts.* Compass Point Books, 2001. ISBN 0756500192. 48 p. Grades 2–5.

Hamanaka, Sheila. *In Search of the Spirit: The Living National Treasures of Japan.* Calligraphy by Ayano Ohmi. Morrow Junior Books, 1999. ISBN 0688146074 (pbk.); 0688146082 (lib. bdg.). 48 p. Grades 4–6.

Jaskol, Julie, and Brian Lewis. *City of Angels: In and Around Los Angeles.* Illustrated by Elisa Kleven. Dutton Children's Books, 1999. ISBN 0525462147. 48 p. Grades 4–6.

Johnson, Sylvia A. *Mapping the World.* Atheneum Books for Young Readers, 1999. ISBN 0689818130. 32 p. Grades 4–6.

Kaplan, William, with Shelley Tanaka. *One More Border: The True Story of One Family's Escape from War-Torn Europe.* Illustrated by Stephen Taylor. Groundwood Books, 1998. ISBN 0888993323. 60 p. Grades 3–6.

Levine, Ellen. *Darkness over Denmark: The Danish Resistance and the Rescue of the Jews.* Holiday House, 2000. ISBN 0823414477. 164 p. Grades 5–up.

Lewin, Ted, and Betsy Lewin. *Gorilla Walk.* Lothrop, Lee & Shepard, 1999. ISBN 0688165095. 48 p. Grades 4–6.

Lourie, Peter. *Mississippi River: A Journey down the Father of Waters.* Boyds Mills Press, 2000. ISBN 1563977567. 48 p. Grades 4–8.

———. *Rio Grande: From the Rocky Mountains to the Gulf of Mexico.* Boyds Mills Press, 1999. ISBN 1563977060. 48 p. Grades 4–6.

Mann, Elizabeth. *Machu Picchu* (A Wonders of the World Book). Illustrated by Amy Crehore. Mikaya Press, 2000. ISBN 0-9650-493-9-6. 48 p. Grades 4–7.

———. *The Panama Canal* (A Wonders of the World Book). Illustrated by Fernando Rangel. Mikaya Press, 1998. ISBN 0965049345 (hc.). 48 p. Grades 4–6.

———. *The Roman Colosseum* (A Wonders of the World Book). Illustrated by Michael Racz. Mikaya Press, 1998. ISBN 0-965049337. 48 p. Grades 3–6.

Matthews, Tom L. *Light Shining Through the Mist: A Photobiography of Dian Fossey.* National Geographic Society, 1998. ISBN 0792273001. 64 p. Grades 4–6.

Millard, Anne. *A Street Through Time: A 12,000 Year Walk Through History.* Illustrated by Steve Noon. DK, 1998. ISBN 0789434261. 32 p. Grades 4–up.

Montgomery, Sy. *The Man-Eating Tigers of Sundarbans.* Photographs by Eleanor Briggs. Houghton Mifflin, 2001. ISBN 0618077049. 57 p. Grades 4–8.

Pandell, Karen. *Journey Through the Northern Rainforest*. Photographs by Art Wolfe. Illustrated by Denise Y. Takahashi. Dutton Children's Books, 1999. ISBN 0525458042 (hc.). Unpaged. Grades 4–6.

Rabinovici, Schoschana. *Thanks to My Mother*. Translated from the German by James Skofield. Dial Books, 1998. ISBN 0803722354. 249 p. Grades 7–up.

Rubin, Susan Goldman. *Fireflies in the Dark: The Story of Friedl Dicker-Brandeis and the Children of Terezin*. Holiday House, 2000. ISBN 0823414612. 48 p. Grades 4–8.

Steele, Philip. *Knights*. Kingfisher, 1998. ISBN 0753451549. 64 p. Grades 4–up.

Tanaka, Shelley. *Attack on Pearl Harbor: The True Story of the Day America Entered World War II*. Paintings by David Craig. Maps by Jack McMaster. Historical consultation by John Lundstrom. A Hyperion/Madison Press Book, 2001. ISBN 0-7868-0736-9. 64 p. Grades 4–8.

———. *In the Time of Knights: The Real-Life Story of History's Greatest Knights*. Illustrated by Greg Ruhl. Diagrams and maps by Jack McMaster. Historical consultation by K. Corey Keeble. A Hyperion/Madison Press Book, 2000. ISBN 0-7868-0651-6. 48 p. Grades 4–6.

———. *Lost Temple of the Aztecs*. Illustrated by Greg Ruhl. Diagrams and maps by Jack McMaster. Historical consultation by Eduardo Matos Moctezuma. A Hyperion/Madison Press Book, 1998. ISBN 0786804416. 48 p. Grades 4–6.

———. *Secrets of the Mummies: Uncovering the Bodies of Ancient Egyptians*. Illustrated by Greg Ruhl. Historical consultation by Dr. Peter Brand. A Hyperion/Madison Press Book, 1999. ISBN 0-7868-0473-4. 48 p. Grades 4–6.

Wadsworth, Ginger. *Tundra Discoveries*. Illustrated by John Carrozza. Charlesbridge, 1999. ISBN 0881068756. Unpaged. Grades 2–5.

Warren, Andrea. *Surviving Hitler: A Boy in the Nazi Death Camps*. HarperCollins, 2001. ISBN 0688174973 (trade); 0060292180 (lib. bdg.). 144 p. Grades 4–8.

Wright, Rachel. *The Viking News*. Consultant: Richard Hall. Candlewick Press, 1998. ISBN 076360450X. 32 p. Grades 4–up.

Wright-Frierson, Virginia. *A North American Rain Forest Scrapbook*. Walker, 1999. ISBN 0802786790 (hc.); 0802786804 (reinforced). Unpaged. Grades 3–5.

CHAPTER 5

American Journeys: U.S. History and the People That Made It Happen

THE AMERICAN EXPERIENCE

Journeys in Time: A New Atlas of American History by Elspeth Leacock and Susan Buckley tells the story of 20 American journeys, a few of the millions of journeys that made the United States of America what it is today. Long, long ago, perhaps as long as 12,000 years, the Anishinabe people migrated from the east coast of the United States to the central Great Lakes area, and the legend of that trip is the first story in *Journeys in Time*. In 1492 Columbus journeyed from Spain across an uncharted ocean to America. The voyage took 33 days, and his sailors threatened to mutiny. It took the Pilgrims in 1620 twice that long. They were originally headed for Virginia, but the *Mayflower* was blown off course.

In 1598 Don Juan de Onate journeyed from Mexico City to what is now New Mexico. Ben Franklin left Boston for Philadelphia in 1723, and Broteer, a six-year-old West African prince, was captured by slave merchants in 1735 and was brought to the new world under deplorable shipboard conditions. He was relatively lucky. Not only did he survive the journey, but he also was able to purchase his freedom 30 years later.

In 1775 Daniel Boone cleared the Wilderness Road, which enabled the population of settlers in Kentucky to increase from 400 to 73,000 in just 15 years. So many journeys were made—cowboys drove cattle, immigrants arrived by the thousands, and African Americans such as Louis Armstrong moved north in a great migration. Even today, migrant workers move continually and new immigrants arrive every day.

The stories here will make you think about the journeys that have changed your life. Where did your ancestors journey from to get to America? Have you yourself made any journeys?

This is a fascinating look at the way the United States grew. Show your audience the map of the migrant workers on page 42.

When talking about ancestors and immigration, tie in *Journey to Ellis Island: How My Father Came to America* by Carol Bierman with Barbara Hehner.

In 1922 a mother and her two children left their miserable life in Russia to come to America. The family's father had been drafted into the Russian army and disappeared. No one knew what had happened to him. Eleven-year old Yehuda, the son, had a finger on his right hand shot off when the family was caught in the middle of a battle. Yehuda's arm had become infected, and doctors were afraid they would have to amputate it.

Yehuda's mother had not allowed the amputation, but his right arm was always in a sling and the doctors advised Yehuda not to move it. Going to America was thus a difficult business. American immigration officials were strict, and they did not want people with serious medical problems to come. Yehuda's mother feared that he might be sent back to Russia, but her elder son was already in the United States and had paid the family's passage. They decided to take their chances.

Yehuda managed to gain admittance to America in a very unusual way. The book's pictures are fun to show the children—almost any will do, but show the one on page 10 of Yehuda and his sister eating their dinner of boiled potatoes and herring—the same dinner they had every single night of the voyage.

When immigrant families arrived at Ellis Island, they were thrilled by the sight of the symbol of the United States. Lynn Curlee writes about the "woman with a torch" in *Liberty*. She is probably the most famous statue in the world, and nearly everyone calls this statue "she"—not "it." Do you know who she is? She is the Statue of Liberty, which stands in New York Harbor. And she is not really American at all. She is French.

The French people gave the Statue of Liberty to the American people to celebrate—although a little late—America's centennial. A French professor came up with the idea, and a young French sculptor was present when he did. That sculptor, Frederic Auguste Bartholde, became obsessed with the idea. He wanted the gift to happen—and he wanted to be the one to make that gift. He designed it over a period of years, and the first thing he finished was the hand holding the torch. For several years, you could pay a nickel in New York City and see just that hand.

The statue was so big it had to be built in pieces, and this book has fantastic pictures that show the process. Show your audience the double-page spread on pages 16 and 17. Can *you* think of any statue that is more famous?

Jefferson's Children: The Story of One American Family by Shannon Lanier and Jane Feldman tells the true story of a rather surprising American family who made a long journey to find out the truth about their ancestors. It is an amazing story that you may have already heard.

Thomas Jefferson was one of the greatest men of all time. Among other things, he was the third president of the United States and the main writer of the Declaration of Independence. In that document he states that all men are created equal, and people have wondered about that phrase for more than 200 years. If all men are created equal, how can anyone own another person? And how could Jefferson himself own slaves?

But he did own them his whole life. And now, within the last few years, DNA testing has proved that Jefferson not only owned slaves, but he had one or more children with one of his slaves, Sally Hemings, a woman who was his wife's half sister.

The descendants of those slave children knew the truth all along. Their parents, great-grandparents, and ancestors all the way back to the children of Sally Hemings told them about it. If they were not aware of their lineage, it was usually because their light complexions enabled them to join white society and they tried to forget about their slave past.

But in November 1998 DNA testing changed everything, and soon many descendants of Jefferson, both black and white, joined in a different kind of family reunion at Jefferson's Virginia home, Monticello.

Shannon Lanier, who wrote this story, is himself a descendant of Sally Hemings, and he is proud of all of his ancestors. He interviewed other members of his extended family (often newly found) to create this fascinating look at a very unusual American family, some of whom still believe that Jefferson would not have had sexual relations with a slave.

Lanier's book is filled with great photographs to show, but be sure to include the one of the newly found family at Monticello on May 15, 1999 (pages 14 and 15).

Americans have always been fascinated with their presidents. Four American presidents have been assassinated in office. Can you name them? Lincoln, Garfield, McKinley, and Kennedy are the answers. In addition, assassination attempts have been made on other presidents: both Roosevelts, Ford, Reagan, Jackson, and Truman. *In the Line of Fire: Presidents' Lives at Stake* by Judith St. George tells us about those attempts and about how the killers and would-be killers breached the security net that usually protects U.S. presidents quite well. It makes for interesting reading.

President Garfield was shot in the back at close range in a train station. This happened in 1881, and at that time we knew relatively little about bacteria and infection. Several doctors attempted to find the bullet, and not all of them washed their hands before touching Garfield. He might have survived with a bullet in him, but he could not survive the infection caused by the unsanitary practices. As it was, he survived for two months but was horribly ill much of the time, during which the country was in a state of suspension.

Something similar happened in the case of President McKinley, who in 1901 was shaking hands at a reception. A man standing in line had his right hand wrapped in a white bandage—a bandage that was hiding a gun. He shot the president at close range. Again, doctors today speculate that McKinley, who stayed alive for 10 days, might have lived if modern medical practices had been followed.

Not only do we read details of these assassinations as well as those of Lincoln and Kennedy, but we also learn about several attempted assassinations, the killers, and would-be killers. If you remember the assassination of President Kennedy or any of the later assassination attempts, tell the audience about them. The book is not heavily illustrated, but the "Wanted for Treason" poster of President Kennedy on page 88 is interesting. This is a good read.

The President Has Been Shot! True Stories of the Attacks on Ten U.S. Presidents by Rebecca Jones is another good book on the same topic. The chapter on Abraham Lincoln is especially interesting. Most people know that John Wilkes Booth shot Lincoln, but other people were involved in the plot as well, and four of them received the death penalty for their crime. One of them was a woman, Mary Surratt, and no one really knows how involved she was in the actual shooting. Also, did you know that Lincoln had a guard that night who should have been sitting outside the door to his theater box, but Lincoln dismissed him and told him to have a seat in the audience? Imagine what might have happened if the guard had prevented the assassination.

This book is a great choice for middle school readers—every chapter has something interesting that even adults probably don't know. The chapter on John F. Kennedy is also quite good. The dramatic photograph on page 102 of Jack Ruby shooting Lee Harvey Oswald is a famous one to show.

Some events in history, such as assassinations, are so surprising or shocking or awful that people remember them for the rest of their lives. Joe Garner has compiled some of these events in *We Interrupt This Broadcast: The Events That Stopped Our Lives . . . from the Hindenburg Explosion to the Death of John F. Kennedy.*

Do you remember where you were when you heard that John F. Kennedy had been shot? Your students don't, but they might remember the death of Princess Diana, the explosion of flight 800, or the Columbine shootings. This oversized book details events in U.S. history that caught people by surprise and made their lives stop momentarily. The book is loaded with photographs and comes with two audio CDs of actual media broadcasts from the time of the incidents. If you are booktalking about disasters, war, or history, this book will make an excellent addition, especially if you can play an audio clip to your listeners. Included in the book are clips from 1937 to 1999, from the dramatic *Hindenburg* explosion to Martin Luther King Jr.'s assassination to the death of John Kennedy Jr.

Many people complain that history books focus primarily on men. Penny Colman set out to balance the scales by writing *Girls: A History of Growing Up Female in America.* Being a girl isn't easy. (Neither is being a boy, but that is not what this book is about.) For most of the history of the United States, women have had few rights. Everything a girl owned belonged to her father until she was married—and then it belonged to her husband. Women were not allowed to vote in most states until 1920. Many people believed it was not important that girls be educated or even learn to read or write. After all, they were going to grow up to be wives and mothers and would not need such skills.

In this fun-to-read book, Penny Colman gives us an overview of what it has been like to be a girl in America. There were rich girls, poor girls, immigrant girls, Native American girls, and slave girls, and she tells us a bit about their lives. Show the picture on page 20 of the toddler getting a permanent in 1938.

Do you like the American Girl books? Or the Dear America books? Or any kind of diary books? If you do, *Real American Girls Tell Their Own Stories* by Dorothy and Thomas Hoobler is for you.

Many diary books (such as the Dear America series) are fiction, stories about girls who never existed. This book includes excerpts of diaries from real girls from colonial times (more than 250 years ago) to the 1950s. A fun one was written in 1881 by Mary

Paxon, who lived in Pennsylvania. She was supposed to write a 130-word personal essay about George Washington's birthday. This is what she wrote. Each word in the diary has a number over it!

> George Washington was tall and not very good looking, he had large hands and a large nose, any way they look big in the pitchures [sic].
>
> When he was 13 years old he made 110 rules for himself to use to learn how to be polite and to behave well. Maybe when I am 13 years old I will make some too only I don't believe I will need so many. 25 or 30 will be enough, I guess. He married Martha Custis and she had been married once before and had plenty of money. He died of laryngittis [sic] and I have had it twice and never died yet. He went to the grave Childless that means he had no children, the only thing he was Father to was his country. (page 25)

Read the real-life diary entries in this book and tie them in with some of the historical diaries published by Capstone Press that are described later in this chapter.

We take our clothes pretty much for granted today, and most of us have quite a few. We have to decide what we are going to wear when we get up every morning, and we usually have several choices. And usually our clothes are clean. This was not always the case, as you will find out in Brandon Marie Miller's *Dressed for the Occasion: What Americans Wore 1620–1970*.

Figure 5.1. *Dressed for the Occasion: What Americans Wore 1620–1970* **by Brandon Marie Miller.**

When Europeans first settled America in the 1600s, and for a long time after, people had very few clothes, and they seldom cleaned them. They might even wash their undergarments, the same underclothing they wore day after day and night after night, only every six weeks or so.

This book gives us a brief but interesting overview of fashion in America over the last 400 years. Here are some examples:

In the mid-1700s men and women wore wigs and powdered them with white flour, sometimes almost a pound per wig. Rooms in which they did this were called powder rooms. Small boys had long hair and wore dresses for much of our history.

The clothing that slaves wore was sometimes awful. One slave said he had "[n]o shoes, no stockings, no jacket, no trousers; nothing but coarse sack-cloth or tow-linen, made into a sort of shirt, reaching down to my knees. This I wore day and night, changing it once a week."

Before sewing machines were invented, it took 14 hours to make a shirt. With a sewing machine, it took only one and one-half hours.

How did jeans become so popular? Who invented them? When were sneakers invented and why were they called that? For a look at a topic that interests everyone—what we wear—check out this book. Show your audience the frontispiece of the woman.

NATIVE AMERICANS

When Columbus sailed to North America, he thought he had reached India, so, of course, he called the people he found there "Indians." Today many people still call them Indians. The new people who came to what is now America called the various groups of Indians by names that were just as poorly descriptive. Charlotte and David Yue, authors of *The Wigwam and the Longhouse*, tell us that "[p]eople who called themselves Wendat, [which means] 'Dwellers on a Peninsula,' were called Huron by the French, using a French term to describe them as 'unkempt boots.' Iroquois was probably a European adaptation of a name meaning 'poisonous snakes' or 'killer people,' used by their enemies for the Hodenosaunee, or 'People of the Longhouse.' Eventually, many of these names replaced the real names of the tribes" (page 5).

The Wigwam and the Longhouse is about the people who lived around the Great Lakes. How did they live? What did they eat? How did they travel? What did they believe? And why did their way of life, once so successful, disappear almost completely? It's a book that makes you think.

Sitting Bull and His World: Tatan'ka Iyota'ke by Albert Marrin is an amazing book but not a fast read. Sitting Bull, member of the Lakota tribe, was born in 1831 and died in almost exactly the same spot 59 years later, the greatest and most famous Native American leader of all time—killed by his own people. During his lifetime, the Lakotas' world was changing beyond all recognition. This was an age of great growth and change for the American nation and a period of terrible hardship for the Native Americans. They were displaced by white settlers who wanted their lands and broke promise after promise in order to get what they wanted.

This book explains many things that are hard to understand—including why people were scalped and why Native Americans had more than one wife. It also explains the relationships among the Native American nations and the enmities among them. And it puts many historical events into context. Custer's last stand, for instance, was not an uncalled-for massacre. There was a good reason for it, and this book explains it. Loaded with black-and-white photographs and sketches, this is a fine read recommended for readers seventh grade and above.

Also for middle-schoolers is *Indian School: Teaching the White Man's Way* by Michael L. Cooper. Imagine that a group of aliens invades your homeland. They kill your people, take away your food and your homes, and then decide to take you to a special school they have built just for the people they have conquered. In that school they take away your clothes, cut off your hair, and forbid you to speak your own language. They make all of the rules and tell you that everything about the way you have lived all of your life is completely wrong. That is how the Native American children who went to "Indian schools," beginning in 1879, were treated. These children left their homes on the Great Plains and took the train east to a boarding school in the small town of Carlisle, Pennsylvania. One of them, an 11-year-old boy named Ota Kte, wrote down his feelings: "I could think of no reason why white people wanted Indian boys and girls except to kill them, and not having the remotest idea of what a school was, I thought we were going east to die" (page 1).

Getting the children's parents to agree to their going to school was not as difficult as you might think. Many parents did not see how they themselves, let alone their children, were going to be able to live. Their way of life had changed so much that survival was almost impossible. Many of the parents believed that the schools would give their children a chance to survive. But what happened at the schools was all too often a sad and terrible event in American history. Read this intriguing book to learn some of the bad things and the occasional good things that happened to the kids who went to these schools. The cover of the book is riveting, as are many of the pictures inside. Somewhat similar to the cover is a before-and-after photo on page 38.

Another tragic episode in Native American history is discussed in Michael Burgan's *The Trail of Tears*. In their own language, the Cherokee, who lived through the incident Burgan describes, call it "the trail where they cried" (page 6). We know it as the "Trail of Tears," and many people consider this event one of the cruelest things the United States government has ever done.

When Europeans first came to what is now the United States, they called the native people "Indians" and viewed them with suspicion, contempt, and fear. As more and more settlers wanted their own land, they realized that a good way to get it was to take it from the natives. The Cherokee were settled in the southeastern United States on good, desirable land. They had developed their own alphabet and were skilled at governing as well. But by the time Andrew Jackson became president, people wanted the land the natives owned. The settlers wanted the Cherokees to leave, so out they went in a brutal, horrifying move. The settlers decided the natives should go to Oklahoma, and to get there the natives traveled 800 miles on foot. A lot of them never made it. The Trail of Tears is something every American should know about. Read this book to find out more. Show the picture of the Cherokee cabin on page 8.

THE FOUNDING OF THE UNITED STATES OF AMERICA

Thirteen years before the Pilgrims landed at Plymouth Rock, English settlers came to America. And they were there to stay, unlike the settlers who had come 20 years earlier to the Roanoke Colony—and disappeared. *The Jamestown Colony* by Brendan January is a first-rate introduction to this period in American history.

In 1607, 105 British citizens arrived in Virginia. They had suffered a great deal on their ocean voyage. One man was locked up in chains because he had complained about the ship's leaders. His name was John Smith, and he became the most famous member of the entire group. When they arrived in Virginia, he became one of the colony's five leaders—and he turned out to be a good one.

Native Americans were both curious and concerned about the arrival of these new people. And they were right to be concerned. At first the settlers were not very good at taking care of themselves. Most of them considered themselves gentlemen, which meant that they were not supposed to have to work. But if no one worked, no crops would be grown, and there would be nothing to eat. Over the next few hard years, matters had to change dramatically.

What England wanted from the colonists was wealth. The settlers needed to find something that would justify their government supporting the colony, and the colonists were hoping for gold. But what they found was tobacco. This is a colorful, intriguing look at a little-known era in American history. Show the picture of John Smith dealing with the Native Americans on page 23.

Marcia Sewall's book *Jamestowne: Struggle for Survival* also details the interesting story of this new colony.

Three ships left England in December 1606, but for the first six weeks of their stormy journey, they did not leave sight of England. Food supplies ran low, and almost everyone was seasick. But in April they finally reached land—what is now Virginia. And there they sought a good place for their settlement, which they called the Jamestown Colony.

How this colony got going and made it through the "Starving Time" is one of the most interesting stories in American history. Read all about it and the dramatic story of how Pocahontas rescued John Smith from a death sentence. Show the picture of that scene on page 27.

Americans know that part of the reason we celebrate the Fourth of July is the writing of the Declaration of Independence. But what do we really know about that document? To find out more, read Russell Freedman's *Give Me Liberty! The Story of the Declaration of Independence.*

Start your booktalk by reading the first two paragraphs on page 1:

> William Gray, a master rope maker, knew there was going to be trouble in Boston that night. He wanted no part of it. As dusk fell, he closed the shutters of his house and shop. After supper, he sent his apprentice, fourteen-year-old Peter Slater, upstairs and locked the boy in his room.
>
> Peter waited until the house was quiet. Then he knotted his bedding together, hung it out the window, and slid to freedom. He wasn't a rope maker's apprentice for nothing.

What happened that night was the Boston Tea Party, the first in a series of rebellious acts that would culminate in the writing of a declaration two and a half years later. And that declaration changed the world.

A group of representatives from each of the 13 British colonies met in Philadelphia and determined that it was not right that a king who was 3,000 miles away could make bad laws and levy unfair taxes. Thomas Jefferson, who actually wrote the declaration, stated (Freedman paraphrases), "Whenever any government fails to protect the rights of its citizens, the citizens have the right to change it or to abolish it and create a new government" (page 71). The men who bravely signed that declaration knew they were risking their homes, their money, and their very lives, for now they were traitors to the king and could be hanged for it.

This is an exciting look at the Declaration of Independence, the most famous document in our country's history. It is loaded with great pictures. Show the one of John Hancock on page 31, and tell your audience why he wrote his name in such large letters on the declaration (so that the king could see it without his glasses).

What really happened at the Boston Tea Party? Why would a bunch of grown men dress up like Native Americans and throw 342 chests of tea into Boston Harbor? *The Boston Tea Party* by Michael Burgan tells the story in an accessible way for elementary school students.

More than 7,000 residents of Boston went to a meeting in the Old South Meeting House on the night of December 16, 1773. They were fighting mad. And they were ready to act on their anger.

In the harbor were three ships loaded with tea. The people of Boston were part of the Massachusetts Colony, and, as in all of the other colonies, their ruler was Great Britain. And the British government wanted them to pay more taxes. Nearly every time that country tried to impose a new tax, the colonists got so upset that the government ended up canceling it. Finally, only one tax was left—the one on tea. But a growing group of people felt that no one should have to pay taxes unless that person also had a say in how those taxes were spent. This group—the patriots—led the crowd.

They dressed up like Native Americans and went to the harbor, where they had the most famous tea party of all time—and didn't even drink any tea. In fact, since that time, tea has not been the most popular hot drink in America. Read about this important and exciting event in U.S. history. Show your audience the picture on page 11 of the tax collector being tarred and feathered. It doesn't look like fun.

A similar book, which might be a good choice for younger readers, is *The Boston Tea Party* by Steven Kroll. It explains the story clearly and concisely, telling about the unfair taxes that the British government placed on items that were imported into the American colonies. We have all heard the famous phrase "No taxation without representation!" Read this book to find out what it means and what happened that famous night in Boston in 1773.

You can't talk about the American Revolution without mentioning its most famous figure and the first president of the United States. George Washington was an amazing man, as you will find out by reading *George Washington* by Cheryl Harness. Because we see his rather stern face everywhere, even on the dollar bills we carry, it is sometimes hard to realize how great he was. But there are many excellent reasons why Washington is so well known.

Washington was born in Virginia in 1732 and knew he wanted to go to sea. His mother said no, so he came up with a substitute ambition. When he was 13 years old, he found his grandfather's surveying tools, and by the time he was 17 he was already a professional surveyor (and in a land that was just beginning to be settled, there was much to survey).

At the age of 21, Washington became an officer in the Virginia militia and went off to fight in the French and Indian War, where he learned that British generals do not always win. Then, for 16 years he farmed—until he was asked to lead an army.

That army had been formed by the Continental Congress, which had gathered in Philadelphia to declare the colonies' independence from Great Britain and its unfair laws. They knew Washington was a great soldier, and so he proved to be.

After the Revolution was over, Washington turned down a chance to be king of the United States. "Even King George III said that if the general could give up a throne, he'd be the greatest man of the whole eighteenth century. George could and did and was" (page 31).

Read all about Washington in this colorful book full of great illustrations by the author, Cheryl Harness. Flip through them to show the audience, and then show the one of the young George hunting on page 5.

A good friend of Washington's was named Lafayette. Have you ever heard of him? A lot of us have, but you probably do not know much about him. He was French, and he fought for the colonies in the American Revolution. Do you know much more than that? If you want to find out more, read *Why Not, Lafayette?* by Jean Fritz.

An excellent writer, Fritz was interested enough in Lafayette to go to his 240th birthday celebration in an American city that was named after him—Fayetteville, North Carolina. After researching this unusual man, she wrote this interesting book about him.

The Marquis de Lafayette was a French nobleman, not quite as important as a duke, but almost, and he was very rich. But from the time he was a small child, he was very concerned about freedom and equality, and he became fascinated when the colonies decided to revolt against Great Britain. Lafayette was 19 years old when he boarded a ship and came to America, leaving his wife and daughter behind.

He immediately got involved in the war and became an officer in the Revolutionary army. He became such a good friend of General George Washington that when Lafayette's first son was born, he was named George Washington. Lafayette helped the new country win that war. When he went back to France, he had many more adventures, including five years spent in a horrible prison during the French Revolution. He even met and liked Napoleon!

When Lafayette was an old man, he came back to America and traveled 5,000 miles throughout it, celebrating the fiftieth anniversary of the Revolution and visiting many of his old friends. Read this book and meet the real man behind the famous name—a man who risked and suffered much because of his belief that people should be free and equal.

The American Revolutionary War took place so long ago that some of us find it hard to imagine. It happened even before photography was invented, so we have no photographs to look at as we do of the American Civil War.

But we can tell what things were like during that time when we read what people who lived then wrote. *A Colonial Quaker Girl: The Diary of Sally Wister, 1777–1778* edited by Megan O'Hara gives a fascinating glimpse into what life was like for a child during the American Revolution. Many teachers are looking for primary source material for upper-elementary and middle school students, and this would be a great choice.

Sally Wister was a Quaker girl who kept a journal or diary in the form of letters to her best friend. Quakers opposed the war, as they oppose all wars, but we know from reading this book that Sally really wanted the American rebels to win. She was forced to leave her home in Philadelphia to escape from the occupying British troops, and she had several encounters with soldiers. These letters are well written and show a portrait of the life of a young American girl during the Revolution.

Imagine not having a microwave oven, a toaster oven, or even an ordinary baking oven. Imagine not having a refrigerator or a grocery store. In colonial America, only about 200 years ago, this was the way it was. People grew or raised their own food, preserved it to eat in the months when there were no crops, and prepared it over a fireplace. That's what life was like for Sally Wister and everyone who lived in colonial times. In *Hasty Pudding, Johnnycakes, and Other Good Stuff: Cooking in Colonial America* by Loretta Frances Ichord, find out what they ate.

Cooking over a fire was difficult because fireplaces were dangerous places with open flames. It was hard to keep fires going, and accidents occurred frequently. Food spilled, or clothing or hair caught on fire. There were no timers, and cooks had to estimate the amount of time needed to cook or bake things.

There was no pizza. There was no fast food. You made your own bread, and any meat you had was from either hunting or killing your own livestock. People relied on the native American foods, for much of what they had been used to in Europe was not available.

Ichord's book is full of fascinating information as well as recipes for food the colonists made that we can duplicate using today's more efficient methods. Some of these recipes would make fun science fair projects.

Show your audience the picture of the icehouse on page 16 and of the Native American popping corn over a fire on page 32. If you are familiar with any of the more unusual foods or have eaten them, be sure to mention them. More on this subject can be found in Susan Dosier's *Colonial Cooking*.

Figure 5.2. *Colonial Cooking* by Susan Dosier.

Not only does this book have some easy recipes, it is full of good information about the early American colonies. Boxed sections highlight in-depth facts about food and people. (Almost all of us know that Squanto befriended the Pilgrims, but we might not realize that he learned English when he was kidnapped by an English captain and taken to England for nine years. He finally earned passage back to North America, only to be captured by slave raiders and taken to Spain to be sold as a slave. When he escaped he fled to England again—and all of this happened *before* the Pilgrims landed!)

Dosier's book has recipes for colonial foods such as mashed pumpkin, country captain, Indian pudding, and Boston baked beans, and there are poems and information about the kinds of foods that were available to the settlers of our new land. It's a colorful and fascinating book. Show the picture on page 15 of the Indian corn, a food the settlers ate in vast quantities.

PIONEERS AND LIFE IN THE 1800s

How would you like to take a trip into the past? Wouldn't it be interesting to live like the pioneers did in the 1800s? *Ultimate Field Trip 4: A Week in the 1800s* by Susan E. Goodman is a true story about a group of kids who did. They spent a week living in the Kings Landing Historical Settlement in New Brunswick, Canada. And they didn't always have an easy time.

First of all, they had no indoor bathrooms. Everyone had to use outhouses, and guess what they sometimes used for toilet paper—corncobs! The girls had to wear dresses all the time. And hats! They all had to work hard to prepare their food and take care of their farm. The girls did not like the fact that they were stuck in the house doing housework while boys were allowed to do many more things. They liked even less the realization that women did not have very many rights in the 1800s and could not even vote.

Going to school was hard, too. The schools were small, and frequently the schoolteacher was not much older than the students and did not know much more either.

This book has good guessing games to play with the pictures of antique objects. You figure out what they were used for. This is fun to read. If you have a small group, show the picture on page 46—a conversation starter for sure.

To learn even more about farm life in the nineteenth century, read *Pioneer Farm: Living on a Farm in the 1880s* by Megan O'Hara.

Pioneer families had to grow most of the food they ate. There were no supermarkets, and most people did not have much money anyway. Children had to work hard to help their families, and this book tells us what it was like to live on a pioneer farm. What did kids wear? What kind of chores did they do? (Remember, there were no dishwashers or washing machines.)

Children like Laura Ingalls lived in much the same way that the kids in this book do. Learn how to play some of the games they played and make some of the crafts they made. A list of Web sites and other historical farms to visit is included. The one featured here is the Oliver Kelley farm near Elk River, Minnesota.

Pioneer children, if they went to school at all, went to one-room schools. This is hard for kids today to imagine, but they'll be able to visualize it better after seeing Raymond Bial's *One-Room School*.

When the western regions of our country were settled, there weren't many towns. And there were no existing schools for the pioneers. They had to find their own land, build their own schools, and hire their own teachers. Because most people, including kids, lived on farms, the students frequently had to walk a long way to get to school. And because the population was small, all of the grades studied together in one room. The school had no playground equipment, and there was no indoor plumbing—probably just a pump and a boys' outhouse and a girls' outhouse. You might be in eighth grade, but the person sitting next to you might be in first grade. And because your teacher was very busy with many different students in different grades, you might end up helping to teach that first-grader.

This book is loaded with pictures of real one-room schools and tells us what they were like. If you, the booktalker, know any stories about them, share them. Stories about your parents and grandparents will make the book come alive. Read the rules for teachers on page 29.

A first-person account of school life in the 1800s is the subject of *A Nineteenth-Century Schoolgirl: The Diary of Caroline Cowles Richards, 1852–1855*. Caroline was 10 years old in 1852 when she began writing a diary. She was living with her grandparents in upper New York State, for her mother had died when she was only six years old. Caroline was lucky. Her grandparents were successful people, so she lived well. Her life was not full of dramatic events, but she participated in small ways in many of the big events that were happening at that time. She saw Susan B. Anthony, who fought for the rights of women (they had almost no rights at that time), and she was interested in abolishing slavery.

The book includes recipes for cooking buckwheat cakes and for making berry ink. Your audience will learn what it was like to live in the 1850s.

Cover up Caroline's hairstyle in the picture on the book's cover. Doesn't she look like she could be a model in the twenty-first century?

The 1800s were years of great movement in the United States. Some people moved west for more land and opportunities, and others went to look for gold. When people think of the Old West, the names they know are usually the names of men. At the time the West was settled, most women had few rights and opportunities. But some women made their own way and accomplished amazing things. Liza Ketchum describes their lives in *Into a New Country: Eight Remarkable Women of the West*.

Two were sisters. Susette and Susan LaFlesche were Native Americans belonging to the Omaha people. Intelligent and determined, they wanted the Omaha to have better lives. Susette was educated much more than most other women at that time, and she fought fiercely to improve living conditions for the Omaha. Susan became a physician and went back to spend her life on the reservation, helping her people.

Biddy Mason was brought to California as a slave—and was freed after a court trial. She became an extremely successful buyer and seller of real estate—and a very wealthy woman. Lotta Crabtree was an entertainer from the time she was five years old. She spent most of her youth entertaining miners and made a fortune in the process. Kate Ryan became famous as Klondike Kate, who turned the Klondike gold rush into a wild success for herself. Mary Tape was a Chinese immigrant who fought like a tiger for the right to have her children receive a good education in America. Susan Magoffin kept a diary when she was just a teenager. In it she describes life on the Santa Fe Trail in 1846. Finally, Bethenia Owens-Adair showed everyone who knew her the incredible things that you can do when you know what you want and are determined to get it. These women are so interesting that you will want to know more about them. Show the photo of Lotta Crabtree on page 37.

Like women, African Americans aren't commonly associated with the westward movement, but they were there. Learn more about their experiences in *Hurry Freedom: African Americans in Gold Rush California* by Jerry Stanley. Not all of them struck it rich. Most of them didn't find gold anywhere except through hard work. But California in the gold rush days presented opportunities to African Americans that were not readily available to them in most other areas of the country.

Perhaps the most amazing story told here is that of Mifflin Wistar Gibbs, who was born in Philadelphia in 1823. When he was eight years old, his father died, and for the next eight years, he drove a doctor's carriage for $3 per month. Mifflin was lucky in one respect. Although the world he lived in merely tolerated African Americans, he had never been a slave. He had seen slavery though, and told his employer that he would kill anyone who made him a slave (page 5).

Thus, by the time he was 20, he was secretly working in the Underground Railroad and spent the rest of his life working for the rights of African Americans. When he was 25, he went to California.

Just getting to California took a huge effort. Slaves were coming to California, taken there by their owners (on the way, some of them escaped and fled to Mexico, where slavery had been illegal since 1824), but Mifflin decided to travel by ship. This was expensive and dangerous, for many people came down with malaria when they made the land crossing over Panama. Mifflin himself became very sick, but he managed make it to San Francisco, where he arrived with only a few cents in his pocket.

Hurry Freedom is the astounding story of how he made lots of money in San Francisco, how he helped other African Americans who came to California, how he finally left the United States in frustration, and how he came back and became the U.S. ambassador to Madagascar. Show his photo on page 4.

Morgan Monceaux is an African American who was fascinated by the Old West. He loved to play cowboys and Indians when he was a kid, and he was surprised to find out that he, like many African Americans, also had Native Americans in his family tree. When he grew up and became a painter, he decided he would like to paint portraits of some of the Native and African-American people who are important in American history. *My Heroes, My People: African Americans and Native Americans in the West* by Morgan Monceaux and Ruth Katcher contains a stunning picture of these significant people and a page or so of information about each of them.

Almost everyone has heard of Montezuma, Pocahontas, Sitting Bull, and Geronimo. *My Heroes, My People* also includes cowboys such as Nat Love, fur traders such as Jim Beckworth, women, criminals, lawmen, and many others. When Ben Hodges, a swindler, died, he was buried in Boot Hill near Dodge City because, as one of the pallbearers explained, "We wanted him where we could keep an eye on him" (page 21).

Another section is on Native Americans, such as Chief Joseph of the Nez Perce, a man of peace who was not treated well by the white people. In 1876 he explained to a U.S. government agent why his people were not bound by an 1863 treaty:

> Suppose a white man should come to me and say, "Joseph, I like your horses, and I want to buy them." I say to him, "No, my horses suit me, I will not sell them." Then he goes to my neighbor and says to him, "Jospeh has some good horses, I want to buy them but he refuses to sell." My neighbor answers, "Pay me the money, and I will sell you Joseph's horses." The white man returns to me and says, "Joseph, I have bought your horses and you must let me have them." If we sold our lands to the government, this is the way they were bought. (page 53)

Learn about some notable and unusual Americans in this colorful book. Show the picture of Chief Joseph on page 52.

The Alaskan and Canadian gold rushes started in 1898. People went a little crazy thinking that they might be able to get rich by heading for the goldfields. Many of them brought along their whole families—so there were many children who participated in one of the most famous gold rushes of all time.

Children of the Gold Rush by Claire Rudolf Murphy and Jane G. Haigh is almost like a photograph album of different kids who were there. Included are all sorts of interesting facts. A list of trail hints has some good booktalk material. People had to travel great distances to get to the goldfields, and this list was distributed to many of them:

- Don't waste a single ounce of anything, even if you don't like it. Put it away, and it will come in handy when you do like it.
- Don't eat ice or snow. Go thirsty until you can melt it.
- No man can continuously drag more than his own weight. Remember that this is a fact.
- Keep your sleeping bag clean. If it becomes inhabited, freeze the inhabitants out.
- A little dry grass or hay in the inside of your mitts, next to your hands, will promote great heat.
- When your nose is bitterly cold, stuff both nostrils with fur, cotton, or wool.
- There are no snakes in Alaska.

Find out what life was like for some real kids not that many years ago.

How did the pioneers travel across the country? They certainly didn't have SUVs to drive. Between 1750 and 1850 the real American "trucks" were Conestoga wagons, and *Conestoga Wagons* by Richard Ammon tells their story.

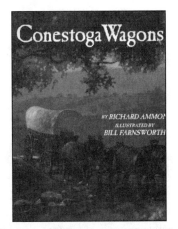

Figure 5.3. *Conestoga Wagons* by Richard Ammon.

Conestoga wagons were built in Lancaster, Pennsylvania, and most of the pioneers traveled between Philadelphia and Lancaster on what is now the Pennsylvania Turnpike. The wagons were made by hand, and one thing that made a Conestoga wagon unique is the floor. It curved inward to help keep the load from moving around in the wagon.

The wagons also had brakes, which was very unusual at that time—but very helpful when going downhill. The men who drove the wagons were called teamsters because they drove teams of horses—and that is where the name of the Teamsters Union comes from.

The horses that pulled the wagons were huge Conestoga horses, which weighed about 1,800 pounds. They wore bells to let people know they were coming—and that is where we get the expression "I'll be there with bells on."

The coming of the powerful steam engine put them out of business, but they are an important part of American history.

This book has beautiful pictures and fascinating information about the wagons. Show your audience the picture of the Conestoga horses.

Along with covered wagons, people associate cowboy hats with the American West. Find out about the inventor of that hat by reading *Boss of the Plains: The Hat That Won the West* by Laurie Carlson.

John Batterson Stetson grew up in a family of hatmakers. His father had a small hat shop in Orange, New Jersey, but John always wanted to go west. It took him quite a while to get his chance, but when he was 29 years old he headed toward Saint Joseph, Missouri, where the West began, and ended up with a group of gold seekers bound for Colorado.

Stetson never found gold, but he did find something better than gold—he found a need. People who lived and worked in the American West needed a kind of hat that was different from what anyone had ever invented, a hat that was sturdy and strong and had a bigger brim than any other hat at that time.

Stetson invented that hat, which we all call a cowboy hat. Eventually his factory in Philadelphia expanded to fill an entire city block—and famous people from everywhere came to get fitted for a Stetson hat. His most famous hat was called "The Boss of the Plains."

Young elementary readers will enjoy this picture book. Tie it in with other books about pioneers or fiction books about the West for a great booktalk.

Bad Guys: True Stories of Legendary Gunslingers, Sidewinders, Fourflushers, Drygulchers, Bushwhackers, Freebooters, and Downright Bad Guys and Gals of the Wild West by Andrew Glass tells about another aspect of the American West. Outlaws, cowboys, gunfighters—almost everybody has heard of the most famous ones, people such as Wyatt Earp, Calamity Jane, Billy the Kid, Jesse James, and Wild Bill Hickok. But what do you really know about them? What did they do?

Some people called Jesse James "America's Robin Hood" because he robbed the rich and gave to the poor, they said. No one ever really saw him do that, but some people believed it. James started out his life of crime in Bloody Kansas, one of the many awful places to live during the Civil War. After the war he and his brother Frank robbed a bank—and everyone in Missouri cheered for them. He and Frank continued robbing, and they murdered a lot of people, too. Finally, the government offered a $10,000 reward for him, and a new member of his gang shot him in the back of the head.

Billy the Kid started out okay—but he didn't live long enough to end up okay. He was only 21 when he died, shot by Sheriff Pat Garrett, who used to be his friend. In his seven-year life of crime, he killed several people and had lots of adventures. But the legends about him were more fiction than fact.

This is a fun book that tells us the true stories of those bad guys you've always read about. Show the audience the picture of Billy the Kid or Jesse James.

Have you heard the phrase "Remember the Alamo"? Do you know anything about it? In February 1836 the small group of people in the Alamo in San Antonio, Texas, knew they were in big trouble. Most of them knew they probably didn't have a chance. And they were right. Learn about their fight for independence in *The Alamo* by Michael Burgan.

They were Texians (Americans living in Texas, which was part of Mexico) and Tejanos (native Mexicans living in Texas). Some were American citizens, of whom Davy Crockett was perhaps the most famous, and a few were African-American slaves.

There had been a fast-growing American colony in Texas since 1820. Mexico had just won its independence from Spain, and Texas became part of one of Mexico's own states. The Mexican government wanted to stop more American settlers from coming in and started taxing those who were there—a lot. But it didn't work. Americans had already shown the world during the Revolutionary War that they did not like unfair taxes.

Tensions increased daily, and by the time of the famous battle of the Alamo, the Americans were just as determined to get their independence from Mexico as they had been to get their independence from Great Britain 60 years earlier. But they had a big fight on their hands first, and this book tells all about it. Show the picture on page 28 of Davy Crockett, who was probably taken out and executed after the defeat.

A pivotal event of the nineteenth century was the American Civil War. Several accessible books tell what those years were like for children on both sides of the battle lines. *Children of the Civil War* by Candice F. Ransom is a good choice for third-through fifth-graders.

In 1861, when the Civil War began, children in both the North and South were automatically involved. Some kids joined the army—see the photo of Johnny Clem on page 11. He was so small that he could fit in a drum, so this 11-year-old became a drummer boy. Later he was promoted to sergeant. Other kids stayed at home but suffered shortages of food, and their houses were sometimes destroyed during the fighting. Some became orphans when their parents were killed.

Perhaps the only children who "won" anything were the slave children. But the masters of many slaves did not bother to tell them that they were free. Even though they were free after the war, they still had to fight to be treated equally. Lots of pictures fill this interesting book.

Fourth-graders on up will enjoy *A Confederate Girl: The Diary of Carrie Berry 1864*, a firsthand account of the war written by a young Southern girl.

Carrie Berry was 10 years old in 1865 when General Sherman and his Union troops came to Atlanta, her hometown. You may have seen a movie called *Gone with the Wind*, and, if so, you may know what happened there. The end of the Civil War was near. The South, or the Confederate states, was losing the war, and General Sherman was determined to end it as quickly as possible. His troops burned most of Atlanta to the ground. And Carrie was there. She was a real girl who kept a real diary. And she had a lot to write about. Being a child in the Civil War was not only dangerous but also frequently boring. Carrie's mother made her stay inside much of the time so she would not get wounded during the battles and the shelling.

This attractive book presents facts about shells, bread riots, and the burning of Atlanta. There are also directions for making your own rag doll and writing your own diary.

For a similar account from the point of view of a child from the North, read *A Civil War Drummer Boy: The Diary of William Bircher 1861–1865*.

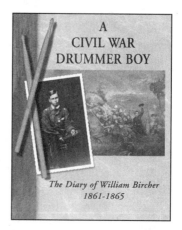

Figure 5.4. *A Civil War Drummer Boy: The Diary of William Bircher 1861–1865* **by William Bircher.**

William Bircher was only 15 years old when he decided to enlist as a drummer boy in the Civil War. Drummer boys, as one of the sidebars in the book tells us, were important. Before there were cell phones and walkie-talkies, drummers communicated orders to the soldiers. When there was thick smoke from gunfire, drumbeats helped soldiers find their units. William probably thought he would have a good time being in the Union army.

He had no idea what he was in for. Frequently there was not enough food and not any water. When his shoes wore out, he wore rags around his feet, but his feet hurt so much he could barely walk. His body was covered with fleas and lice because he was unable to take any baths. When he was finally allowed to go on leave to visit his home in Saint Paul, he got to sleep in a bed for the first time in two years!

He saw horrible things in the war—people dead and dying and people who had been horribly wounded. He kept a diary of his experiences.

The book includes a recipe for making hardtack, which the soldiers ate often (it sounds pretty awful) and information about the diseases that killed many soldiers. More died from disease than from wounds they received in battle.

Megan O'Hara is the editor of another real diary from the 1800s. *A Whaling Captain's Daughter: The Diary of Laura Jernegan, 1868–1871* is about a girl who was only six years old when she went on a whaling expedition. Her father, a ship's captain, wanted to take his family with him because he knew he would be gone for months. Laura's parents gave her a journal so she could write down what happened each day. Some days she did not write much—only what the family ate.

But Laura, like everyone else aboard a whaling ship, had a lot of adventures. Some people called the whaler she was on—the *Roman*—a "lady ship," which meant a ship with the captain's wife and possibly children on it. They had to endure the scary, dangerous whale chases and also the terrible mess and smell of the whale oil being boiled out of the blubber.

Page 16 has a great photograph of scrimshaw portraits of Laura's parents. The sailors would take a whale's tooth and make things out of it, usually carving pictures on it. The portraits of Laura's parents are amazing.

Read this book and ask the kids whether they would have liked to be on a whaling ship. It sounds as though it might have been pretty boring most of the time. This book ties in closely with Jim Murphy's *Gone A-Whaling: The Lure of the Sea and the Hunt for the Great Whale* (Chapter 1).

Also by Megan O'Hara, *General Store: A Village Store in 1902* tells about daily life many years ago. In 1902 there were no supermarkets, and most towns had only one store, a general store, which carried just about anything you might need.

This is the story of a little girl's trip to the store with a basketful of eggs and a list of things that her family needed. It is filled with other interesting information, too, such as the fact that, because there were no refrigerators, food spoilage was a serious problem. Sometimes there were insects in the food you bought. Storekeepers tried to be very careful, but it was difficult to prevent the bugs from getting into the food.

The pictures in this book were taken at the Meighen store near Preston, Minnesota. The book includes Web sites and a list of other places in the United States where you can visit old general stores.

THE AFRICAN-AMERICAN EXPERIENCE

African-American soldiers have had a hard time of it in the United States armed forces until quite recently. Reading some parts of *The Black Soldier: 1492 to the Present* by Catherine Clinton might make you angry. One very upsetting story starts in the last paragraph of page 45 and continues to page 46. Read it aloud. In summary, in 1906 black infantrymen at Fort Brown, Texas, were harassed and attacked by whites whenever they went into the nearby town of Brownsville. Finally, they fought back, and one white person was killed. Newspaper reporters said this proved that African Americans should not be in the military. Authorities were unable to find the few men responsible for the killing, and ultimately President Theodore Roosevelt gave dishonorable discharges to 160 black soldiers, including six Medal of Honor winners.

The military didn't become integrated until Harry Truman became president, about 40 years later. Even then, blacks were often treated unfairly and found it difficult to get promotions. Before that time, black soldiers were kept separate from white soldiers, although their commanding officers were usually white.

We know that a black man arrived with Columbus in 1492, and we know that African Americans have been in our armed forces throughout our history, no matter how unfairly they were treated. This is a fascinating but appalling story. There are pictures of African-American soldiers throughout the book. Show the one of General Colin Powell on page 142.

It is a terrible thing to be a slave. Can you imagine not having any rights? Slaves had none. The people who owned them could do anything they wanted to them. They could beat them, hurt them, separate them forever from their families, and treat them like animals. Read about this appalling chapter in U.S. history in *Slave Young, Slave Long: The American Slave Experience* by Meg Greene.

The first slaves arrived in Virginia a year before the pilgrims landed at Plymouth Rock. About 20 of them were brought over from Africa, and at first they were not condemned to be slaves for life. They could work or earn money to pay for their freedom. But by the late 1600s slavery was a permanent condition. Slaves were brought by the hundreds and thousands from Africa in horrifying conditions. They were packed into ships, sometimes chained at the neck and legs, with only about 18 inches of space in which to move. They were fed very little, and many died on the trip. Some became so depressed that they chose to die. In fact, less than half of the people who were brought from Africa became effective workers. If they did not die on the journey, they were sometimes permanently crippled from the ordeal.

Life on a plantation was, for most of them, almost as bad as the voyage. Some attempted to escape but suffered terrible penalties if they were caught. A few who rebelled endured even more dreadful penalties.

Slave Young, Slave Long is full of photographs of slaves and descriptions of the life they led. Show the picture of the slave family in their decrepit cabin on page 48.

The brave people in Dennis Brindell Fradin's *Bound for the North Star: True Stories of Fugitive Slaves* all had one thing in common: They hated being slaves and were determined to gain their freedom.

Figure 5.5. *Bound for the North Star: True Stories of Fugitive Slaves* **by Dennis Brindell Fradin.**

Running away from slavery was about the scariest a thing a person could think of. If you were caught, you would almost certainly be beaten, probably sold into worse conditions than you had lived in before, and maybe even be killed. Most likely you could not read—because it was illegal to teach slaves how to read. You probably did not even have a map and knew only to look for the North Star. You might not have any knowledge of geography. One slave was a few miles away from a free state when someone convinced him that he should go south. He did just that and ended up in New Orleans, thinking he would be able to go to England, where slavery was illegal.

A few of the people in these stories are famous. Almost everyone has heard of the amazing Harriet Tubman. Eliza Harris became famous for crossing the partially frozen Ohio River, the boundary between the slave state of Kentucky and the free state of Ohio, with her baby in her arms. Harriet Beecher Stowe wrote a story called *Uncle Tom's Cabin* about this incident. Another slave, Margaret Garner, killed her children rather than have them returned to slavery, and her life story was the basis of the famous book (and movie) *Beloved* by Toni Morrison.

People who are desperate can become very creative. Two of the stories in the book are about slaves who packed themselves into boxes and shipped themselves to freedom. One is about a free African American living in Saratoga Springs, New York, who was kidnapped by slavers and sold into slavery in the Deep South—where he stayed for 12 years.

The descriptions of slave life are horrifying. Show the picture on page 22 of the woman wearing a contraption of bells and horns so she cannot escape—or sleep.

Anne Rockwell writes about a very famous escaped slave in *Only Passing Through: The Story of Sojourner Truth*. Read this quote (from the first page) to start your booktalk:

> Strangers stared while the auctioneer poked and pointed at the girl with his stick—showing how tall and strong she was. He promised that since she was only about nine years old and already so tall, she'd soon be able to do the work of any man.

This slave girl, called Isabella, was for sale, but nobody wanted to buy her. The auctioneer finally threw in a flock of sheep, and then someone bought her. Her new owner spoke English and she spoke only Dutch, so he would whip her when she did not understand what he wanted her to do.

Isabella was a very angry girl who did her best to obtain her freedom. And she did. She became one of the greatest women in American history. Find out what happened in this moving, colorful book. Show the picture on the first page of Isabella being auctioned.

Elizabeth Dana Jaffe's *Sojourner Truth* is an easier-to-read biography of that amazing American woman, Sojourner Truth.

Around 1797 she was born a slave in the state of New York. Her family called her Belle, but she had no last name. Her owner was Dutch, so that was the language she grew up speaking. Although she eventually learned to speak English, Belle always spoke with a Dutch accent.

Life was hard for slaves. Seven of her brothers and sisters had been sold away from their parents. Belle's turn came when she was 11. Her new owners beat her to make her speak English, which no one had ever taught her. She was sold twice more, and when her fourth owner broke his word that he would let her go free, she ran away. And that was just the beginning. Belle became famous and traveled throughout the United States. She met Abraham Lincoln, and she wrote the story of her life.

Find out why she changed her name and what happened when you read this interesting book. Show the picture of the photograph of Sojourner Truth with Abraham Lincoln on page 24.

Everybody has a personal story, but Clara Brown had many incredible stories to tell. Read about her in *Aunt Clara Brown: Official Pioneer* by Linda Lowery.

Clara Brown was a slave. She had lived in Kentucky, Kansas, Missouri, and Virginia. She had been sold many times, but in 1856 when her owner died, she managed to purchase her freedom with money she had made and saved by working very hard. Perhaps the worst thing that happened to her was that her daughter Eliza had been sold away from her when Eliza was only 10 years old.

In 1859, at age 57, Brown went west to Colorado. She found work doing laundry for gold hunters, but what she went through to get to Colorado and to the goldfields is almost unbelievable. She was hoping that she would find Eliza there.

Brown made and lost a good deal of money. And throughout her life she kept looking for Eliza. Read this wonderful book to discover what happened. Show your audience the picture on page 17 of Brown walking 680 miles to Colorado.

For a rare firsthand account of an African-American girl in the mid-1800s, read *A Free Black Girl Before the Civil War: The Diary of Charlotte Forten, 1854* edited by Christy Steele with Kerry Graves.

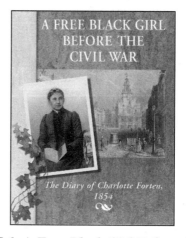

Figure 5.6. *A Free Black Girl Before the Civil War: The Diary of Charlotte Forten, 1854* **edited by Christy Steele with Kerry Graves.**

Charlotte Forten was 16 years old in 1854, and her life was extraordinary. She was free and African American. Her father wanted her to be well educated, so he sent her to live with family friends in Salem, Massachusetts, where she was able to go to a school in which white people and African Americans were educated together. But just being black was very hard for anyone at that time. On July 17 she wrote : "I long … to dwell … far from the land, my native land—where I am hated and oppressed because God has given me a dark skin. How did this cruel, this absurd prejudice ever exist? How can it exist? When I think of it a feeling of indignation rises in my soul too deep for utterance" (page 20).

An especially hard thing for Charlotte Forten to observe was the capture and return to slavery of Anthony Burns, a slave who had run away from his plantation and ended up in Boston, which was in a free state. He was sent back to slavery in irons after a trial that many considered unfair. This is a fascinating look at another era.

African Americans have a long history of fighting against injustice. Many have dedicated their lives to helping others overcome prejudice and oppression, and white people have also joined in the struggle. Levi Coffin is one of them, and Gwenyth Swain tells his story in *President of the Underground Railroad: A Story About Levi Coffin*.

Levi Coffin fought injustice almost his entire life. He put his money where his mouth was. He was an amazing man who did his best to fight slavery and to help runaway slaves escape. Someone said he was the "president of the Underground Railroad." Although the Underground Railroad was not an official organization and certainly had no officers, Coffin deserved the honor.

He was born in North Carolina and had often seen slaves mistreated. He saw parents sold away from their children, husbands sold away from their wives, and horrible punishments inflicted on slaves, who had no legal rights of any sort. In fact, slaves had no rights whatsoever. Their owners could do whatever they wanted to them.

Coffin believed this was wrong. He and his family were Quakers, and Quakers did not believe in slavery. When he was just a teenager, he begged neighbors not to remove a runaway slave from her family—and actually convinced them.

When Coffin grew up and got married, he knew he did not want to live in a slave state. In 1824 he moved to Indiana, on the frontier, and there he protected runaway slaves who came looking for shelter. He estimated that he helped about 3,000 slaves to escape their bondage. This is an incredible story about a man who is not as well known as he ought to be.

The problems of African Americans did not end with the abolishment of slavery. New forms of oppression and injustice took its place, and people continued to struggle for equality. *Ida B. Wells: Mother of the Civil Rights Movement* by Dennis Brindell Fradin and Judith Bloom Fradin is a fine biography about a great woman crusader.

Figure 5.7. *Ida B. Wells: Mother of the Civil Rights Movement* by Dennis Brindell Fradin and Judith Bloom Fradin.

Do you think that anyone has ever been burned at the stake in the United States of America? More than one person has, and these people were usually guilty of only one "crime": the fact that they were African Americans.

One woman led a crusade to stop this from happening. Her name was Ida B. Wells, and she was born a slave in 1862. She had little education, but when she was still in her teens and responsible for bringing up her younger brothers and sisters after her parents were killed in a typhoid epidemic, she discovered that she was good at writing. And perhaps the most important thing she decided to write about was lynching.

Lynching began to be common in the 1870s. A group of white people, often involving the Ku Klux Klan, would sometimes break into a jail and capture a black prisoner, take him out, and, if he was lucky, hang him. If he was not so lucky, they might torture him, burn him at a stake, gouge out his eyes, or do other painful things to him before he died.

Many people loved to go see lynchings. Often people knew in advance that one was going to take place. Thousands of people would come to the town where it was going to take place, and they acted as though it were a carnival and had a good time. People sent each other postcards showing the lynched people.

Ida Wells hated this situation and became very interested in it when a good friend of hers was lynched. What was his crime? He and his two partners opened a grocery store in a black neighborhood in Memphis. The owner of a nearby white grocery store was angry because his business suffered—so the three black grocery store owners were lynched.

Wells wrote about this incident very convincingly. She spent her life working for justice and equal rights for African Americans. She was a truly great American, and this biography is a must for middle school students.

Osceola Mays was more than 90 years old when *Osceola: Memories of a Sharecropper's Daughter*, collected and edited by Alan Govenar, was written. The daughter of a sharecropper, she was born in east Texas in 1910. Sharecropping meant that her father farmed the land of another man, usually a white man, and the two shared the harvest. Mays's father got only one-third of the crop, and their family was always poor. They had no money at all, for the man who owned the land they farmed paid them in his own coin, which they had to use to buy food and supplies. They always owed money.

Mays's grandmother was a slave. She was 10 years old when she was freed, but she remembered that part of her life well and told Osceola about it. Osceola Mays got her name from a Native American, a man who "stretched his tent" (page 11) near her house. She liked his name but not her own, so she took his instead.

Being a sharecropper's daughter was not easy, but Mays was loved by her mother and her father and was grief-stricken when her mother died after childbirth.

Filled with songs and poems Mays remembered from her childhood, this stunning book will open your eyes to a different time and way of life. The illustrations are beautiful. Show the picture of the man Osceola Mays named herself after on page 12, and read "The Black Man's Plea for Justice" that starts on page 57.

Framed in fiction, *If a Bus Could Talk: The Story of Rosa Parks* by Faith Ringgold tells the true story of Rosa Parks, whose act of courage helped to change a United States law.

Parks was born in Alabama in 1913. She remembered being very scared when the Ku Klux Klan, a group of white men who hated African Americans, would ride past her grandparents' farm. Sometimes her whole family slept in their clothes in case the Ku Klux Klan set fire to their house and they had to escape. African Americans were treated unfairly by almost everyone at that time. When young Rosa went to school, there was only one teacher for every 50 or 60 children. All of the African-American children were in one school, one that ran only five months of the year and had only the first six grades. The white children had much smaller classes, and their school was open for nine months and went through the twelfth grade.

When Parks grew up, she got a job in a department store in Montgomery, Alabama, but taking the bus to work was a problem. Black people were allowed to sit only in the back of the bus. They were permitted to sit in the middle section if no whites were sitting in those seats, but they had to move if whites wanted to sit there. They were prohibited from sitting in the same row with white people. In addition, bus drivers were often very mean to black people.

Parks married a man who was very active in the National Association for the Advancement of Colored People (NAACP). Soon she, too, became active in that cause and began fighting for her rights and those of all black people. On December 1, 1955, a bus driver told Parks to give her seat to a white man, but Parks said no. The police took her to jail, and soon trouble broke out all over the South. Read this wonderful book to find out what happened to this courageous woman. Show the picture of the Ku Klux Klan riders early in the book.

Ruby Bridges tells her own amazing story in *Through My Eyes*, a beautiful book full of photographs. In 1960 Bridges was the first "Negro," as she tells us African Americans were called at the time, to integrate the William Frantz Public School in New Orleans, Louisiana. She was six years old and in the first grade. Every day four United States marshals escorted her to school so that she would not be hurt by the screaming, abusive mobs of white people who did not want public schools integrated. The hatred in their faces in the photos is horrifying to see, especially on the day they displayed a black doll in a coffin.

Because most white children refused to attend the school, little Ruby was the only child in her class. She and her teacher, a young woman from Boston named Barbara Henry, were alone together all year long. Going to school every morning was an ordeal. Ruby's father was even fired from his job because his child was going to a white school. What Ruby did that year helped pave the way for more racial equality in the United States. Fortunately, Ruby was too little at the time to understand why people hated her so much. Show your audience the cover of the book and the photo on page 21 of the crowd holding the doll in the coffin.

To introduce *Malcolm X: A Fire Burning Brightly* by Walter Dean Myers, read this paragraph: "To come right down to it, if I take the kinds of things in which I believe, then add to that the kind of temperament that I have, plus the 100 percent dedication I have to whatever I believe in—these are ingredients which make it just about impossible for me to die of old age."

The man who said that was Malcolm X, an African American who believed that African Americans should use force and even violence, if necessary, to achieve the rights that had been denied to them since they were brought to America as slaves.

Malcolm X was born Malcolm Little in Omaha, Nebraska. He was only six when his father was found crushed to death under a trolley. Some people said he had been murdered because people did not like his opinion that black people should stand up for their rights. When Malcolm's mother became ill, Malcolm and his siblings were sent to foster homes. Malcolm knew he was smart, but by the time he was 18 he was in trouble, and, a few years later, he landed in jail. There he started reading, and what he read changed his life.

It was a short life, but it was one that made a remarkable difference. Read this book to learn about this amazing man. Show your audience the illustration of Malcolm reading in prison.

There are few better writers for young people than Walter Dean Myers. When he tells a story, you know it will be a good one. And when he tells the true story of one of his own heroes, as he does in *The Greatest: Muhammad Ali*, you know it will be hard to put down.

Muhammad Ali was born in Louisville, Kentucky, in 1942. He was black, and his family didn't have much money. He grew up knowing he would not have the same opportunities as white kids did. He could not go to the same schools they went to, eat at the same restaurants, use the same rest rooms, or even drink from the same water fountains.

Muhammad's name wasn't Muhammad then. It was Cassius Clay. But when he grew into a talented, good-looking young man, he got rid of his old name, the one he called a slave name, and became a Muslim. Then he chose a new name for himself.

Muhammad started learning to fight when he was 12 years old and his bicycle was stolen. He took boxing lessons and worked harder than anyone else. In addition, he was quicker than everyone else—and very handsome and proud of himself and his black heritage. In America in 1960, even after he won a gold medal in the Olympics, this was not considered normal behavior. It was actually very unusual, and many white people, and even many African-American people, disliked it.

How Muhammad Ali became the world heavyweight champion, broke some laws, was persecuted, and eventually lost his crown after having what would probably have been his three best years stolen from him makes an unforgettable story. Myers also tells us what kind of a man his hero was and still is and of the effects the sport of boxing has on the people who participate in it. Show your audience the photo of young Cassius Clay facing the heading of Chapter 1.

For another inspiring true story, you can't beat *The Riches of Oseola McCarty* by Evelyn Coleman. Oseola McCarty was an African American who lived with her grandmother in Hattiesburg, Mississippi. She was born in 1913, a time when life was very hard for poor African Americans in the United States and especially in the South. "Jim Crow" laws were enforced there, and their only purpose was to keep African Americans from having the same opportunities and education as white people. Many African-American women saw little of their own children because they spent most of their time doing housework for white employers.

Oseola McCarty knew she was lucky because her grandmother washed clothes for a living, and she washed them at home—which meant she could spend time with her children and grandchildren. When Oseola was 12, she dropped out of school to help her family, and she, her aunt, and her grandmother loved to work together.

McCarty also did something else very unusual. She started putting the money she earned into a savings account and never took any of it out. By the time she was an old woman, she was able to start a college scholarship fund so young African-American students could go to the University of Southern Mississippi in Hattiesburg. By that time she had saved more than $150,000. McCarty became famous and even received a medal from the president of the United States.

BIBLIOGRAPHY

Ammon, Richard. *Conestoga Wagons*. Illustrated by Bill Farnsworth. Holiday House, 2000. ISBN 0823414752. Unpaged. Grades 3–5.

Berry, Carrie. *A Confederate Girl: The Diary of Carrie Berry 1864*. Edited by Christy Steele with Anne Todd, foreword by Suzanne L. Bunkers. Content Consultant: Frank Wheeler, Former Associate Director, Georgia Historical Society. Blue Earth Books, 2000. ISBN 0736803432. 32 p. Grades 4–up.

Bial, Raymond. *One-Room School*. Houghton Mifflin, 1999. ISBN 0395905141. 48 p. Grades 4–6.

Bierman, Carol, with Barbara Hehner. *Journey to Ellis Island: How My Father Came to America*. Illustrated by Laurie McGaw. A Hyperion/Madison Press Book, 1999. ISBN 0786803770. 48 p. Grades 4–6.

Bircher, William. *A Civil War Drummer Boy: The Diary of William Bircher 1861–1865*. Edited by Shelley Swanson Sateren, foreword by Suzanne L. Bunkers. Content consultant: Hampton Smith, reference archivist, Minnesota Historical Society. Blue Earth Books, 2000. ISBN 0736803483. 32 p. Grades 4–up.

Bridges, Ruby. *Through My Eyes*. Articles and interviews compiled and edited by Margo Lundell. Scholastic, 1999. ISBN 0590189239. 64 p. Grades 4–6.

Burgan, Michael. *The Alamo* (We the People). Compass Point Books, 2001. ISBN 0756500974. 48 p. Grades 3–7.

———. *The Boston Tea Party* (We the People). Compass Point Books, 2001. ISBN 0756500400. 48 p. Grades 2–5.

———. *The Trail of Tears* (We the People). Compass Point Books, 2001. ISBN 0756501016. 48 p. Grades 4–up.

Carlson, Laurie. *Boss of the Plains: The Hat That Won the West*. Pictures by Holly Meade. DK, 1999. ISBN 0789424797. 32 p. Grades 2–4.

Clinton, Catherine. *The Black Soldier: 1492 to the Present*. Houghton Mifflin, 2000. ISBN 039567722X. 117 p. Grades 4–8.

Coleman, Evelyn. *The Riches of Oseola McCarty*. Illustrated by Daniel Minter. Whitman, 1998. ISBN 0807569615. 48 p. Grades 3–5.

Colman, Penny. *Girls: A History of Growing Up Female in America*. Scholastic Reference, 2000. ISBN 0590371290. 192 p. Grades 5–8.

Cooper, Michael L. *Indian School: Teaching the White Man's Way*. Clarion Books, 1999. ISBN 0395920841. 104 p. Grades 5–8.

Curlee, Lynn. *Liberty*. Atheneum Books for Young Readers, 2000. ISBN 0689828233. 42 p. Grades 4–7.

Dosier, Susan. *Colonial Cooking* (Exploring History Through Simple Recipes). Consultant: Melodie Andrews, Professor of Early American History, Minnesota State University, Mankato. Blue Earth Books, 2000. ISBN 0736803521. 32 p. Grades 4–up.

Fradin, Dennis Brindell. *Bound for the North Star: True Stories of Fugitive Slaves*. Clarion Books, 2000. ISBN 0395970172. 206 p. Grades 5–8.

Fradin, Dennis Brindell, and Judith Bloom Fradin. *Ida B. Wells: Mother of the Civil Rights Movement*. Clarion Books, 2000. ISBN 0395898986. 178 p. Grades 5–up.

Freedman, Russell. *Give Me Liberty! The Story of the Declaration of Independence.* Holiday House, 2000. ISBN 0823414485. 90 p. Grades 4–8.

Fritz, Jean. *Why Not, Lafayette?* Illustrated by Ronald Himler. G. P. Putnam's Sons, 1999. ISBN 039923411X. 87 p. Grades 4–8.

Garner, Joe. *We Interrupt This Broadcast: The Events That Stopped Our Lives . . . From the Hindenburg Explosion to the Death of John F. Kennedy.* Updated second edition. Sourcebooks, 2000. ISBN 1-57071-535-1. 169 p. Grades 5–up.

Glass, Andrew. *Bad Guys: True Stories of Legendary Gunslingers, Sidewinders, Fourflushers, Drygulchers, Bushwhackers, Freebooters, and Downright Bad Guys and Gals of the Wild West.* Doubleday, 1998. ISBN 0385323107. Unpaged. Grades 3–7.

Goodman, Susan E. *Ultimate Field Trip 4: A Week in the 1800s.* Photographs by Michael J. Doolittle. Atheneum Books for Young Readers, 2000. ISBN 0689830459. 50 p. Grades 4–7.

Govenar, Alan (editor). *Osceola: Memories of a Sharecropper's Daughter.* Illustrated by Shane W. Evans. Jump at the Sun/Hyperion Books for Children, 2000. ISBN 0786804076 (hc.); 0786825777 (lib. bdg.). 64 p. Grades 4–up.

Greene, Meg. *Slave Young, Slave Long: The American Slave Experience.* Lerner, 1999. ISBN 0822517396. 88 p. Grades 4–8.

Harness, Cheryl. *George Washington.* National Geographic Society, 2000. ISBN 0792270967. 48 p. Grades 3–6.

Hoobler, Dorothy, and Thomas Hoobler. *Real American Girls Tell Their Own Stories.* Atheneum Books for Young Readers, 1999. ISBN 0689820836. 104 p. Grades 4–6.

Ichord, Loretta Frances. *Hasty Pudding, Johnnycakes, and Other Good Stuff: Cooking in Colonial America.* Illustrated by Jan Davey Ellis. Millbrook Press, 1998. ISBN 0761303693. 64 p. Grades 4–6.

Jaffe, Elizabeth Dana. *Sojourner Truth* (Compass Point Early Biographies). Compass Point Books, 2001. ISBN 0756500680. 32 p. Grades 2–5.

January, Brendan. *The Jamestown Colony* (We the People). Compass Point Books, 2001. ISBN 0756500435. 48 p. Grades 2–5.

Jones, Rebecca. *The President Has Been Shot! True Stories of the Attacks on Ten U.S. Presidents.* Dutton Children's Books, 1996. ISBN 0-525-45333-4. 134 p. Grades 5–8.

Ketchum, Liza. *Into a New Country: Eight Remarkable Women of the West.* Little, Brown, 2000. ISBN 0316495972. 135 p. Grades 4–8.

Kroll, Steven. *The Boston Tea Party.* Illustrated by Peter Fiore. Holiday House, 1998. ISBN 0823413160. Unpaged. Grades 1–3.

Lanier, Shannon, and Jane Feldman. *Jefferson's Children: The Story of One American Family*. With photographs by Jane Feldman. Introduction by Lucian K. Truscott IV. Historical essays by Annette Gordeon-Reed and Beverly Gray. Random House, 2000. ISBN 0375805974. 144 p. Grades 5–8.

Leacock, Elspeth, and Susan Buckley. *Journeys in Time: A New Atlas of American History*. Illustrations by Rodica Prato. Houghton Mifflin, 2001. ISBN 0395979560. 48 p. Grades 4–8.

Lowery, Linda. *Aunt Clara Brown: Official Pioneer* (On My Own Biography Grades 2–3). Illustrations by Janice Lee Porter. Carolrhoda Books, 1999. ISBN 1575050455 (lib. bdg.); 1575054167 (pbk.). 48 p. Grades 2–3.

Marrin, Albert. *Sitting Bull and His World: Tatan'ka Iyota'ke*. Dutton Children's Books, 2000. ISBN 0525459448. 246 p. Grades 7–up.

Miller, Brandon Marie. *Dressed for the Occasion: What Americans Wore 1620–1970*. Lerner, 1999. ISBN 0822517388. 96 p. Grades 4–8.

Monceaux, Morgan, and Ruth Katcher. *My Heroes, My People: African Americans and Native Americans in the West*. Portraits by Morgan Monceaux. Frances Foster Books/Farrar, Straus & Giroux, 1999. ISBN 0374307709. 64 p. Grades 4–8.

Murphy, Claire Rudolf, and Jane G. Haigh. *Children of the Gold Rush*. Roberts Rinehart, 1999. ISBN 1570982570. 82 p. Grades 5–up.

Myers, Walter Dean. *The Greatest: Muhammad Ali*. Scholastic, 2001. ISBN 0590543432. 172 p. Grades 4–8.

———. *Malcolm X: A Fire Burning Brightly*. Illustrated by Leonard Jenkins. HarperCollins, 2000. ISBN 0060277076. Unpaged. Grades 3–5.

O'Hara, Megan (editor). *A Colonial Quaker Girl: The Diary of Sally Wister, 1777–1778*. With foreword by Suzanne L. Bunkers. Content consultant: J. William Frost, Jenkins Professor of Quaker History and Research, and Director, Friends Historical Library, Swarthmore College. Blue Earth Books, 2000. ISBN 0736803491. 32 p. Grades 4–7.

———. *General Store: A Village Store in 1902*. Blue Earth Books, 1998. ISBN 1560757235. 32 p. Grades 3–5.

———. *Pioneer Farm: Living on a Farm in the 1880s*. Blue Earth Books, 1998. ISBN 0516212532. 32 p. Grades 3–5.

——— (editor). *A Whaling Captain's Daughter: The Diary of Laura Jernegan, 1868–1871*. Foreword by Suzanne L. Bunkers. Content consultant: Judy Downey, Librarian, New Bedford Whaling Museum, New Bedford, Massachusetts. Blue Earth Books, 2000. ISBN 0736803467. 32 p. Grades 4–7.

Ransom, Candice F. *Children of the Civil War* (Picture the American Past). Carolrhoda Books, 1998. ISBN 1575052415. 48 p. Grades 3–5.

Richards, Caroline Cowles. *A Nineteenth-Century Schoolgirl: The Diary of Caroline Cowles Richards, 1852–1855*. Edited by Kerry A. Graves, foreword by Suzanne L. Bunkers. Content consultant: Wilma T. Townsend, Curator, Ontario County Historical Society, Canandaigua, New York. Blue Earth Books, 2000. ISBN 0736803424. 32 p. Grades 4–up.

Ringgold, Faith. *If a Bus Could Talk: The Story of Rosa Parks*. Simon & Schuster Books for Young Readers, 1999. ISBN 0689818920. Unpaged. Grades 2–5.

Rockwell, Anne. *Only Passing Through: The Story of Sojourner Truth*. Illustrated by R. Gregory Christie. Alfred A. Knopf, 2000. ISBN 0679991867. Unpaged. Grades 2–5.

St. George, Judith. *In the Line of Fire: Presidents' Lives at Stake*. Holiday House, 1999. ISBN 0823414280. 144 p. Grades 4–8.

Sewall, Marcia. *Jamestowne: Struggle for Survival*. Atheneum Books for Young Readers, 2001. ISBN 0689818149. 40 p. Grades 3–5.

Stanley, Jerry. *Hurry Freedom: African Americans in Gold Rush California*. Crown, 2000. ISBN 0517800942. 86 p. Grades 5–8.

Steele, Christy, with Kerry Graves (editor). *A Free Black Girl Before the Civil War: The Diary of Charlotte Forten, 1854*. Consultants: Daniel Gross, Director, Beverly Historical Society, Beverly, Massachusetts, and Mary-Ellen Smiley, Curator, Wenham Museum, Wenham, Massachusetts. Blue Earth Books, 2000. ISBN 0736803459. 32 p. Grades 4–7.

Swain, Gwenyth. *President of the Underground Railroad: A Story About Levi Coffin* (A Creative Minds Biography). Illustrations by Ralph L. Ramstad. Carolrhoda Books, 2001. ISBN 1575055511. 64 p. Grades 4–6.

Yue, Charlotte, and David Yue. *The Wigwam and the Longhouse*. Houghton Mifflin, 2000. ISBN 0395841690. 118 p. Grades 4–6.

CHAPTER ___ 6

Innovators: Artists, Inventors, Amazing Achievers, and Feats of Technology

ARTISTS

In *Michelangelo*—a gorgeous picture book written for upper-elementary to middle school students—Diane Stanley describes one of the greatest innovators of all time. He was born in 1475—17 years before Christopher Columbus discovered a new land—and lived for almost 90 years. What he did during that time is still viewed with awe today.

Michelangelo was only one of his names, but it is the one we all know. He wanted to be a sculptor. He *always* wanted to be a sculptor, but he was not always able to be in charge of his own life. In Italy at that time, which we call the Renaissance, great artists were often not allowed to make their own professional decisions. Today artists create works of art and sell them. During the Renaissance, artists were frequently employed by rich people called patrons, who told the artists what works to make.

Michelangelo had to fight to become an artist. His family was not rich, but they had enough money to think that no member of their family should have to work with his hands. He must have been determined because he managed to obtain an apprenticeship with a famous artist. He showed so much promise that in a short time he went to live in the home of the ruler of Florence, Lorenzo di Medici. We know Michelangelo had a bad temper and once got into a fight with another apprentice, who punched him in the nose and wrecked any chance of his ever being handsome.

He studied hard. He dissected corpses to see how the body was made so that he could sculpt it accurately. He worked constantly but, in spite of that, was almost always short of money.

The work of art he became most famous for was one he did not even want to create. Do you have any idea what that was?

Diane Stanley illustrates her book with wonderful pictures. Show the one of Michelangelo sculpting a snowman by the order of the ruler of Florence. And if you have ever personally seen any of Michelangelo's works, be sure to tell the audience about your experience.

Adults will know this next famous American artist, but children may need the introduction found in *Norman Rockwell: Storyteller with a Brush* by Beverly Gherman. Rockwell was a man who did his own thing. He did not much care what art critics thought—and they kept saying they did not think much of the pictures he painted. But people who were not art critics loved Rockwell's paintings. What he did that was so different from what other artists were doing was to tell a story in each picture.

Rockwell was a scrawny kid who tried to be a bodybuilder but didn't succeed. He was much better at drawing and painting, and when he was very young he sold his first painting—to the *Saturday Evening Post*, one of the most popular magazines in the United States. He went on to paint 332 covers for the magazine over many, many years.

There are excellent pictures here of some of his greatest paintings. See what you think of them. Show the cover and also the picture on page 40, which caused trouble for him with many of his fans.

A different kind of artist is profiled in *Now You See It—Now You Don't: Rene Magritte* by Angela Wenzel. Magritte was a painter who died about 30 years ago. When you look through this book, you will find a different view of the world. Magritte saw things in his own way (we all do), but his way was really unusual.

Take a good look at the picture on the front cover. Then check the ones on pages 7 and 13. Looking through this book will really make you think.

The Boy Who Loved to Draw: Benjamin West by Barbara Brenner is another story about an artist. Benjamin West, born in 1738, was the tenth child of a Pennsylvania family. A preacher said about him, "This boy will do great things someday." So everyone watched him, waiting for greatness.

This prediction began coming true when he was seven years old. He had to watch his infant niece one day, and, while he was staring at her, he decided to draw her picture. He took his father's quill pen and did just that, delighting his mother and his sister. Later, a Native American friend, Gray Wolf, taught him how to make red and yellow paint. His mother gave him something for blue paint, but he had a problem. He did not have a brush. He did not even know that a brush was what he needed to put the paint on the picture. What West did in trying to make one is part of this great, true story. Show your audience the picture of West with Gray Wolf and of West's infant niece.

What Do Illustrators Do? by Eileen Christelow is not only an interesting book, but it could also inspire a student to think about a career in art.

When you look at a picture book, do you ever think about the fact that someone worked hard to create it? Someone had to decide how the pictures were going to look, how big they were going to be, what colors to use, and then draw the pictures. If the pictures illustrate a story, the person who created them had to decide which parts of the story to illustrate.

This book tells us about this process. It shows us two illustrators. Each of them is going to illustrate the story of *Jack and the Beanstalk*. Because they are busy, they make their pets leave. The dog and the cat get together and tell us how the illustrators work.

For the booktalker, this is a wonderful opportunity to use different versions of the same folktale or fairy tale to demonstrate how differently illustrators see the same thing. The candy house from different editions of *Hansel and Gretel* illustrates this point well. You will never look at a picture book in the same way after you read this.

On page 31, the same illustration is shown using three different types of color. And on the next page the same illustration is shown with no black lines. Fascinating.

In Real Life: Six Women Photographers by Leslie Sills is not only a book about six outstanding photographers who just happened to be women, it also shows us what first-rate photography is. "Cameras," says the author, "do copy what is in front of the lens, and so, in that sense, photographs show what is real. They are simultaneously, however, creations of the artist's intentions and unconscious mind" (page 5).

Three of the photographers are still working today. Carrie Weems, an African American, like many great photographers, tells stories with her photos. Elsa Dorfman uses a huge, extremely detailed Polaroid camera to take portraits of her subjects. A bonus here is a portrait Dorfman took of the author, her son, and his dog. Cindy Sherman's photographs are probably the most famous of the three. She takes photographs using herself as a model, and they tell intriguing, often mysterious, stories.

Dorothea Lange's astonishing photographs revealed the plight of the poverty-stricken people who came to California looking for work during the Great Depression. Lola Alvarez Bravo, a citizen of Mexico, put together photo montages in surprising new ways.

It is hard to decide which of these many fine photos to show your audience, but Sherman's photo of herself on page 68 will certainly arouse curiosity.

Elizabeth Partridge writes more about the life of a photographer in *Restless Spirit: The Life and Work of Dorothea Lange*. You may recognize the famous photograph of the migrant-worker mother on page 4—it was taken by Lange during the Great Depression.

Dorothea Nutzhorn was born in 1895 in Hoboken, New Jersey. Her grandparents were German immigrants. When she was seven years old, she came down with polio, which left her with a limp that made her the subject of ridicule by other children. Her attempts to rid herself of the limp lasted many years but were unsuccessful. Dorothea's parents were well-off, but when she was 12 years old, her father deserted the family and apparently was never heard from again. Dorothea, her brother, and her mother went to live with her mother's parents, and Dorothea's mother got a job as a librarian in the lower East Side, where Dorothea then went to school. Dorothea changed her last name to Lange, her mother's maiden name, for she had no desire to associate herself with her absent father.

Lange wanted none of the traditional professions open to women, which were few. Instead, wanting to be a photographer, she applied for and got a job assisting Arnold Genthe at his studio. She learned what was to become her trade and at age 22 decided to travel around the world with her best friend Fronsie. They made it only as far as San Francisco, where a pickpocket stole all of their money. They both found work the next day, Lange at the photo-finishing counter of a department store.

In California she met the man, 20 years older than she, who became her first husband, Maynard Dixon, a painter. Their marriage was fraught with difficulties caused by financial worries, his frequent absences, and their apparent inability to prioritize spending time with their two sons, who were frequently farmed out to friends.

Lange became famous for her work during the depression, when a government agency hired her to photograph migrant workers, which she did to great effect. She took the time to get to know her subjects and then took her photos. During this time, she met Paul Taylor, who was also working with the government and the migrant workers, and they fell in love. She divorced Maynard and married Paul (complicating her life even further because he himself had children, who were soon equally neglected) in 1935. It was a genuine love match that stood the test of time.

Lange photographed the Japanese in the detention camps during World War II and later traveled around the world taking photographs. She died of cancer in 1965.

The author of this book is the daughter of one of Lange's assistants, Ron Partridge. There are photographs of the author as a child with Lange, and Partridge adds her personal recollections at the end of the book.

Another groundbreaking photographer is featured in *Margaret Bourke-White: Her Pictures Were Her Life* by Susan Goldman Rubin. Margaret Bourke-White was born in 1904, a time when women were expected not to have careers. Instead, they were expected to get married and have children, and caring for husband and offspring would be their "career." Bourke-White was different. She knew she wanted to do something that she dearly loved to do, and her first choice was to become a herpetologist, an expert on snakes. That did not work out, so her second choice was photography. She went to college, took classes in photography, and immediately starting taking photographs that were strikingly different from what everyone else was doing. She was fascinated by architecture, industry, and machines, and she photographed them in unusual ways. Soon people were buying her photographs, and by the time she was in her mid-twenties Henry Luce asked her to take photographs for *Fortune*, a new magazine he was starting. This worked out well, and when Luce started another new magazine a few years later, called *Life*, Bourke-White had found the work that would bring her lasting fame. As a photographer for the highly regarded, hugely popular magazine, she traveled all over the world, taking pictures of World War II, famous people such as Gandhi, and human beings living and working in terrible conditions everywhere—photographs that made people think and then work to correct injustices.

The subtitle of this book is very important. Bourke-White's pictures were indeed her life. Outside of her photos and her work, her life, which was marred by two divorces and her constant need to put her work first, was not a happy one. For almost the last 20 years of her life, she was not able to work as she wished, for she was living with Parkinson's disease.

This is a story that will hold your interest from beginning to end. Show your audience some of Bourke-White's famous photos—the one on page 57 is stunning, and even kids will probably recognize the famous one on pages 74 and 75.

Another woman who made her mark in the arts is in the subject of *Tallchief: America's Prima Ballerina* by Maria Tallchief with Rosemary Wells. Maria Tallchief, who was born on an Osage Indian reservation in Fairfax, Oklahoma, in 1925, became the most famous American ballerina in history. Although she grew up during the Great Depression of the 1920s, Tallchief was very lucky, for her father, a full-blooded Osage, who looked "just like the Indian on the buffalo-head nickel," was a very wealthy man. Oil had been discovered on the reservation, and all of the people who lived there became rich.

Tallchief loved music and she loved to dance. She took dancing lessons as a small child, but when she was eight years old, her family moved to Los Angeles, where she began to study ballet seriously. Her teacher, Madame Nijinska, was the sister of one of the most famous dancers of all time. How Tallchief decided to become a dancer and the choices she made along the way make for an excellent story. Show your audience the picture on page 7 of Tallchief dancing and on page 17 of her waiting for the bus like a dancer.

Savion: My Life in Tap by Savion Glover and Bruce Weber is a biography of a true innovator. Your students may not know the name Savion, but maybe they have seen him dancing in a Coca-Cola commercial, at the Winter Olympics, in an MTV video, or in the opening credits for ABC's *Monday Night Football*. Savion Glover has made tap dancing cool again. Just reading this energetic book might make you hear the rhythms of jazz, hip-hop, rock and roll, rap music, and the blues. Although still in his twenties, Savion is best known as the choreographer of the Broadway hit *Bring in 'da Noise. Bring in 'da Funk*. This show seeks to portray African-American history and racism through Savion's feet. Show your listeners the picture on page 59 of Savion when he was on *Sesame Street*, and then show them on page 79 what he looks like now. Both informative and inspiring, this would be an excellent choice for a middle school biography assignment.

Start your booktalk for *Sebastian: A Book About Bach* by Jeanette Winter by reading the frontispiece. "The first *Voyager* spacecraft was launched in 1977. On the spacecraft there is a recording of sounds from Earth. Should the spacecraft encounter any life beyond our galaxy, the first sound that will be heard is the music of Johann Sebastian Bach."

Wow! Who on earth was Johann Sebastian Bach? Younger elementary kids can find out in this interesting book. Have any of you ever heard of Bach? Do any of you know any music he wrote? Even if you do not, you'll probably recognize some of it. (If you are able to, hum or play your favorite Bach music.)

Johann Sebastian Bach was born more than 300 years ago, descended from a long line of musicians. He was brilliant and dedicated most of his life to writing music—although he also married and had 20 children. What was he like? How did he write his music? Read this fun book to learn about him. Show children the illustration of Bach in prison because he did not ask permission to change jobs.

Figure 6.1. *Sebastian: A Book About Bach* **by Jeanette Winter.**

Middle school students, especially those with an interest in music, may enjoy *Clara Schumann: Piano Virtuoso* by Susanna Reich. Clara Wieck (pronounced Veek) was an extraordinary child and an even more extraordinary woman. In a time when women were treated more or less as the possessions of first their fathers and then their husbands and when few women had careers outside the home, she became famous as one of the finest pianists who ever lived.

Born to musical parents in Leipzig in 1819, Clara was trained from early childhood to play the piano brilliantly. Her father was a renowned musician who spent much time with her and, in fact, focused his life on her. When she fell in love with another gifted student, a musician named Robert Schumann, her father initially forbad them to marry. Their efforts to continue the relationship eventually triumphed in their marriage, and they had several children together. In an era when people frowned upon women appearing pregnant in public, Clara kept on playing the piano and supporting her family even during her pregnancies. When she was 35 years old, her work became even more difficult, for her husband was committed to an insane asylum, where he died two years later.

Clara Schumann was completely responsible for her children's welfare, for the family's income, and for conducting her own career. It is fascinating to read this biography and compare her life with women's lives today. Show your audience the photo of Schumann taken in 1845, when photography had just been invented.

Have you heard of jazz music? One of the all-time great jazz musicians is profiled in *Once upon a Time in Chicago: The Story of Benny Goodman* by Jonah Winter.

Figure 6.2. *Once upon a Time in Chicago: The Story of Benny Goodman* **by Jonah Winter.**

Benny Goodman grew up poor. Very poor. He lived in Chicago, and his father was a Jewish immigrant who worked hard to support his family. But he had a very large family—12 children—and made barely enough money to support them all. He wanted his children to have a better life, and he took three of his boys to the local synagogue to play in the boys' band there. Benny got a clarinet, and what he did with that clarinet still amazes everyone who hears his music. Show your audience the picture of Goodman "playing and playing until everyone in the world had heard his beautiful music."

Although you may never have heard an orchestra playing in person, for sure you have often heard them in movies, on the radio, and on TV. An orchestra can make beautiful music, and *The Story of the Incredible Orchestra: An Introduction to Musical Instruments and the Symphony Orchestra* by Bruce Koscielniak tells you how that happens.

Four hundred years ago there were no orchestras. Small groups of musicians played together and did not make a very big sound. Then an organist in Venice wrote a piece of music with different parts for various instruments, and the group that played it became the first orchestra. Over the years more instruments were invented and perfected. For instance, Antonio Stradivari, who lived from 1644 to 1737, made such fine violins that they are still considered the finest ever.

The Story of the Incredible Orchestra gives descriptions of the sounds the instruments make and tells what the instrument maker had to do to get that sound. If you would like to play an instrument, or already do, or if you just like music, this is a great book for you. Show any of the lovely two-page spreads.

A whole different world of music is described in *Shout, Sister, Shout! Ten Girl Singers Who Shaped a Century*. Author Roxane Orgill goes through the decades of the last century and profiles women such as Sophie Tucker, Bessie Smith, Ethel Merman, Judy Garland, Bette Midler, and Madonna. Your students will be familiar with Judy Garland, who played Dorothy in the *Wizard of Oz*. It is said that Garland could look at a script once and have it memorized instantly. She seems sweet in the *Wizard of Oz*, but she was actually quite temperamental. Page 51 tells about one difficult episode when she refused to come out of her dressing room for hours. At that time, MGM studios regularly dispensed drugs to its stars. MGM made Garland take diet pills, which kept her from sleeping, and then she was given sleeping pills that made her groggy. In the mornings she took pills to wake up. This dangerous problem, which began when she was only 15, plagued Garland her for the rest of her life. The best photographs to show are on pages 50 and 56.

All of the women singers profiled in this book are interesting, and the types of music they are known for encompass jazz, musical theater, folk, gospel, and pop music. Encourage your readers to learn about someone new.

Frank O. Gehry: Outside In by Jan Greenberg and Sandra Jordan tells about an artist of an entirely different kind—an architect. You have probably never seen anything remotely like a Frank Gehry building—unless you have seen a Frank Gehry building. He thinks differently and has a unique way of seeing things.

Gehry designs buildings, and the most famous one he has designed so far is the Guggenheim Museum in Bilbao, Spain. Everyone has fallen in love with that strange, startling, and unusual building. (Show some of the pictures, for instance, those on page 36.)

Gehry grew up in Canada, and, when he was very small, a fortune-teller told his mother that he was going to be an architect. He did not even know what that meant. But he did not want to design buildings that looked like every other building. He believes that straight lines are neither necessary nor desirable in every building, and what he has done with curved lines is incredible. Take a look at this neat book with its great photos.

Ask whether anyone has seen a Gehry building, and tell them if you have. Show the picture of the binoculars building on page 28 and of the Fred and Ginger building on page 31.

INVENTORS AND INVENTIONS

Have you made any mistakes today? Most people have, but it is heartening to learn that many great inventions actually started out as mistakes.

Mistakes That Worked by Charlotte Foltz Jones describes a few dozen mistakes that turned out surprisingly well. Popsicles. Potato chips. Tea bags. Penicillin. Chocolate chip cookies. Post-It notes. All of them happened because someone was trying for or doing something else.

Brown'n'serve rolls are delicious, and they are a lot faster than making bread and letting it rise for hours. How were they created? A volunteer fireman was called to a fire and took some half-baked rolls out of his oven when he was leaving. When he got back, he was not sure whether to throw them away—but he decided to put them back in the oven. They were delicious, and a popular new food item was born.

If you have ever read stories about sickness and injury in history, you may already know that penicillin is one of the greatest discoveries ever made. How it was discovered makes a fine story—Alexander Fleming accidentally contaminated an experiment he was conducting and discovered that the contaminant was virtually a miracle drug.

Ivory soap is fun because it floats. But the reason it floats is that too much air had been put in the soap mixture in one batch. Amazingly, people liked the floating soap, and Ivory became a very profitable product. You won't be able to read just one of these stories that make inventions fun for young readers.

Kids will definitely relate to the inventions described in *Toys! Amazing Stories Behind Some Great Inventions* by Don L. Wulffson. Legos. Mr. Potato Head. Raggedy Ann. Parcheesi. Checkers. These are a few of the many famous toys this delightful book describes.

How were the world's most famous toys invented? Some of them have been around for a long, long time. The seesaw, or teeter-totter, was apparently invented in ancient Rome and was used during gladiatorial games. Each end had a basket on it, and a clown got into each basket. Then a hungry tiger that had not been fed for days was released. Whenever one of the clowns hit the ground, the tiger ran toward it. That clown pushed up—and the tiger ran to the other clown. This went on and on until one of the clowns got too tired—and the tiger had fresh clown for dinner.

The Chinese invented playing cards about 1,000 years ago. More than 100 million decks a year are sold in the United States today. Hobby horses have been around for thousands of years, as have checkers and toy soldiers.

The Trivial Pursuit chapter gives us some great trivia about toys and games, but there is more spread throughout the entire book. What, for instance, do you think the three best-selling board games in the United States are? If you guessed Monopoly first, Scrabble second, and Parcheesi third, you are right. You cannot go wrong with this book.

Some of the stories you'll read about in *The Kid Who Invented the Trampoline: More Surprising Stories About Inventions* by Don L. Wulffson are almost unbelievable. But believe them—because they are true.

Do you know that the first false teeth were made from the teeth of dead people? They were fastened in the mouths of living people with bands of gold. Later, teeth were made from wood, leather, cows' teeth, and tusks. Celluloid teeth, which were tried in the nineteenth century, had a big drawback—they could catch on fire!

Makeup was invented thousands of years ago, and people all over the world used it. In eighteenth-century Europe, some people shaved off their own eyebrows and instead attached fake ones made of mouse skin!

We are very lucky to have flush toilets and toilet paper today. "In the nineteenth century, carriages often had 'carriage pots' built in under the seats. People lifted the seat cushion, sat on a board below it and relieved themselves into the pot through an opening in the board" (page 91). And people would toss the chamber pots full of their waste into the streets.

The first toilet paper for sale arrived in 1857. It wasn't a hit. People preferred to use old newspapers and things such as corncobs. They thought it was a waste of money to use clean paper. Even today, only about 30 percent of the world's people use toilet paper.

The first real toothbrushes more or less like the ones we have today were invented in China in 1498. Almost 300 years later, they came into common use in Europe. Toothpaste was then invented, and "[u]rine, as an active component in toothpastes and mouthwashes, continued to be used into the eighteenth century. Incidentally, urine *does* contain natural cleansing and whitening chemicals" (page 97).

Find out about armor, erasers, vacuum cleaners, contact lenses, and lots of other interesting inventions. And learn why some of the first baby bottles became known as "murder bottles." As you might have noticed, some of these stories are unpleasant, but kids love this kind of information. Pair this book with some of the other "gross" books from Chapter 7 for an irresistible booktalk. Show the picture on page 37 of George Washington's false teeth.

I Wonder Why Zippers Have Teeth and Other Questions About Inventions by Barbara Taylor is full of intriguing information about inventions from today and throughout history. Did you know that the first false teeth were made of ivory or bone? The bone, unfortunately, turned brown and rotted. And paper straws were invented to keep liquids cooler. When you do not touch your glass with your warm hands, your beverage will stay cold longer. Safety pins were invented almost 200 years ago, but they were not an original idea. They were copied from clasps the ancient Egyptians used. Lipstick in stick form has been around for less than 100 years, but lip color has been around for thousands of years. This book is great fun to browse through.

Women have invented many good things, as you'll find out when you read *Girls Think of Everything: Stories of Ingenious Inventions by Women* by Catherine Thimmesh. If you like chocolate chip cookies, thank the woman who made the first batch, almost by mistake. Instead of melting the chocolate she was using first, as the recipe called for, she just broke up the chocolate and threw it in the batter—and everyone fell in love with the best cookies they had ever tasted.

Women came up with the ideas for windshield wipers (it was really hard to see without them when you were driving in rain or snow), Scotchgard (which makes it easy to wipe up stains), square-bottomed paper bags (such as the kind we get our groceries in), and the Snugli, for carrying babies safely and easily. A schoolgirl came up with the idea for ways to write in the dark. Even the endpapers of this book have the names of women and their inventions.

Tell your listeners about an amazing inventor using Kathryn Lasky's *Vision of Beauty: The Story of Sarah Breedlove Walker*. When Lasky was a little girl, she wanted to have a lemonade stand. One day she walked into the kitchen with a jar full of money, and her mother said, "Goodness, Kathryn, maybe you'll grow up to be the next Madam Walker." All of her life, Lasky was fascinated by Madam C. J. Walker, for good reason—she was an amazing woman.

Sarah Breedlove was never a slave, but her parents were. She was born in 1867, two and one-half years after the end of the Civil War, and the only difference between slaves and most free African Americans at that time was that, as Lasky says, free people could dream. But Sarah and her family were desperately poor, and by the time she was seven years old she was an orphan. She and her older sister did laundry for white people day and night just to make enough money to eat. By the time she was 14 years old, she was married, and a few years later, she was a widow. She still did laundry for a living, but she managed to save some money.

One day she heard Mrs. Booker T. Washington speak to a group in St. Louis. She greatly admired Mrs. Washington and wished she could look just as attractive. Especially her hair looked wonderful. Sarah's hair was in bad shape, so bad that she was going bald—and she was only 37 years old. She decided to do something about it. And what she did made her a wealthy woman.

Tie this book in with *Ida B. Wells* by Judith Bloom Fradin and Dennis Brindell Fradin (Chapter 5). Madam Walker gave $5,000 to the antilynching fund of the National Association for the Advancement of Colored People (NAACP), which was Ida Wells's number-one cause. Flip through the book to show your audience the many colorful illustrations.

A very well known inventor is described in *Always Inventing: A Photobiography of Alexander Graham Bell* by Tom L. Matthews. The Scottish-born Bell was inventing things by the time he was 11 years old, when he created a tool to take husks off of wheat kernels. But his real interests were teaching speaking and doing public speaking himself. He began to study this, but his future was partially shaped by two family tragedies: the deaths from tuberculosis of his brothers Melville and Edward. In an attempt to get away from Scotland's cold, wet climate, which people believed made the disease worse, Alex's father moved his family to southern Ontario (Canada) when Alex was 20 years old.

Bell got a job teaching in Boston at a school for people who were deaf and could not speak. There he met a student, Mabel Hubbard, who had become deaf when she contracted scarlet fever at the age of five. Eventually Alex fell in love with and married Mabel, and it is clear that they remained in love all of their lives. Show your audience their wedding photos on page 32 and the joyful photo on page 59 of them in old age. Mabel was an expert lip reader, but after they had grandchildren, she would sometimes cover her eyes and tell the grandchildren that she could not "hear" them!

Bell's most famous achievement, the invention of the first workable telephone, came partially as a result of an accident. He misunderstood the function of another invention and, based on that misunderstanding, decided to try to make the telephone work in a certain fashion. Many inventors at the time were trying to make a workable telephone, but Bell was the first one to get it right. The first words ever transmitted over a telephone were from Bell to his assistant, Thomas Watson, who was in the next room. He said, "Mr. Watson—come here—I want to see you."

Bell became world famous for his invention, but he never stopped inventing and made many other wonderful creations. He also never lost his interest in teaching deaf people and became one of Helen Keller's dearest friends. She even dedicated her autobiography to him. This book is illustrated with many excellent photographs. Show your audience the one on page 27 of the first working telephone.

For more details on this useful invention, read *The Telephone* by Sarah Gearhart. We are used to getting information very quickly today and to talking to our friends almost whenever we feel like it. Thanks to the telephone, we can call people, e-mail them, and send faxes.

Not much more than 100 years ago, if people left their homes overseas and immigrated to the United States, most of them never again got to see or talk to the families they had left behind. To us today, that is almost unimaginable.

Alexander Graham Bell is credited with the invention of the telephone, but he was really the one who had the best patent for the particular equipment that was needed. He was one of many who worked at improving the speed and accuracy of communication. In 1843 a young American named Samuel Morse got permission to run an experimental telegraph line along the tracks of the railroad between Baltimore and Washington, D.C. His telegraph was a staggering improvement over long-distance communications of the past. But it had its drawbacks. For one thing, it was very expensive. In 1876, the year Bell invented the telephone, it cost 75 cents to send 10 words by telegraph—more than most people made in half a day.

And in March of that same year, Alexander Graham Bell succeeded in talking to his assistant in another room over a telephone. By May, that phone was ready to be exhibited publicly, and less than two years later the first commercial telephone exchange opened in New Haven, Connecticut, with 21 subscribers. We all depend on the telephone and use it often. This is a surprising look at how it became the incredible electronic device it is today.

If you know anything about Robert Fulton, it is probably that he invented the steamboat. But that is wrong. He did not invent the steamboat. To find out why we think he did, read the colorful *Robert Fulton: From Submarine to Steamboat* by Steven Kroll.

Robert Fulton was born in Pennsylvania in 1765 and loved to paint and design things. When he was only 14 years old, he designed an air gun to help out with the American Revolution. When he was 22, he went to England, carrying a letter to Benjamin West (see *The Boy Who Loved to Draw: Benjamin West* earlier in this chapter). Fulton became a student of the famous painter, but five years later he decided he wanted to be an engineer rather than an artist. He designed a submarine, which was not a success, but then he became interested in steamboats. Robert Fitch had already invented the steamboat, but Fulton met a wealthy American who had the rights to control steamboat traffic in New York State waters. He was on his way. How he succeeded and how superior steamboats were to ordinary riverboats are things you'll learn when you read this book. Show the picture of Fulton with his air gun design.

David A. Adler has written numerous biographies accessible to young readers. *A Picture Book of George Washington Carver* tells the story of a man who was born a slave on a Missouri farm. Carver never knew exactly when he was born, but he knew it was sometime near the end of the Civil War. He lost both of his parents by the time he was a toddler, and he and his brother were raised by their former owners, who were kind to them.

Carver's ill health made it hard for him to work around the farm, so he had plenty of free time. He explored the land and the flowers and animals around him. He desperately wanted to get an education, and in spite of many obstacles, he did.

How he got his education and how he decided to spend his life helping his own African-American people—and what he did to help them—makes for a fascinating story. He even refused an offer of a high-paying job from the famous inventor Thomas Edison. Read about what he did and how he did it. Show your group the picture of Carver with Edison.

AMAZING ACHIEVERS

Helen Keller is the heroine of many young readers. Her triumph over incredible disabilities is universally admired, and many know the story of how Annie Sullivan taught Helen her first word—*water*. *The World at Her Fingertips: The Story of Helen Keller* by Joan Dash is a new biography that will appeal to middle school students and will take them beyond that famous day to the rest of Keller's long life. Of course, her early years are fascinating, but what she did later is also remarkable. After she learned to understand sign language she went on to study French, German, Greek, and Latin, among other subjects. She graduated from Radcliffe, the most prestigious college for women in the United States. Then she spent her life as an activist, performer, speaker, and world traveler. You'll learn a lot about her and her gifted teacher, Annie Sullivan. This ALA Best Book for Young Adults makes a great read for pleasure and for the inevitable middle school biography assignments.

Joan of Arc by Diane Stanley is an exciting book. Who has ever heard of Joan of Arc? If you have, do you know why she is famous? Do you know how she died? Do you know why she had to die? Do you know that there is no one in all of recorded history who is at all similar to Joan, a poor girl who could neither read nor write and who lived in a small village in France?

From the time she was a young teenager, Joan heard voices, voices of the saints she loved, voices that told her that she alone could save her country and her king. She listened to the voices for four years and then decided it was time to act. She cut off all of her hair and went to the town to which the voices directed her, looking for help. Why would anyone believe her? How could this happen?

She knew she would know her king the minute she saw him, although she had never seen a picture of him. The king had never been crowned, for the war that was ripping France apart had prevented him from reaching the cathedral where coronations always took place.

How Joan found her king and her army and what she did with them has fascinated people for more than six centuries. Read all about it in this amazing book appropriate for fifth- through eighth-graders.

Josephine Poole's *Joan of Arc*, written for upper-elementary school students, also tells what may be the most astonishing true story ever. The voices Joan heard told her to form an army, and to do this she had to see the king. She was 17 years old and very poor. How could she create an army and see the king? Joan's life and horrible death make an unforgettable story. The pictures in this fine book are lovely.

Joan of Arc is also mentioned in *Lives of Extraordinary Women: Rulers, Rebels (and What the Neighbors Thought)* by Kathleen Krull. Start your booktalk by reading aloud the quote on the first page: "Well-behaved women rarely make history" by Laurel Thatcher Ulrich, an American historian.

Right away we realize that the women we are going to read about in this book are definitely not well behaved. In fact, the reason they are still famous, some hundreds or even thousands of years after their deaths, is that they did not behave well.

You will seldom find a group of more interesting women than the ones described here, although you may not have heard of them all. Some of them, such as Wilma Mankiller, Rigoberta Menchú, and Aung Suu Kyi, are still alive. Have you ever heard of them? Do you know who they are?

Following are other tidbits to share from this unique book:

- The one woman in history who has fascinated people probably more than any other is Joan of Arc. More than 10,000 books have been written about her.

- Queen Elizabeth I loved presents and parties and owned the first wristwatch. Historians believe she may be the most effective ruler Britain has ever had.

- Harriet Tubman dressed up in a man's suit after she left her husband to escape from slavery. She went back down south 19 times to help other slaves escape.

- Jeanette Rankin was the first congresswoman. Which bathroom should she use? There were none for women. She was the only person in Congress who voted against the United States entering World War II after the attack on Pearl Harbor.

- Golda Meir, the first woman prime minister of Israel, was born in Russia and grew up in Milwaukee.

• Eva Perón and her husband owned 63 cars and lived a fabulously wealthy existence in Argentina—but she also helped poor people enormously.

Humorous and delightful illustrations by Kathryn Hewitt add to the enjoyment. This is a fun book and you will learn new things by reading it. Show the picture of Joan of Arc on page 18.

Another gossipy book by Kathleen Krull is *They Saw the Future: Oracles, Psychics, Scientists, Great Thinkers, and Pretty Good Guessers*. This book makes you wonder. Are there really people who know what is going to happen next? It certainly would seem that there have been some. Krull says that the most famous prediction of all is the one Jeane Dixon made—that a young, blue-eyed president, elected in 1960, would die violently in office. She had made her first prediction about this 11 years before the event and continued making it right up to a few minutes before it actually happened. One reason this prediction is so famous is that so many people heard it before John F. Kennedy was assassinated. Jeane Dixon became wildly famous throughout the world, but a lot of her predictions did not come true.

All through history people have claimed to be able to see the future. In ancient Greece, it was the Oracle at Delphi. In ancient Rome, it was the Sibyls. People would travel great distances to see them and to have their futures predicted. The Maya, in Central and South America, also made many predictions, and their calendar is considered by some to be the best ever made.

Leonardo da Vinci was so far-seeing that science fiction novels have been written claiming he must have been an alien. He drew pictures of submarines, bifocals, armored tanks, and flying machines—hundreds of years before they were invented. Many consider him the greatest genius the world has ever known.

Because of Nostradamus, who lived in France in the 1500s, the word "prediction" came about. He predicted many things, but like many famous augurs, many of his statements are open to interpretation. To put it another way, "Most Nostradamus experts seem to think that around half of his predictions have come true. The trouble is that they disagree about which predictions apply to which events" (page 55). Edgar Cayce was called "America's sleeping prophet." He would go into trances and predict many things, none of which he recalled when he awakened. He became very popular and had followers everywhere. This intriguing book will give you a great deal to think about and to tell your friends.

Another intriguing character has been dead for more than 70 years, but it really doesn't matter. If you ask anyone to name the most famous magician ever, the answer will almost always be Houdini. Learn more about him in *Spellbinder: The Life of Harry Houdini* by Tom Lalicki.

Figure 6.3. *Spellbinder: The Life of Harry Houdini* **by Tom Lalicki.**

Houdini's real name was not Houdini at all. It was Erich Weiss, and he was born in Hungary in 1874. His family moved to Appleton, Wisconsin, when Erich was very small, and he grew up there. (Appleton has a wonderful museum where you can see his handcuffs and many of his tricks.) Houdini grew up poor. When he was 12, he ran away from home in hopes of making a fortune—but did not succeed. But by the time he was 18, he was performing magic shows. No one really knows how he got interested in or started doing magic.

Weiss changed his name to Houdini after his hero, the great magician Robert Houdin. Then he decided to become the greatest, most famous magician ever. And he did it.

Houdini was an interesting fellow who adored his wife and mother and took good care of them both all of his life. But he was obsessed with tricks—learning new ones, improving them, and always being faster and better and more interesting than his many imitators.

Houdini was a genius at getting publicity. He became an expert at breaking out of locks and handcuffs. Whenever he went to a different town in Europe, he said, the first thing he did was to break out of jail—while police watched. He developed water tricks in which he would be locked up (sometimes in a straitjacket) and then submerged in ice-cold water. Many people came to watch him perform partly because they thought he would probably die during one of his tricks. His death, at the age of 52, was directly related to one of the illusions he performed. Show your audiences the photo of him, nearly naked, on page 15.

This next achiever made her mark in the water, but in a very different way. The first two paragraphs of *America's Champion Swimmer: Gertrude Ederle* by David A. Adler are a perfect way to start the booktalk.

"In 1906 women were kept out of many clubs and restaurants. In most states they were not allowed to vote. Many people felt that a woman's place was in the home. But Gertrude Ederle's place was in the water."

Gertrude Ederle was born that year in New York City and did not start swimming until she was seven years old. She had almost drowned when she fell into a pond, so her father taught her how to swim. She became incredibly good at it—so good that when she was 18, she was chosen for the U.S. Olympic team. And then she decided to do something that no woman—and very few men—had ever done: swim the English

Channel between England and France. Ederle was an amazing athlete, and this is a wonderful book. Show the picture of her eating during her Channel swim.

Russell Freedman writes about another outstanding athlete in *Babe Didrikson Zaharias: The Making of a Champion.* Zaharias was born in 1911. Or 1913. Or maybe even 1915. You could never be sure with Babe. Like her father, she was a good story-teller, and she loved to make a good story even better. People were not always sure what was the truth and what was a story, but it is a fact that Babe Didrikson Zaharias was one of the greatest athletes who ever lived. She was good at almost every sport she tried. In many cases, she was the best—at least for a while.

To quote the dust jacket, "She was an All-American basketball player, an Olympic gold medallist in track and field, and a championship golfer who won eighty-two amateur and professional tournaments. She also mastered tennis, played exhibition baseball, and was an accomplished diver and bowler. Six times she was voted the 'Woman Athlete of the Year' by the Associated Press."

But Babe hardly ever had it easy. She was named Mildred, the sixth of seven children of a Texas family of Norwegian immigrants. They were poor, and during the Great Depression, when Babe began to be well known, she sent her family most of the money she made.

As a child, Zaharias was an incredible athlete. When it came time to pick sides for games, girl or not, Babe was chosen first. By the time she was a junior in high school, she was so good that a Texas firm recruited her to work for them and play on their women's basketball team. But she still had a lot to put up with. Times were different then. Read aloud the four paragraphs that start on page 84. Thankfully, times have changed a good deal.

Another innovative woman is profiled in *Fly High! The Story of Bessie Coleman* by Louise Borden and Mary Kay Kroeger. The first African American ever to get a pilot's license was Bessie Coleman, who was enormously determined.

She was the tenth of 13 children, and her parents, who were terribly poor, could neither read nor write. But they helped Bessie go to school, even though she could not go all of the time because she had to help with the farmwork. Bessie walked four miles both to and from school, and she was able to rent books from a small library wagon. When she got older, she walked five miles each way to pick up dirty laundry for her mother to wash and press.

When Coleman was 23, she moved from Texas to Chicago, where she believed opportunities would be better. In 1919, after her brothers came home from World War I, she heard about the women pilots in France. She worked hard to save money to travel to France because *she* wanted to be a pilot, too. She found a flying school, which she had to walk nine miles each way to attend, but she earned her pilot's license.

Back in the United States she started flying in air shows, but planes then were not very safe, and Coleman died in a tragic accident at a young age. Show the picture of Coleman getting books from the library wagon and of her in her aviator uniform.

Jane Addams is an American woman who dedicated her life to helping people. In 1931 she became the first American woman to win the Nobel peace prize. Learn about her work by reading *A Personal Tour of Hull House* by Laura B. Edge.

In 1889 Jane moved into a mansion in Chicago. Once elegant, the neighborhood had fallen on hard times, and now Hull's House, as the mansion was then called, looked out of place among its shabby neighbors.

The neighbors were mainly immigrants, newcomers to America who were able to afford only the cheap, shabby, flimsy housing that had been erected for them. Their lives were hard, and the hours they worked were long. They were poor, but they wanted to get ahead. They needed help.

And Addams provided that help. She and several of her friends and helpers eventually created a new, much larger Hull House, as they called it, where immigrants and poor people could come for help of all sorts. At Hull House, a bustling hub of activity, they were treated with kindness and respect.

This book takes a typical day in Hull House in 1908 and describes what happened there. It's a great way to learn about a small part of our nation's history. Show the frontispiece photo of the Hull House expansion and the one on page 4 of the original Hull House.

FEATS OF TECHNOLOGY

Building Big by David Macaulay goes into detail about some significant feats of technology. This book will appeal to your future engineers, architects, and kids with lots of curiosity. If they want to know how bridges, tunnels, dams, domes, and skyscrapers are built, this is the book. Pair it with books in this chapter about skyscrapers, or with *The World of Architectural Wonders* (Chapter 4). It details the construction of many specific structures, so if you live near the Golden Gate Bridge, the Astrodome, Hoover Dam, the United States Capitol, the Sears Tower, or other landmarks, this book will be of particular interest to your students.

Great Buildings by Anne Lynch spans the history of buildings from early civilizations through today's industrial world. Colorful illustrations show the Forbidden City in China, the Hagia Sophia in Istanbul, the Taj Mahal in India, the palace at Versailles, the Casa Milá in Spain, the Sydney Opera House in Australia, and much more. Pick any of the colorful two-page spreads and tell your audience about these marvelous structures. Future architects will eat it up.

Younger readers will appreciate *Dig a Tunnel* by Ryan Hunter. People probably dug the first tunnels after they saw the ones that animals dug. They found a lot of uses for them, as this book shows. Prisoners dig tunnels to escape. Bank robbers dig tunnels to get in. Miners dig tunnels to find minerals. Diamond-mining tunnels in South Africa are so deep that the rock walls are hot. This book tells about the world's most famous tunnels and shows how tunnels are dug today. Show your audience almost any of the pictures in this colorful book to attract their interest.

Have you ever wished you could ride in a rescue helicopter or control a crane or drive a tow truck? If you like trucks and machines and easy-to-read books, the following titles are for you. The series "Big Machines at Work" by Hal Rogers includes four titles—*Tow Trucks, Rescue Helicopters, Graders,* and *Cranes.*

Figure 6.4. *Tow Trucks* **by Hal Rogers.**

You will learn how these vehicles work and the names of the different parts of the machines and see pictures of the vehicles in action. Almost any picture is guaranteed to please younger boys.

Have you ever wanted to build an igloo? If you follow the directions in Ulli Steltzer's *Building an Igloo*, you just might be able to do it. In simple text and photos, Steltzer shows two Inuit men building a traditional igloo. Tookilkee Kiguktak and his son live in northern Canada, and, like other Inuit today, they live in a house. But when they go hunting they build igloos for shelter. Any of the photographs in this book would be good to show a group of listeners. Can you imagine living in such a cold climate?

Most children have never seen a cable car, but they were an important means of transportation in our history. *Cable Cars* by Lola M. Schaefer provides an introduction to this mode of transportation for early elementary school students.

Only one city in the world has cable cars. Do you know what it is? Other cities used to have them, but only one is left. Why do you think that is? Read this interesting book to learn that 13.5 million people ride those cable cars in that one city every year and other fun facts about them.

Most of us do not live in cities that have subways, but the cities that do have them are crazy about them. Subways are a great way to travel through a crowded area. Young readers can find out more by reading *Subways* by Allison Lassieur.

A subway is a train that runs underneath the ground, although some subways go both underneath and on top of the automobile traffic. The first subway was opened in London in 1863. Charles Pearson, a city planner in London, thought the trains would be a huge help. Streets were horribly crowded and subways could avoid all of the traffic. Now more than 50 cities in the world have subway systems, and in New York City more than 4 million people a day take the subway.

Older readers can learn more about subways in *Tunnels, Tracks, and Trains: Building a Subway* by Joan Hewett. Los Angeles is building a subway system that will take 20 years to complete. Hewett and her photographer husband, Richard, documented a year and a half in the building process of this subway. On pages 30 and 31 you can show the model of how the subway station will look when it is completed. Then show how the subway tunnel looks while under construction (pages 22 and 23). It is an amazing process.

The urban landscape is dominated by tall buildings called skyscrapers, which are relatively new in our history. *Skyscrapers: How America Grew Up* by John B. Severance explains the development of these fascinating feats of technology.

There have been tall buildings throughout history. The Great Pyramid of Cheops is as high as a 50-story building. Medieval cathedrals were very tall, as were Hindu temples and Mayan pyramids. But our definition of a skyscraper is quite complex. To be workable, skyscrapers require steel structures, elevators, telephones, modern plumbing, and electric lighting. No one wants to climb up 20 flights of stairs to go to work—and then climb down and back up to go to the bathroom. Think about it.

Even the first elevators were not safe enough to be put in tall buildings. If the rope holding them broke, they would crash into the floor. Not a good thing. When the safety brake was invented in 1854, that solved that problem.

Companies wanted to have their offices in downtown areas. There was not enough room there for nearly all the offices that were required. Downtown could spread out only so far, but it *could* go up. And that is why we have skyscrapers.

This book tells the fascinating story of how that all happened. Many people believe that the Chicago fire of 1871 really got skyscrapers going. Many buildings had to be replaced, so architects began to design skyscrapers to replace them. They flourished in other cities, too. New York City had dozens, including the one that is still the most famous in the world, the Empire State Building. How city planners made regulations to make the skyscrapers work makes for a fine read. Show the picture of the Flatiron building on page 54.

TV and movie buffs will love Jake Hamilton's *Special Effects in Film and Television*. Published by Dorling Kindersley, this oversized book is filled with fascinating facts and stunning visuals. Students could casually browse or dig deep into the text to learn more about filming techniques. The picture of the ape head on pages 24 and 25 makes for a good visual aid. This animatronic head was worn by an actor, and every twitch of the face was controlled remotely. It is also fun to show the makeup job shown on pages 34 through 37. Watch the actor go from a normal guy to an intergalactic warrior. Another interesting spread to show is on pages 42 and 43. The stunt person in the small photo really is on fire—he's wearing fireproof clothing with a prosthetic head and hands. The flames must be put out within 20 seconds though, because that's the longest the stuntman can hold his breath. Show a few photos and this book will sell itself.

Technological gadgets can be lots of fun, and students who read *Night Stalkers Special Operations Aviation* by Andrea L. Weiser will want their own night vision goggles.

The name "Night Stalkers" is a nickname. During the Persian Gulf War, specially trained U.S. soldiers guarded trade ships—and used special glasses called night vision goggles to watch for enemies in the dark. What kid hasn't dreamed of having an invention like this? That's how Night Stalkers got their name.

Only men can be Night Stalkers, and they go through a very tough training called Green Platoon training. Night Stalkers take part in dangerous missions. They frequently fly helicopters to support soldiers on the ground. Sometimes, while they are flying, enemies shoot at them.

Take a look at this colorful Capstone Press book with its photos and lists of Web sites. Show your audience the photo of training on page 40.

BIBLIOGRAPHY

Adler, David A. *America's Champion Swimmer: Gertrude Ederle*. Illustrated by Terry Widener. Gulliver Books Harcourt, 2000. ISBN 0152019693. Unpaged. Grades 1–3.

————. *A Picture Book of George Washington Carver*. Illustrated by Dan Brown. Holiday House, 1999. ISBN 0823414299. Unpaged. Grades 2–4.

Borden, Louise, and Mary Kay Kroeger. *Fly High! The Story of Bessie Coleman*. Illustrated by Teresa Flavin. Margaret K. McElderry Books, 2001. ISBN 0689824572. Unpaged. Grades 2–4.

Brenner, Barbara. *The Boy Who Loved to Draw: Benjamin West*. Illustrated by Oliver Dunrea. Houghton Mifflin, 1999. ISBN 0395850800. Unpaged. Grades 2–4.

Christelow, Eileen. *What Do Illustrators Do?* Clarion Books, 1999. ISBN 0395902304. 40 p. Grades 1–3.

Dash, Joan. *The World at Her Fingertips: The Story of Helen Keller*. Scholastic, 2001. ISBN 0-590-90715-8. 235 p. Grades 5–8.

Edge, Laura B. *A Personal Tour of Hull House*. Lerner, 2001. ISBN 0822535823. 64 p. Grades 4–7.

Freedman, Russell. *Babe Didrikson Zaharias: The Making of a Champion*. Clarion Books, 1999. ISBN 0395633672. 192 p. Grades 5–8.

Gearhart, Sarah. *The Telephone* (Turning Point Inventions). Fold-out illustration by Toby Welles. Atheneum Books for Young Readers, 1999. ISBN 0689828152. 80 p. Grades 5–8.

Gherman, Beverly. *Norman Rockwell: Storyteller with a Brush*. Atheneum Books for Young Readers, 2000. ISBN 0689820011. 58 p. Grades 4–8.

Glover, Savion, and Bruce Weber. *Savion: My Life in Tap*. William Morrow, 2000. ISBN 0-688-15629-0. 77 p. Grades 6–up.

Greenberg, Jan, and Sandra Jordan. *Frank O. Gehry: Outside In*. DK, 2000. ISBN 0789426773. 48 p. Grades 4–8.

Hamilton, Jake. *Special Effects in Film and Television*. DK, 1998. ISBN 0-7894-2813-X. 62 p. Grades 4–8.

Hewett, Joan. *Tunnels, Tracks, and Trains: Building a Subway*. Photographs by Richard Hewett. Lodestar, 1995. ISBN 0-525-67466-7. 48 p. Grades 4–7.

Hunter, Ryan. *Dig a Tunnel*. Illustrated by Edward Miller. Holiday House, 1999. ISBN 0823413918. Unpaged. Grades K–3.

Jones, Charlotte Foltz. *Mistakes That Worked*. Illustrated by John O'Brien. A Doubleday Book for Young Readers, 1991. ISBN 0385320434 (pbk.). 82 p. Grades 4–6.

Koscielniak, Bruce. *The Story of the Incredible Orchestra: An Introduction to Musical Instruments and the Symphony Orchestra*. Houghton Mifflin, 2000. ISBN 0395960525. Unpaged. Grades 3–5.

Kroll, Steven. *Robert Fulton: From Submarine to Steamboat*. Illustrated by Bill Farnsworth. Holiday House, 1999. ISBN 0823414337. Unpaged. Grades 2–4.

Krull, Kathleen. *Lives of Extraordinary Women: Rulers, Rebels (and What the Neighbors Thought)*. Illustrated by Kathryn Hewitt. Harcourt, 2000. ISBN 0152008071. 95 p. Grades 4–8.

————. *They Saw the Future: Oracles, Psychics, Scientists, Great Thinkers, and Pretty Good Guessers*. Illustrated by Kyrsten Brooker. Atheneum Books for Young Readers, 1999. ISBN 0689812957. 108 p. Grades 5–8.

Lalicki, Tom. *Spellbinder: The Life of Harry Houdini*. Holiday House, 2000. ISBN 082341499X. 88 p. Grades 4–8.

Lasky, Kathryn. *Vision of Beauty: The Story of Sarah Breedlove Walker*. Illustrated by Nneka Bennett. Candlewick Press, 2000. ISBN 0763602531. Unpaged. Grades 3–5.

Lassieur, Allison. *Subways*. Bridgestone Books, an imprint of Capstone Press, 2000. ISBN 0736803645. 24 p. Grades 1–3.

Lynch, Anne (consulting editor). *Great Buildings*. Time-Life Books, 1996. ISBN 0-8094-9371-3. 64 p. Grades 4–up.

Macaulay, David. *Building Big*. Houghton Mifflin, 2000. ISBN 0-395-96331-1. 192 p. Grades 6–up.

Matthews, Tom L. *Always Inventing: A Photobiography of Alexander Graham Bell*. National Geographic Society, 1999. ISBN 0792273915. 64 p. Grades 4–6.

Orgill, Roxane. *Shout, Sister, Shout! Ten Girl Singers Who Shaped a Century*. Margaret K. McElderry, 2001. ISBN 0-689-81991-9. 148 p. Grades 5–8.

Partridge, Elizabeth. *Restless Spirit: The Life and Work of Dorothea Lange*. Viking, 1998. ISBN 067087888X. 122 p. Grades 5–8.

Poole, Josephine. *Joan of Arc*. Illustrated by Angela Barrett. Research by Vincent Helyar. Alfred A. Knopf, 1999. ISBN 0679890416. Unpaged. Grades 3–6.

Reich, Susanna. *Clara Schumann: Piano Virtuoso*. Clarion Books, 1999. ISBN 0395891191. 118 p. Grades 5–8.

Rogers, Hal. *Cranes* (Big Machines at Work). The Child's World, 2000. ISBN 1567666515. 24 p. Grades 1–3.

————. *Graders* (Big Machines at Work). The Child's World, 2000. ISBN 1567666531. 24 p. Grades 1–3.

————. *Rescue Helicopters* (Big Machines at Work). The Child's World, 2000. ISBN 1567666574. 24 p. Grades 1–3.

————. *Tow Trucks* (Big Machines at Work). The Child's World, 2000. ISBN 1567666582. 24 p. Grades 1–3.

Rubin, Susan Goldman. *Margaret Bourke-White: Her Pictures Were Her Life.* Photographs by Margaret Bourke-White. Henry N. Abrams, 1999. ISBN 0810943816. 96 p. Grades 5–up.

Schaefer, Lola M. *Cable Cars.* Bridgestone Books, an imprint of Capstone Press, 2000. ISBN 0736803610. 24 p. Grades 1–3.

Severance, John B. *Skyscrapers: How America Grew Up.* Holiday House, 2000. ISBN 0823414922. 112 p. Grades 4–8.

Sills, Leslie. *In Real Life: Six Women Photographers.* Holiday House, 2000. ISBN 0823414981. 80 p. Grades 4–8.

Stanley, Diane. *Joan of Arc.* Morrow Junior Books, 1998. ISBN 068814330X. Unpaged. Grades 5–8.

———. *Michelangelo.* HarperCollins, 2000. ISBN 0688150861. Unpaged. Grades 4–8.

Steltzer, Ulli. *Building an Igloo.* Henry Holt, 1995. ISBN 0-8050-3753-5. Unpaged. Grades K–3.

Tallchief, Maria, with Rosemary Wells. *Tallchief: America's Prima Ballerina.* Illustrations by Gary Kelley. Viking, 1999. ISBN 0670887560. 28 p. Grades 3–5.

Taylor, Barbara. *I Wonder Why Zippers Have Teeth and Other Questions About Inventions.* Kingfisher, 1995. ISBN 185697670X. 32 p. Grades 1–4.

Thimmesh, Catherine. *Girls Think of Everything: Stories of Ingenious Inventions by Women.* Illustrated by Melissa Sweet. Houghton Mifflin, 2000. ISBN 0395937442. 58 p. Grades 4–8.

Weiser, Andrea L. *Night Stalkers Special Operations Aviation* (U.S. Army Special Operations Command). Capstone Press, 2000. ISBN 0736803386. 48 p. Grades 4–up.

Wenzel, Angela. *Now You See It—Now You Don't: Rene Magritte.* Prestel-Verlag, 1998. ISBN 379131873X. 28 p. Grades 2–5.

Winter, Jeanette. *Sebastian: A Book About Bach.* Browndeer Press/Harcourt Brace, 1999. ISBN 015200629X. Unpaged. Grades K–3.

Winter, Jonah. *Once upon a Time in Chicago: The Story of Benny Goodman.* Pictures by Jeanette Winter. Hyperion Books for Children, 2000. ISBN 0786804629. Unpaged. Grades 1–3.

Wulffson, Don L. *The Kid Who Invented the Trampoline: More Surprising Stories About Inventions.* Dutton Children's Books, 2001. ISBN 0525466541. 128 p. Grades 4–8.

———. *Toys! Amazing Stories Behind Some Great Inventions.* Illustrations by Laurie Keller. Henry Holt, 2000. ISBN 0805061967. 137 p. Grades 4–8.

CHAPTER 7

Biggest, Fastest, Weirdest, Grossest: Quirky Books Kids Love

FUN FACTS

DK Factastic Book of 1001 Lists by Russell Ash is a book that kids will run for. Reading this book is like eating peanuts—you just can't stop. The book is full of fun lists and illustrations, so you will learn all sorts of information. How many letters are mailed per person per year in the United States? Try 686. That's a lot, but it cannot compete with the Vatican, where 9,545 letters a year are mailed per person. Of course, most of that is church mail.

What is the largest nonfood crop in the world? Cotton, followed by tobacco, and then rubber. How did the Alaskan city "Nome" get its name? Someone wrote on a map "Name?" not knowing what the town name was, and someone else misread it, and it has been "Nome" ever since. The longest river in the world is the Nile. The world's biggest pizza measured almost 123 feet around. This is great to browse through and will attract the most reluctant reader.

Also by Russell Ash and equally appealing is *The Top 10 of Everything 2001*. This book will certainly rival the color version of the *Guinness Book of World Records* as the most popular book in the library. Kids and adults will not be able to put it down. On page 49 is a photograph of an enormous snail that will amaze your audience. Also, on pages 44 and 45 see whether your students can list the most popular dog and cat names in the United States. Once they are warmed up, have them name the top boys' and girls' names in the United States and Canada, as well as the most popular surnames in the United States (page 61). Movie and music fans will love the entertainment chapters. Can your students name the yearly recipients of MTV's "Best Video" award (page 192)? The sports section is also great. Did you know that Michael Jordan once scored 69 points in a single basketball game (page 244)? This book is also a great source of trivia questions for classroom or library challenges. As new annual editions come out, you will want to have them in your library for browsing.

Yet another book of facts from DK is *Ultimate Sports Lists* by Mike Meserole. This will appeal to your hard-core sports fans. Chapters include football, baseball, basketball, hockey, golf, tennis, the Olympic games, soccer, auto racing, and horse racing. Some of the most fun facts are in the "Miscellaneous" chapter. Can you guess the top-grossing contemporary sports movies (page 212), the athlete most frequently on the cover of *Sports Illustrated* (page 217), or the most popular participation sport in the United States (page 217)?

You'll have a blast when you start looking through the *Scholastic Book of World Records* by Jennifer Corr Morse. It's jam-packed with colorful photographs and information. There are records of all sorts. Which country do you think eats the most chocolate per person? Would you believe the United States is not even in the top three? The answer is Switzerland.

Do you know that one of the world's billionaires will not even be 18 years old until 2003? Her name is Athina Onassis Roussel, and her very wealthy grandfather left all of his money to her mother, who died and left it to her. There is a section of U.S. records as well. See what unusual thing your state is tops at. (Minnesota has the coldest city in the United States—International Falls. Hmm, what about Alaska?) Which state has produced the most presidents? (Answer: Virginia.) Which state has the most farmland? (Answer: Texas.) You won't be able to put this one down.

Even young kids love to know facts, and Robert E. Wells's *What's Faster than a Speeding Cheetah?* has some good ones. On the first page we learn that a human being might at times be able to run as fast as 15 miles per hour. But an ostrich, which can run about 45 miles per hour, is the fastest two-legged runner in the world. But if there were ever a race, a cheetah would win for sure, for a cheetah can run up to 70 miles an hour—more than a mile a minute. The cheetah is the fastest runner on Earth.

But that word "runner" is the catch. What animals and what things do you think can go faster than a mile a minute? Read this book to learn some great facts. Show your audience that first picture.

Biggest, Strongest, Fastest by Steve Jenkins provides the basis for a great animal booktalk. Each spread asks a question, making this book a great guessing game. What is the biggest land animal? (African elephant) What is the strongest animal for its size? (the ant) What is the smallest bird? (the bee hummingbird, which weighs less than a dime) The longest animal? (the sun jellyfish, which can grow to more than 200 feet long) Kids will learn a lot from looking at the neat pictures. Once you get started you will probably have to read the whole book.

For an extended booktalk, try this method. As you ask questions, show the kids related books about the various animals. Gather together some attractive books about elephants, ants, and the other animals in the book, put them in order and out of sight of the kids, and pull them out at just the right time. It's a great way to introduce younger kids to the animal books and a variety of others in your library.

Also by Steve Jenkins, and equally attractive, is *Hottest Coldest Highest Deepest*. What is the longest river in the world? Do you want to guess? It is the Nile. Using this book is a fun way to introduce books on the subjects that are the answers to the questions, plus it will intrigue your listeners. What is the world's oldest and deepest lake? Lake Baikal in Russia is almost one mile deep in one spot—but Lake Superior is the world's largest freshwater lake. The hottest spot in the world is in the Sahara Desert, but the hottest spot in the United States is in Death Valley. The windiest spot on Earth is on top of Mount Washington in New Hampshire. A wind of 231 miles per hour was recorded there. This is a very fun, attractive book. Kids will want to see the beautiful artwork up close.

Another book with some guessing game potential is *Everyday Mysteries* by Jerome Wexler. It is full of photographs of things we see every day, but each one is seen from an unconventional angle. Some are surfaces close up, some are cross sections, some are silhouettes, and others are edges. This book needs no booktalk—just show some of the pictures and let your audience guess what they are seeing. Some are easy to figure out, but others, like the watermelon close up and the potato chip edge, will be harder to guess. This colorful book won't take long to get through but is fun for browsing and will engage your more reluctant readers.

Sometimes the things we take for granted can turn out to be very interesting. Peter Kent proves this in *Hidden Under the Ground: The World Beneath Your Feet*. Most of us don't think much about what may lie in the ground beneath us, but this book will start you wondering. Many animals live underground. Prisoners are often kept underground. Hell, they say, is under the ground. Underground is a good place to hide if you want to do something secret. Much of what makes your city run is underground.

This is a great book for browsing. Start with the section on page 9 on "Subterranean Celebrities." Then proceed through the two-page spreads, each filled with fascinating facts and a "try to find an object" game, starting with "Afterlife Underworlds," moving on to "Caves and Caverns," continuing to "Animal Underworld," including "A Subterranean Tomb," "Dungeons," "Digging for Minerals," and so on. Fascinating pieces of information pop up all over. Did you know that Winston Churchill once hid in a coal mine after he escaped from a POW camp during the Boer War? The rats there ate his candles. Show any of the two-page spreads—and read some of the amazing information.

Aki Nurosi has written a book that's fun to look at. *Colorful Illusions: Tricks to Fool Your Eyes* is easy to booktalk—just show some of the illusions and ask kids the questions on the facing pages. Each one corresponds to an answer key in the back of the book that explains what's happening. The author is a professor of graphic design, so these optical illusions deal with how the eye sees color.

Good illusions to show to a group are on pages 23 and 29. If you're using PowerPoint for your booktalk, you could scan in one of the illusions and show it on the screen for a better view.

A LITTLE BIT GROSS

Nothing grabs reluctant readers like something a little bit gross, and *Mummies, Bones and Body Parts* by Charlotte Wilcox fills the bill perfectly. Behind the excellent photographs lie great life-and-death stories and fascinating science.

Scientists can learn a great deal from human remains—mummies, bones, and body parts. This book describes how many human remains have been found around the world, about how their bodies got to the places where they were found, and about the possible lives of the people whose remains were studied.

Human remains are frequently preserved by mummification, sometimes deliberately and sometimes accidentally, by freezing, and by lying in places like peat bogs. Many of the bodies found in peat bogs (show the photo of the one on page 21) look like they were just put there recently, but they may really be hundreds or even thousands of years old.

One interesting story here is about the influenza epidemic of 1918, which killed thousands of people all over the world. Scientists have never understood why it became so deadly. But in 1997 pathologists dug up the bodies of four people who died of the disease in Alaska, where, of course, it is very cold. One of the bodies was well enough preserved that tissues containing the flu virus were removed and are currently being studied. So dead bodies can help humankind even years after their burial. Fascinating!

Have you read *Yuck! A Big Book of Little Horrors* by Robert Snedden or *Yikes: Your Body, up Close* by Mike Janulewicz? If you liked those books, you'll have a lot of fun with *Youch! It Bites: Real-Life Monsters, up Close* by Trevor Day. It has great photographs and good information about bugs, snakes, and other animals that can hurt human beings.

Did you know that only the female mosquito is out to get your blood? Male mosquitoes live on just flower nectar.

Laura Ingalls didn't like stinging nettles. You will understand why when you see the picture of the one in this book.

And a jellyfish is definitely more dangerous to people than a shark.

Maybe the yuckiest insect of all is the deer tick, but read this book and decide for yourself. Just flip through it and show your audience the pictures. It will sell itself.

A similar title from Seymour Simon called *Out of Sight: Pictures of Hidden Worlds* shows views seen only through telescopes and microscopes. The close-up of the tapeworm (which can live in some animals and even in humans) is a good one to show. Also, the photograph of the bullet going through the Queen of Hearts playing card is intriguing. It was taken with an electronic strobe that gives off light for one-millionth of a second.

You can't go wrong showing your audience any of the pages in this attention-grabbing book. Pair it up with *Lots and Lots of Zebra Stripes: Patterns in Nature* (Chapter 2), a similar book, for an even better booktalk.

Marilyn Singer's *Bottoms Up! A Book About Rear Ends* deals with another topic that most people consider yucky. As Singer says, this is not a book about pooping.

Like Singer, many of us have seen the swollen, bright red bottoms of female baboons in photos or in zoos. But most of us, unlike Singer, never look for more information. What she learned is that animals do many interesting things with their behinds.

Chickens lay eggs, as many as 351 a year! Bees sting. A forceps fish fools predators with the fake eyes on its rear end. Everyone knows what skunks do. Spiders spin. And many animals greet and check each other out by sniffing there. The colorful illustrations will entertain even the most reluctant reader.

Burp! The Most Interesting Book You'll Ever Read About Eating by Diane Swanson is what it says it is—a very interesting book about eating, which is something almost everyone likes to do. You can amaze your friends with some of the facts that you learn, such as these:

- Some people have disorders that make them want to eat peculiar things, like clay or metal.
- In 1980 a 19-year-old boy, Jay Gwaltney, ate an entire birch tree about 11 feet tall. It took him 89 hours.
- People who live in cold places usually eat more food than people who live in warmer ones. They need lots of food to keep their body temperature up.
- People have about 16 million smell sensors. Rabbits have 100 million!
- When you were born, all of your baby and adult teeth were hidden in your gums—although they were not fully formed yet.
- Your blood has to travel through approximately 60,000 miles of vessels—more than two times a trip around the Earth.
- Everyone carries around about a cup of gas in the digestive system. The problem is that we normally pick up about 10 cups of gas a day. It has to get out somehow!
- In ancient Rome, people used to eat huge feasts. When they were full, a servant would tickle inside their throat with a feather. They would throw up, and then they could eat some more.

Show the picture on page 36 of the man's throat being tickled.

Kids love bathroom habits, and what better subject to get their attention than the toilet? Patricia Lauber's *What You Never Knew About Tubs, Toilets, and Showers* makes great reading for elementary students. All these bathroom fixtures center around cleanliness. One reason the people who live in the wealthy countries of the world are lucky is that they can be clean. Most of us like being clean. But it wasn't always that way.

No one knows when human beings started washing up. We do know that the first human beings went to the bathroom wherever they happened to be—and a lot of people still do it that way. But by the time ancient people started writing their history down, practically everyone thought it was a good idea to be clean. It helped that they had running water and good plumbing—without those, being clean isn't easy to do. Drains that take away waste are another good thing.

The Romans, the Greeks, and the Egyptians loved to bathe, and many of them did not need the privacy that a lot of us want. Most of us would rather not be naked in front of strangers or sit down and go to the bathroom next to a row of other people doing the same thing.

Around the world, many people wanted to be clean, but in Europe in the Middle Ages a lot of them didn't seem to want to be clean. The first immigrants to what would become the United States were very dirty!

This is a really fun book with lots of colorful pictures. Show your audience the one of Ben Franklin in his slipper bath and of King Louis XIV of France using his closestool (basically, a toilet) as a throne on which he could receive visitors!

HIGH-SPEED DAREDEVILS

Every school has some kids (usually boys) who just want to read about dirt bikes or motorcycles or other high-speed sports. Fortunately, Capstone Press has many high-interest/low-reading-level books that will appeal to elementary as well as middle school students.

Bicycle Stunt Riding by Jason Glaser is one of those. The first dirt bikes were really small motorcycles. Bicycle motocross (BMX) first became popular in the 1970s. The first real bicycles sturdy enough for stunt riding and freestyling were built by a bicycle company called Haro in 1983. Today many people do stunt riding, and stunt-riding competitions take place throughout North America. This book tells you how to get started and provides information about safety and competitions, as well as addresses and Web sites.

Enduro Racing by Steve Hendrickson will satisfy young motorcycle enthusiasts. When most people think of races, they think "the fastest person or animal will win." But when it comes to enduro races, they would be wrong. The fastest racers do not always win these types of motorcycle races. Instead, the most accurate racer wins. Racers who complete a course too fast or too slow will not will the race.

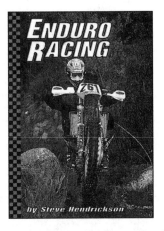

Figure 7.1. *Enduro Racing* **by Steve Hendrickson.**

Enduro racing takes place on paths rather than on racecourses. Most are narrow dirt paths with room enough for only one motorcycle. Throughout the race, racers must show up at checkpoints, and they must arrive there at just the right time—neither too late nor too early. If they arrive at the wrong time, they are penalized. Because the path is so narrow, the racers cannot all start at once. Instead, a few at a time start.

Enduro racing is controversial. Some people consider it bad for the environment. But it looks like a lot of fun for the people who do it. Show the picture on page 44.

Also by Steve Hendrickson is *Supercross Racing*. Supercross is a type of motorcycle racing that owes its beginnings to motocross racing. In motocross racing, the spectators cannot see the entire race, although they may be able to see a part of it. But supercross races take place in stadiums, where everyone in the crowd can see the whole event.

Figure 7.2. *Supercross Racing* **by Steve Hendrickson.**

Supercross racing makes use of many obstacles that make it more exciting. Short, steep bumps about five feet apart are called whoops, which is short for whoop-de-doos. Tabletops are large bumps with flat tops, and doubles are two large bumps in a row. A triple is a series of three large bumps that can launch riders more than 40 feet into the air.

Hendrickson's book gives information on skills, stunts, and companies that sponsor supercross races. Great color photos show lots of action. Show the ones on pages 4 and 45.

For those who can't get enough of racing, try Steve Hendrickson's *Land Speed Racing*. The main reason land speed racers compete is to see how fast their vehicles can go. And they do not race on racecourses. Instead, they use large, flat areas, such as dry lake beds or the Bonneville Salt Flats. Dave Campos, who set a record speed of more than 322 miles per hour there in 1990, was the world record holder at the time this book was written.

Just qualifying to race is not easy, and the rules may surprise you. The dangers are scary, too. All drivers must wear fireproof suits because after a motorcycle crashes, it is sometimes difficult to get off and very dangerous for the driver if the motorcycle catches on fire. If you like motorcycles and racing, this book is for you.

Dirt Track Racing by Ed Youngblood has color photographs that show the history of dirt track racing, which is one of the oldest types of motorcycle racing in North America. It began in the early 1900s.

By 1908 a special kind of track called a velodrome was built for the sport. This track was made of wood with steep, banked corners and looked something like an oval bowl. In 1912 one racer reached a speed of 100 miles per hour, an incredible velocity for that time. But by the mid-1920s those tracks were gone because they were hard to maintain, and the high speeds had caused so many accidents.

This book has all sorts of interesting information about dirt track motorcycles. For instance, they use special soft tires that provide better traction—and these tires usually wear out after only one race. Also, the fuel has more oxygen than regular gasoline and costs four times as much. Show the picture of a racing helmet, which covers just about everything, on page 24.

Also by Ed Youngblood is *Superbike Racing*. Superbike motorcycles are specifically designed just for superbike racing, which the American Motorcycle Association developed in 1976.

This book includes the history, with photographs, of the first motorcycles, which were really steam-powered engines attached to bicycles. This was not a good thing. Steam-powered engines not only got very hot, they also let off steam—and riders could easily get burned. Often the rider's seat was directly above the engine. Motorcycles have come a long, long way.

This book has excellent color photos and information. One surprising fact is that racing teams warm up their motorcycles' tires before a race. A tire heater looks like an electric blanket. A cold tire cannot race at full speed—it might even fall apart. And riders must wear full-coverage helmets—ones that cover the rider's entire head. Sometimes riders look like they are related to Darth Vader. Show your audience the photo on page 10 of the early motorcycle and the one on page 26 of the rider with the full-coverage helmet.

Jason Glaser's *Bungee Jumping* describes a different type of daredevil. Bungee jumping is a sport that has caught on in the United States only in the last few years. You should be in reasonably good physical condition and weigh more than 75 pounds if you are going to try it. What you do is jump off a high place, but you are attached by a stretchy rope—called a bungee—that prevents you from hurting yourself. The scary part is that you dive head first!

Bungee jumping started on Pentecost Island, near Australia, where men in the Bunlap tribe tie strong vines to their ankles and jump from towers.

This book is full of fun photos and neat ideas, including Web sites and snail-mail addresses. Do you know anyone who has ever bungee jumped?

MYSTERIOUS HAPPENINGS

Eerie, spooky color photographs grab your attention when you open *Ghosts of the West Coast: The Lost Souls of the Queen Mary and Other Real Life Hauntings* by Ted Wood. Upper-elementary students love ghost stories, and Wood's book is full of them.

The *Queen Mary*, now a hotel in Long Beach, California, is perhaps the most famous haunted ship in the world. The ship, which is three football fields long and 12 stories high, seems to be home to a lot of ghosts. Perhaps the saddest ones are those of the sailors from the British ship *Curacao*. The *Queen Mary* collided with this ship, cutting it in half, during World War II. Three hundred thirty-eight men were killed, and people say that their groans and shrieks can still be heard near the collision point.

Spanish monks haunt some of California's beautiful missions. Kate Morgan shot herself in the head on the beach at the Hotel del Coronado in San Diego in 1892—or maybe she didn't. Maybe her husband murdered her. In any case, Kate haunts her old room, number 3312.

Convicts, imprisoned in Alcatraz, the most horrible prison in the United States, still haunt their former cells. And Sarah Winchester in San Jose was convinced that she must keep adding on to her house or she would die. She was terrified of the ghosts of the people who had been killed with her husband's Winchester rifles, and for 38 years she built and built. She even hid from the ghosts by sleeping in a different bedroom every night! When she died, she left behind a 160-room house. Kids love ghosts, and this is a great book for browsing.

Most people enjoy a mystery, and nothing beats a real one that has never been solved. Maybe someday someone *will* solve it, and it would most likely happen by reading. A really strange mystery is told in *The Wolf Girls: An Unsolved Mystery from History* by Jane Yolen and Heidi Elisabet Yolen Stemple.

Reverend Joseph Singh was a missionary in India. He ran an orphanage, and in 1921 a local doctor came to examine two orphan girls. Singh at first told the doctor the girls had been left at the orphanage doorstep the year before. The girls were in such horrible shape, unconscious and barely breathing, that the doctor asked a lot of questions. And Singh gave him some very surprising answers.

The girls, he said, who were about two and eight years old, had been living with jungle wolves. They had been raised by the wolves and barely acted like human beings. They walked on all fours, growled, and refused to wear clothing.

The doctor told everyone about this, and Reverend Singh became famous, which seemed to please him. He wrote a book about finding the girls, the younger of whom had by now died, and told the awful story of their capture.

No one is really certain whether Reverend Singh was telling the truth or what he thought was the truth, or whether he was trying to make a good story even better. People have made up all sorts of theories, and you can find some of them on a two-page spread near the end of the book. Read this with your friends and then see what *you* think—and whether you all agree. Show the picture of Reverend Singh feeding the younger girl while the older one lies in a cage.

Also by Jane Yolen and Heidi Elisabet Yolen Stemple is *The Mary Celeste: An Unsolved Mystery from History*. One of the best mysteries ever is still waiting for someone to solve it. And it really happened.

In December 1872 sailors on the American ship *Dei Gratia*, in the middle of the ocean, spotted something unusual in the distance. It was another ship, but something about it was strange. As it drew close, the crew of the *Dei Gratia* recognized her as another American ship, the *Mary Celeste*, but they couldn't see anyone on board. They boarded the *Mary Celeste* and were bewildered by what they found. There should have been 10 people on board, but everyone was gone. Everything was in perfect order, except that some of the ship's tools were missing, but there was a six-month supply of food and freshwater, and everything looked normal, or as sailors say, "shipshape."

What had happened? What was going on? Captain Morehouse of the *Dei Gratia* was sick at heart, for the night before the *Mary Celeste* had sailed, he had had dinner with its skipper, his friend, Captain Briggs. Briggs was taking his wife and two-year-old daughter on the trip with him, although his son was left back home in school.

Where was everybody? What had happened? By the law of the sea, the *Dei Gratia* now owned the *Mary Celeste*. They towed it to port, but by the time they took the matter to court, they made almost no money on it.

More than 100 years later, we are still baffled by this mystery. At the end of the book, the authors offer us some of the theories about what happened and ask questions about each one. Take a look at them. Read the facts. What is your theory? Maybe someday someone will solve this mystery, and, who knows, it could be you!

Nothing is quite so tantalizing as a good historical mystery, and they don't get much better or more famous than the one about Atlantis. *Atlantis: The Lost City?* by Andrew Donkin will tell you more.

Almost everyone has heard of Atlantis. But we don't really know much about it. Only one person in all of history has actually claimed that such a place existed and was destroyed. That person was Plato, an ancient Greek and one of the greatest thinkers of all time. He told the story of a fantastic, beautiful city built by an advanced civilization and described it fairly thoroughly. What we don't know is whether he was telling the truth he believed or whether he was telling a fable, a story that has a moral.

In any case, people have been looking for and thinking they may have found the real Atlantis for thousands of years. The first place they think it may be is under the ocean. But some people think it is in America, or in Antarctica, or in Crete—it just depends. Many of the theories are presented in these books. What do *you* think? Show the two-page spread on pages 12 and 13.

POTPOURRI

Some books defy categorization, but they're so much fun they deserve to be booktalked and enjoyed by kids. The topics of these potpourri books range from twins to gargoyles to the tooth fairy. The one thing they share is their universal appeal to nonfiction readers.

No one would ever want to go to prison, but as bad as prisons in the United States are today, prisons in other times were even worse. *Go to Jail! A Look at Prisons Through the Ages* by Peter Kent presents the history of prisons in a high-interest book accessible to upper-elementary students.

How would you like to be shut away in a stinking prison hulk, a rotting, smelly ship in which you wear heavy leg irons but are taken out during the day to work on building sites? Prisoners like this were always cold and damp, and one in every four died. In England, prisoners were housed in hulks from 1776 to 1857.

Or would you rather be alone all of the time and never speak to anyone else? Even when you went to church, you sat in a section by yourself, where you could not even see anyone else. Some of these prisoners were so lonely that they went insane. How would you like to be imprisoned in a cathedral spire where the ringing of the bells would make you deaf?

This book is full of interesting information about prisons, including illustrations of famous prisoners on the end pages and a "find the prisoner" game you can play on every two-page spread. One problem: No prison of the past was nearly as clean as these look, but kids will have a grand time.

Donna M. Jackson's mother was a twin, and, like many of us, she has always been interested in twins. She starts her book *Twin Tales: The Magic and Mystery of Multiple Birth* with the story of Brielle and Kyrie Jackson, who were born prematurely in 1995. Each was placed in her own warming bed.

The smaller one, Brielle, had a great deal of trouble. Her blood oxygen level was low, and eventually she started turning bluish gray. Suddenly the hospital nurse got an idea. She asked the babies' parents if she could put the twins in the same bed. Brielle started getting better almost immediately. Show the wonderful photo of tiny Kyrie with her arm around Brielle in that bed (page 6).

Twins such as Kyrie and Brielle often share a special bond. One man even formed a group for twin survivors—people whose twin has died. He remembers well when his own twin brother died from electrocution in an accident more than 50 years ago. The surviving twin felt as though he had been electrocuted himself.

About one-third of all twins are identical twins. Jackson tells us that identical twins share the same genes and frequently have much in common, even when they are not raised together and do not even know that their twin exists.

There are lots of good twin stories in this book, and it ends with a famous one. In Auschwitz, the infamous Nazi concentration camp in World War II, Dr. Josef Mengele performed horrifying experiments on twins. We read the story of Miriam and Eva Mozes, who were subjected to his torturous treatments, and we see the old photo of them being liberated from Auschwitz in 1945—and again in the same place, when they returned in 1991. Show your audience these photos on pages 46 and 47.

Twins are a popular topic, and you can read more about them in Daniel Jussim's *Double Take: The Story of Twins*. Most of us are not twins, so there is something fascinating about people who are. To quote the author on page 2:

> Twins have something that most people want—they grow up with constant companionship so they're hardly ever lonely. They have a soul mate who understands them when no one else can. But they face unique challenges also. For while the world—always comparing—sees a single pair, twins are two, too. They must develop a sense of themselves as individuals. They must understand that their tastes and talents, whether running marathons or playing piano, won't always be shared.

You will discover how twins form and how a pregnancy of twins (or even more than twins) is difficult for the mother. You will be intrigued by how things can go wrong with twin births and even with twins in the womb. *Double Take* has wonderful stories of twins, such as the one about the two Russian preschoolers who lived in a group home. They had been injured before they were born, in their mother's womb. Three of their four legs had to be amputated. They had no artificial limbs.

A man in Illinois read a story about them and became intrigued. He had been in the Vietnam War and had lost a leg himself. He became convinced that he should adopt the Russian boys and help them. And he did! Show your audience the photograph of them on page 14.

Studies of twins have helped scientists learn about how our heredity contributes to who we are. This is a fascinating book.

Younger readers who want to read about the subject can enjoy *Twins!* by Elaine Scott. What would it be like to have a twin? Maybe you have one or know someone who does. Do you think it would be fun to have a brother or sister so close to you? Or might it not be fun to always have to share your birthday? Of course, sometimes older brothers or sisters of twins can get pretty sick of having twins as siblings. This fun book has great pictures and information about twins.

Gargoyles are popular right now. Do you know what they are? "A gargoyle is a stone statue that is weird or strange-looking" (page 8). If you have a little one at home you'll want to bring it in when you booktalk *Gargoyles: Monsters in Stone* by Jennifer Dussling. This book tells young readers about gargoyles and is great fun to read.

Gargoyles were especially popular during the Middle Ages. They were carved high up, near the very top of churches. No one is sure why they were put there, but we know that they were useful—they served as drains.

> They were like fancy, funny drainpipes. Rain ran through the pipes in their bodies. Then it shot out their mouths. That is how gargoyles got their name. "Gargoyle" comes from a French word that means "throat." And think about it. Gargoyle sounds a lot like the word "gargle." And that is what gargoyles did. They held water in their mouths. Then they spit it out. (page 22)

Experts think some gargoyles looked like real people their carver knew. Read this to find out some great information.

Behold … the Dragons! by Gail Gibbons is a fun book about dragons, animals that never existed. So why do people all over the world tell stories about them? Gibbons gives us fascinating pictures and interesting information. She tells us that people made up stories to explain things they could not understand, events like volcanic eruptions and earthquakes.

The word "dragon" comes from the Greek word "drakon," which means "a huge snake with piercing eyesight." Experts on dragons classify them into five groups: serpent dragons, semidragons, classical dragons, sky dragons, and neodragons. There are stories about dragons—stories such as Hercules and the many-headed hydra, *Beowulf*, and Saint George and the dragons. Show your audience pictures of any of the various types of dragons or any of the book's illustrations that appeal to you.

For a different sort of imaginary creature, read *Santa Who?* by Gail Gibbons. A lot of kids love Santa Claus. But who is he? Where did he come from? How did he get his name? Gail Gibbons writes wonderful books that are easy to understand and fun to read. In this one, she tells us about one of many kids' favorite people.

The first time Christmas gifts were given was more than 2,000 years ago at the birth of Jesus Christ, according to the Bible. But about 1,700 years ago, Saint Nicholas lived in the land now called Turkey. He loved children and gave many gifts to poor people. People started saying that presents were really from Saint Nicholas. His feast day was on December 6, so that became a big gift-giving day—until about 500 years ago, when some religious leaders said it was wrong to celebrate the holidays of saints. After that, people started giving gifts at Christmas. But Saint Nicholas became part of that holiday, too. Read about how Saint Nicholas became Santa Claus and about how children around the world get their presents. Show your audience the two-page spread of Washington Irving's version of Santa Claus as depicted in *Knickerbocker's History of New York*.

And while talking about Santa Claus, mention *Throw Your Tooth on the Roof: Tooth Traditions from Around the World* by Sally B. Beeler. In the United States, many of us know what happens when you lose a baby tooth. It's a good deal! Put your tooth under your pillow, and, while you are sleeping, the tooth fairy will come and take it away, leaving you money. But in other parts of the world, different things happen. Some countries have a tooth mouse instead of a tooth fairy. The Native American Yupik mother wraps up a baby tooth in food and then feeds it to a female dog. In some countries, a little girl's tooth is made into an earring. In many countries, children throw their tooth on the roof of a house. In Vietnam, you throw your lower tooth on the roof and your upper tooth under the bed. Take a look at this fun book. Maybe next time you lose a tooth, you will want to try something different with it. Show the children any of the two-page spreads, making sure to show the one on the second-to-the-last page picturing the entire mouth.

And speaking of teeth, you might not much like going to the dentist, but after you read *Toothworms and Spider Juice: An Illustrated History of Dentistry* by Loretta Frances Ichord, you will realize how lucky we are today. For most of history, there were no dentists, and people suffered a great deal of pain from toothaches and cavities and teeth that were worn down from chewing the stones that were ground up with their flour. We know these things because teeth last much longer than most other parts of the body, and scientists can examine the teeth in skeletons and learn what the people ate.

One amazing thing that was commonly believed was that toothaches were caused by worms that lived in the tooth. People believed that pain was caused by the worm moving around. Scientists now believe that the pulp in a tooth looks sort of like a worm and that is why people thought there were worms inside the teeth.

This book is filled with fascinating facts. Look at the picture on page 15 of a child suffering from a toothache. As the caption says, no one knows why people used to wear a handkerchief tied around their head when they had a toothache, but it accomplished one thing—it let everyone know that the person wearing the handkerchief had a toothache!

Another fact: "The first urine of the morning was used as a medical mouthwash from ancient times through the eighteenth century" (page 19).

And during the Renaissance, there were professional "tooth-drawers" who pulled out teeth. "Even the honest tooth-drawers had limited skills and were capable of tearing large pieces of bone off with a tooth, breaking jaws, and causing facial deformities" (page 37).

The Hindus of India were the first people to use toothbrushes—starting about 4000 B.C. They made their brushes from fresh twigs.

This book is fun to read, especially if you are not squeamish.

Open Wide: Tooth School Inside by Laurie Keller is a fun and funny book about teeth for much younger readers.

Grown-ups have 32 teeth, and younger kids have primary or baby teeth. How should we take care of them? What does each kind of tooth do? What makes them hurt? How do they get fixed? What is the best way to take care of our teeth so that they will last a long time? There are great illustrations and fun photographs in *Open Wide*. Check out the one of the holey, green teeth!

Young children will also enjoy reading about the world of sleep in *Bedtime!* by Ruth Freeman Swain. Every being in the world needs to sleep, but not everyone, now and throughout history, sleeps in a bed. Do you sleep alone? With your whole family? With a brother or sister? You probably have soft, comfortable pillows for your head.

Bedtime! shows other ways of going to bed. Ancient Egyptians slept on wooden bed frames strung with cords to let air pass through. They had hard headrests instead of pillows and used netting to protect themselves from mosquito bites.

In Central and South America, many people used hammocks—and modern people copied them. Many people have hammocks in their yards. One bed in England was big enough for 10 or 12 people to sleep in. Show your audience any of the colorful pictures in the book.

Do you know anyone who lives on a farm? For much of the history of the United States, most people lived on farms. Now most people live in cities and towns. Find out what it was like to live on a farm by reading *Century Farm: One Hundred Years on a Family Farm* by Cris Peterson.

The Peterson family has been living on the same Wisconsin farm for more than 100 years. Mr. Peterson's great-grandfather first bought the farm, and then his son, and his son, and *his* son, Mr. Peterson, have farmed the same land. Many things have changed since the farm's beginning. Pictures show the way the farm was in the early days and the way it is today. If you have ever wondered what it is like to live on a family farm, this book will show you.

The many photos in *Century Farm* are colorful and appealing. Show your audience the color photo of the Peterson kids and the photo of making cookies—some things happen everywhere.

Money is always an interesting topic for kids, and you can read about it in Amy Nathan's *Kids' Allowance Book*. What do you think is the average allowance for kids your age? Do you get one? Do you think they are a good idea?

According to this book, the average allowance for kids ages 9–10 is $3 and ages 11–14 is $5. But frequently their allowance is not their only income from their parents. Some get extra money for doing chores, baby-sitting, and other tasks around the house. Others negotiate or get money on an as-needed basis.

How do you go about asking for a raise? Nathan gives helpful tips for this and for saving and spending your money, as well as information about what other kids do.

If I Were President by Catherine Stier explains some exciting things about having the most important job in the country. Do you think you could ever be president of the United States? Not yet, for sure. A person has to be at least 35 years old, be born a citizen of the United States, and have lived in the United States for at least 14 years to qualify. That includes a lot of people.

The president has to work very hard, first just to get elected and then to take care of the country and make the right decisions. But the president has help, especially from the members of the cabinet, a group of advisors the president selects to help run the nation.

The president also has some very fun things to do, including going to movies or going bowling without leaving the White House, having your own chef, throwing out the first pitch of the baseball season in the spring, and having your own private airplane. Read this fun book and find out what the president does. Show the picture of the first pitch.

If you think being president is the job for you, you'll need a strategy for getting elected. Getting to be the president of the United States is not easy, but Judith St.

George's book *So You Want to Be President?* tells us about some of the men who have become our presidents, and some of the things they have in common—and don't have in common at all.

The best name for a U.S. president must be James because six presidents had that name. Can you name them? There were four Johns, four Williams, three Georges, and two Franklins. How about them?

Eight presidents were born in log cabins, and one pretended that he had been, although he was really born in a mansion.

The biggest president was William Howard Taft, who weighed more than 300 pounds, and the tallest was Abraham Lincoln, who was six feet, four inches. The smallest was James Monroe, who weighed only 100 pounds.

Reading this book is like eating peanuts. It won't take long, and you will start telling everyone you know about the fun things you have read. Show the picture on page 27 of one of Theodore Roosevelt's sons, who once took a Shetland pony upstairs in the White House elevator.

Have you ever wanted to go to Alaska? Well, if you can't go there, the next best thing might be to make some of the snacks in *Moose Racks, Bear Tracks and Other Alaska Kidsnacks: Cooking with Kids Has Never Been So Easy* by Alice Bugni. It's the brightest, most appealing children's cookbook imaginable. The author has worked extensively with children, and her recipes have huge appeal. Show your audience the fun, yummy-sounding recipes. Each has one colorful page to itself, and most are quite simple and relatively safe to prepare. Once kids see it, this book will never stay on the shelf in the library.

Speaking of food, *Let's Make Butter* by Eleanor Christian and Lyzz Roth-Singer has great photos and a fun experiment to do. Do you know where butter comes from? Do you know that making it can be hard work? This would be a great thing to try at home. Show the double-page spread on pages 2 and 3. Younger kids will find this book enjoyable.

Peanut Butter Party: Including the History, Uses, and Future of Peanut Butter by Remy Charlip is a very silly book. As the author tells us, peanut butter is a sticky subject. This is more of a party than any accurate information about the history or uses of peanut butter.

Remy Charlip loves peanut butter, and so do a lot of us. Did you know that Americans tend to be crazy about peanut butter, and when we move across the ocean, our families and friends have to mail it to us because people in most other countries do not like it?

Charlip has some fun and crazy uses for peanut butter. He gives us directions for making ghost toast, name game, art galleries, and peanut butter sculptures, among other things. He gives you ideas for putting on peanut butter shows and includes scripts for the skits. The most famous rhyme in the book is the one you may already know:

A peanut sat on a railroad track
His heart was all aflutter.
A train came by the track. Clack! Clack!
Choo! Choo! Peanut butter!

Show your audience the "More Art Gallery" picture.

Some people say peanut butter tastes good with bananas, which is the subject of *Bananas!* by Jascqueline Farmer.

Almost everyone likes bananas. For one thing, they are probably the easiest fruit of all to eat. They come in their own container, a beautiful yellow peel, and they don't drip and are not sticky. Plus they taste good. The average American eats 28 pounds of bananas every year.

Banana plants grow up to 30 feet tall in one year, but they are in fact herbs, not trees, even though they look like trees. What looks like a tree is really leaves wrapped closely together. You will never see a piece of furniture made out of banana wood—because there is no such thing.

Bananas are very unusual. Sometimes they produce new varieties, which is called *sporting*. This seems to happen almost by accident. The most famous example of sporting happened in 1836, when yellow bananas first appeared. The original bananas were only red and green!

There are over 500 different kinds of bananas, but the one most of us are familiar with is the Cavendish.

Read William Cole's poem "Banananananananana" on the fourth-to-the-last page and show the picture of part of the world's longest banana split (more than four and one-half miles) on the second- and third-to-the-last pages.

Almost everyone likes apple pie, apple juice, apple cider, apple dumplings, and just plain apples. When we like someone, we might say that they are the apple of our eye. *Apples* by Gail Gibbons gives us neat information about apples. They are not a native American food. Settlers brought apples with them from Europe, and Native Americans liked them and took them west and planted them.

Do you have a favorite kind of apple? The most popular one is the Red Delicious, which had its beginning in 1881 on an Iowa farm. More than 2,500 varieties of apples are grown in the United States today.

Can you think of someone who became famous for planting apple trees? His name was John Chapman, but people called him Johnny Appleseed. He traveled through the frontier planting apple trees wherever he went. Read this book for some fun information about a food that tastes good and is very good for you. Show the picture of Johnny Appleseed.

BIBLIOGRAPHY

Ash, Russell. *DK Factastic Book of 1001 Lists*. DK, 1999. ISBN 0789434121 (pbk.); 0789437694 (hc.). 208 p. Grades 4–up.

———. *The Top 10 of Everything 2001*. DK, 2000. ISBN 0-7894-5960-4. 288 p. Grades 5–up.

Beeler, Sally B. *Throw Your Tooth on the Roof: Tooth Traditions from Around the World*. Illustrated by G. Brian Karas. Houghton Mifflin, 1998. ISBN 0395891086. Unpaged. Grades K–3.

Bugni, Alice. *Moose Racks, Bear Tracks and Other Alaska Kidsnacks: Cooking with Kids Has Never Been So Easy.* Illustrated by Shannon Cartwright. Paws IV, published by Sasquatch Books, 1999. ISBN 1570612145. Unpaged. Grades 2–6.

Charlip, Remy. *Peanut Butter Party: Including the History, Uses, and Future of Peanut Butter.* Tricycle Press, 1999. ISBN 1883672694. Unpaged. Grades 1–4.

Christian, Eleanor, and Lyzz Roth-Singer. *Let's Make Butter.* Yellow Umbrella Books, 2001. ISBN 0736807284. 17 p. Grades 1–3.

Day, Trevor. *Youch! It Bites: Real-Life Monsters, up Close.* Designed by Mike Jolley. Simon & Schuster Books for Young Readers, 2000. ISBN 0689834160. Unpaged. Grades 2–6.

Donkin, Andrew. *Atlantis: The Lost City?* DK, 2000. ISBN 0789466821. 49 p. Grades 3–5.

Dussling, Jennifer. *Gargoyles: Monsters in Stone* (All Aboard Reading). Illustrated by Peter Church. Grosset & Dunlap, 1999. ISBN 0448419610 (pbk.). 48 p. Grades 1–3.

Farmer, Jascqueline. *Bananas!* Illustrated by Page Eastburn O'Rourke. Charlesbridge, 1999. ISBN 088106114X. Unpaged. Grades 2–4.

Gibbons, Gail. *Apples.* Holiday House, 2000. ISBN 0823414973. Unpaged. Grades 1–3.

———. *Behold ... the Dragons!* Morrow Junior Books, 1999. ISBN 068815526X (trade); 0688155278 (lib. ed.). Unpaged. Grades 1–4.

———. *Santa Who?* Morrow Junior Books, 1999. ISBN 0688155286 (trade); 0688155294 (lib. ed.). Unpaged. Grades 1–4.

Glaser, Jason. *Bicycle Stunt Riding.* Capstone Press, 1999. ISBN 0516217798. 48 p. Grades 4–8.

———. *Bungee Jumping.* Capstone Press, 1999. ISBN 0736801685. 48 p. Grades 4–8.

Hendrickson, Steve. *Enduro Racing* (Motorcycles). Consultant: Hugh Fleming, Director, AMA Sports, American Motorcyclist Association. Capstone Books, an imprint of Capstone Press, 2000. ISBN 0736804773. 48 p. Grades 4–8.

———. *Land Speed Racing.* Consultant: Hugh Fleming, Director, AMA Sports, American Motorcyclist Association. Capstone Books, an imprint of Capstone Press, 2000. ISBN 0736804765. 48 p. Grades 4–8.

———. *Supercross Racing.* Capstone Press, 2000. ISBN 073680479X. 48 p. Grades 4–up.

Ichord, Loretta Frances. *Toothworms and Spider Juice: An Illustrated History of Dentistry.* Millbrook Press, 1999. ISBN 0761314652 (lib. bdg.). 96 p. Grades 4–8.

Jackson, Donna M. *Twin Tales: The Magic and Mystery of Multiple Birth.* Megan Tingley Books/Little, Brown, 2001. ISBN 0316454311. 48 p. Grades 5–8.

Jenkins, Steve. *Biggest, Strongest, Fastest.* Ticknor & Fields, 1995. ISBN 0395697018. 32 p. Grades 1–3.

———. *Hottest Coldest Highest Deepest.* Houghton Mifflin, 1998. ISBN 0395899990. 32 p. Grades 1–3.

Jussim, Daniel. *Double Take: The Story of Twins.* Viking, 2001. ISBN 0670884529. 96 p. Grades 4–7.

Keller, Laurie. *Open Wide: Tooth School Inside.* Henry Holt, 2000. ISBN 0805061924. Unpaged. Grades 1–3.

Kent, Peter. *Go to Jail! A Look at Prisons Through the Ages.* Millbrook Press, 1997, 1998. ISBN 0761304029. 30 p. Grades 3–6.

———. *Hidden Under the Ground: The World Beneath Your Feet.* Dutton Children's Books, 1998. ISBN 0525675523. 33 p. Grades 3–6.

Lauber, Patricia. *What You Never Knew About Tubs, Toilets, and Showers* (Around the House History). Illustrated by John Manders. Simon & Schuster Books for Young Readers, 2001. ISBN 0689824203. Unpaged. Grades 2–4.

Meserole, Mike. *Ultimate Sports Lists.* DK, 1999. ISBN 0-7894-3753-8. 224 p. Grades 4–up.

Morse, Jennifer Corr. *Scholastic Book of World Records* (A Georgian Bay Book). Scholastic Reference, 2001. ISBN 0439219620. 320 p. Grades 4–up.

Nathan, Amy. *Kids' Allowance Book.* Illustrations by Debbie Palen. Walker, 1998. ISBN 0802786510; 0802775322 (pbk.). 86 p. Grades 4–6.

Nurosi, Aki. *Colorful Illusions: Tricks to Fool Your Eyes*, with Mark Shulman. Sterling, 2000. ISBN 0-8069-2997-9 (trade); 0-8069-6097-3 (pbk.). 80 p. Grades 4–up.

Peterson, Cris. *Century Farm: One Hundred Years on a Family Farm.* With photographs by Alvis Upitis. Boyds Mills Press, 1999. ISBN 1563977109. Unpaged. Grades K–3.

St. George, Judith. *So You Want to Be President?* Illustrated by David Small. Philomel, 2000. ISBN 0399234071. 54 p. Grades 1–4.

Scott, Elaine. *Twins!* Photographs by Margaret Miller. Atheneum Books for Young Readers, 1998. ISBN 0-689-80347-8. 40 p. Grades K–2.

Simon, Seymour. *Out of Sight: Pictures of Hidden Worlds.* SeaStar Books, 2000. ISBN 1-58717-012-4. Unpaged. Grades 1–6.

Singer, Marilyn. *Bottoms Up: A Book About Rear Ends.* Henry Holt, 1997. ISBN 0805042466. 32 p. Grades 3–5.

Stier, Catherine. *If I Were President.* Illustrated by DyAnne DiSalvo-Ryan. Whitman, 1999. ISBN 0807535419. Unpaged. Grades K–3.

Swain, Ruth Freeman. *Bedtime!* Illustrated by Cat Bowman Smith. Holiday House, 1999. ISBN 0823414442. Unpaged. Grades 1–3.

Swanson, Diane. *Burp! The Most Interesting Book You'll Ever Read About Eating* (Mysterious You). Illustrated by Rose Cowles. Kids Can Press, 2001. ISBN 1550745999 (hc.); 1550746014 (pbk.). 40 p. Grades 4–8.

Wells, Robert E. *What's Faster than a Speeding Cheetah?* Whitman, 1997. ISBN 0807522805 (hc.); 0807522813 (pbk.). Unpaged. Grades 1–3.

Wexler, Jerome. *Everyday Mysteries*. Dutton Children's Books, 1995. ISBN 0-525-45363-6. Unpaged. Grades 1–5.

Wilcox, Charlotte. *Mummies, Bones and Body Parts*. Carolrhoda Books, 2000. ISBN 1575054280. 64 p. Grades 4–7.

Wood, Ted. *Ghosts of the West Coast: The Lost Souls of the Queen Mary and Other Real Life Hauntings*. Walker, 1999. ISBN 0802786685 (hc.); 0802786693 (reinforced). 48 p. Grades 4–6.

Yolen, Jane, and Heidi Elisabet Yolen Stemple. *The Mary Celeste: An Unsolved Mystery from History*. Illustrated by Roger Roth. Simon & Schuster Books for Young Readers, 1999. ISBN 0689810792. Unpaged. Grades 2–5.

———. *The Wolf Girls: An Unsolved Mystery from History*. Illustrated by Roger Roth. Simon & Schuster Books for Young Readers, 2001. ISBN 0689810806. Unpaged. Grades 2–5.

Youngblood, Ed. *Dirt Track Racing*. Consultant: Hugh Fleming, director, AMA Sports, American Motorcyclist Association. Capstone Books, an imprint of Capstone Press, 2000. ISBN 0736804749. 48 p. Grades 4–8.

———. *Superbike Racing*. Capstone Press, 2000. ISBN 0736804781. 48 p. Grades 4–up.

Author Index

Title Index